Nigel Phin
2006

Prophets, Cults and Madness

Prophets, Cults and Madness

Anthony Stevens
and
John Price

Duckworth

First published in 2000 by
Gerald Duckworth & Co. Ltd.
61 Frith Street, London W1D 3JL
Tel: 020 7434 4242
Fax: 020 7434 4420
Email: enquiries@duckworth-publishers.co.uk
www.ducknet.co.uk

A catalogue record for this book is available
from the British Library

ISBN 0 7156 2940 9

Typeset by Ray Davies
Printed in Great Britain by
Redwood Books Ltd, Trowbridge

Contents

For Stephanie Cole,
Patron of the Schizophrenic Fellowship,
fine actress and dear friend

Preface

In the past decade the new disciplines of evolutionary psychology and evolutionary psychiatry have begun to explain many things about human behaviour that previously baffled us. Now, for example, we have a pretty good idea why people become depressed or sadomasochistic, or develop phobias about heights, snakes, spiders, and wide open spaces.[1] We know why men are particularly jealous when their partners are physically unfaithful, whereas women get more upset about emotional infidelity.[2] We know why mothers become bonded to their infants,[3] why step-parents can on occasion be so unkind, and why Cinderella was not invited to the ball.[4] But there are still a lot of things about human behaviour that do not make sense – the ubiquitous existence of religious belief systems, for example, with their paradoxical combination of high moral aspiration with fanaticism, intolerance, and prejudice; the occurrence of intense patriotism linked with xenophobia, armed conflict, terrorism, and genocide; or the tendency of large numbers of people all over the world to go so far beyond the bounds of reason as to be classified as mad. Can the evolutionary perspective throw more light on these matters than social and cognitive scientists have previously envisaged? Our shared belief that it can has encouraged us to write this book. In particular, it may help us to find answers to the following intriguing and deeply puzzling questions:

(1) *Cults*: Why do people – admittedly rather odd ones – suddenly receive a 'revelation' which revolutionizes their view of the world and alienates them so profoundly from their former community that they can no longer participate in it as useful members? And why do some of them achieve recognition as prophets or gurus? Why do so many people, especially young ones, abandon their families, their jobs and the beliefs they grew up with so as to attach themselves to these

charismatic individuals and endorse the bizarre teachings they promulgate, even though they may appear insane to outsiders?

(2) *Religion*: Why is it that all societies known to anthropology have religions, and why do so many people, two centuries after the Enlightenment and a century after Nietzsche announced the death of God, remain religious?

(3) *Madness*: Why does a significant proportion of the population of every country in the world suffer from a condition in which they develop delusions, hear voices, and become alienated from their families and friends? We know that there is a strong hereditary element in schizophrenia, yet people suffering from this disorder have fewer children than normal. Because of this lower fertility, schizophrenia should have disappeared many generations ago, yet, in the course of their lifetime, one per cent of people in every human population in the world continue to suffer from the disorder. How is this possible?

(4) *Credulity*: Why do so many people believe in extraordinary things which require the denial of natural science – things like poltergeists, psi-phenomena, alien abductions, ghosts, astral travel, crop circles, transfers of energy between people and things, time travel, the transmigration of souls and so on? Why should the propensity to believe in such improbabilities have evolved? Is it possible that people compete more effectively in the struggle for existence if their behaviour is based on such irrational premises?

(5) *Widespread hypofunction*: This state was summed up by Georgei Ivanovitch Gurdjieff's disciple, A.R. Orage, who declared that 'The vast majority die without realizing more than a fraction of their powers. Born millionaires, they die in poverty.' Why should this view be so frequently expressed and widely accepted – namely, that the majority of human beings are half asleep, that they function like automata, and that they need some special training or processing to 'wake them up', so that they may be raised to a more desirable level of consciousness and effective living?

(6) *Armed conflict, ethnic cleansing and genocide*: Why is it so common for human groups to attack and massacre their neighbours, sometimes deliberately killing off whole populations?

(7) *Racial prejudice*: Why are we so often particularly hostile to people who are unlike ourselves? Why do many human communities

Preface

have customs, and sometime even laws, which forbid sexual union or marriage with people of different race, religion or colour?

(8) *Group narcissism*: Why does every human community, tribe, or nation tend to think it is the best, marked out and chosen by the gods as 'special', believing that the rest of the world is populated by barbarians?

These are questions to which, with the present state of knowledge, we can give only inadequate answers. Yet these typically human characteristics represent extreme dangers for humankind, now that the means of mass destruction are becoming ever more readily available to fanatical individuals or groups. We are not alone in believing these to be the crucial issues of our time, and this book has been written in the hope that examining them in an evolutionary context may promote a deeper understanding of them. It is possible, after all, that the effort to comprehend them may serve to heighten our collective sense of responsibility for the destiny of our planet, and enable us to reduce in some measure the number of human calamities that previous generations would have blamed on God.

Acknowledgements

We should like to thank the American Psychiatric Association, Washington DC, for permission to quote from the Diagnostic and Statistical Manual of Mental Disorders, Fourth Edition.

Our special thanks go to Norma Luscombe for wordprocessing numerous drafts of our manuscript with her unique combination of patience, good humour, and painstaking professionalism. We are also grateful to our editor, Martin Rynja, for the enthusiastic care and attention he has devoted to every stage of the publication of the book.

Wide is the gate and broad is the way that leadeth to destruction, and many there be that go thereat.

Matthew, 7:13

1

Charismatic Leaders
and Their Cults

The most common of all follies is to believe passionately in the
palpably not true. It is the chief occupation of mankind.

                                                          H.L. Mencken

In the late 1980s, a group of New Age travellers took up residence in
a disused quarry on a bleak cliff a few miles north of Land's End, the
westernmost promontory of England. What had brought them there
was the conviction that they were about to witness a most miraculous
event: Lyonesse, an Arthurian city of legendary beauty, was going to
rise up out of the sea. Its emergence would herald the beginning of a
neo-Celtic Golden Age. There would be a great deluge to cleanse the
land of cars and other ecological disasters. Then, when the flood
waters had subsided, a new social order would emerge: marriage
would be abolished, all women would be shared and the homeless
given splendid accommodation.

How could they believe anything quite so fantastic? The answer is
that they were participating in an ancient process which seems to
possess an inherent dynamic all its own, for it has been repeated
countless thousands of times in every part of the planet where human
communities have been established: they had formed a cult round an
inspired leader. The leader in this instance was called 'Holy John'.

Holy John had discovered his vocation while serving a prison term
for a drugs offence: he had a vision in which a Great Earth Goddess
called 'The Lady' appeared to him together with her consort, Pan, and
told him to go to the far end of Cornwall, where Lyonesse was
destined to arise in all its glory and the New Age at last would begin.

When, on his release from prison, John arrived in the Cornish
village of St Just, his extraordinary ideas, bizarre behaviour and

outlandish dress made him an object of curiosity: 'Like Mick Jagger on a bad acid trip, dressed as an Apache', commented one local. However, attracted by his eloquence and his message, an assortment of disaffected drop-outs began to gather round him and absorb his teaching. His eccentric but magnetic personality seemed to inspire absolute belief in his prophecies. It was said that he could induce trance states in his devotees, enabling them to leave their bodies and travel on the 'astral plane'. 'As the intensity of their belief grew', William Shaw tells us in his book, *Spying in Guru Land* (1994), 'people began witnessing strange things. They saw mystical ships or submarines floating off the coast; they saw UFOs. For about two years, disbelief evaporated and was replaced by faith in John's phantasmagorical world. "It was like living in a legend", one of them says.'

But it didn't last. The magic evaporated in a manner which, as we shall see, is typical of many such cult-centred communities. John made the mistake that prophets find so hard to resist: he announced the date when the predicted event would occur and the city of Lyonesse would break through the waves. Needless to say, it failed to oblige. As a result, John's followers began drifting away, though some remained in the area, reluctant to abandon their glorious vision or give up the fellowship of the cult.

The disillusionment experienced by cult members when their leader makes a prophecy that fails to be realized is so common a phenomenon that it has been given a name: apocalyptic disappointment. Usually, but not invariably, it marks the beginning of the end of the cult, some ending with a bang rather than a whimper. Most notorious in this regard were the cults founded by Jim Jones and David Koresh. The tragic history of these examples is too well known to require any detailed account here, but their salient characteristics will be rehearsed later because they throw light on what we might call 'the natural history' of cults and their leaders, though by no means all of them end so apocalyptically.

In 1997, for example, Chen Hon-Ming, known to his followers as Teacher Chen, moved his Taiwanese cult of 150 members en masse to Dallas, Texas, in order to prepare for the end of the world which he had predicted would occur on a certain date. When the day passed without incident, Chen showed a degree of humility rare among prophets in his embarrassing position. 'God has communicated to me that those of us who preach the gospels must have the courage to face the scoffing and laughter of people,' he told his followers. 'Even so, my prediction that God would broadcast live on Channel 18 Television last week has not been realized, nor has He made the personal visit to Dallas which I prophesied. In fact, His conduct so far has not been at all encouraging.' In suitably chastened terms he continued: 'Regrettably, it appears that everything I have preached to you over the past four years has turned out to be shit. God did not appear on Channel 18 Television on March 21st. The sun has not disappeared. There has not been a nuclear holocaust, and we have not been rescued by flying saucers and taken to another planet. I give up.'[1]

The majority of prophets are less humble than Chen, and find reasons to justify the failure of their prophecy to come true. In his book *Father and Son* (1907), Edmund Gosse recalled, 'My father awaited with anxious hope "the coming of the Lord", an event he still frequently believed to be imminent. He would calculate, by reference to the prophecies of the Old and New Testament, the exact date of this event; the date would pass without the expected Advent, and he would be more than disappointed – he would be incensed. Then he would understand that he must have made some slight error in calculation, and the pleasures of anticipation would recommence.'

The extraordinary thing is that in these circumstances leaders of cults are able to retain the credulity and loyalty of a section – often a large section – of their followers. One such was a Maori prophet called Rua, who prophesied that King Edward VII would arrive in New Zealand on a date in June 1906. He would bring with him a gift of £3 million to enable Rua and his followers to buy back the Maori lands which had been taken from them by the whites. With more than a thousand people he went on the appointed day to wait on the beach where the King was due to arrive. When he failed to appear, many began drifting away, but more than half of them loyally accompanied Rua on a long march into the Urawera Mountains, where they established a farming community. Rua had many children, and remained the respected elder of the commune which flourished until it was attacked and overwhelmed by the police in 1916 (Webster, 1980).

What is it about such leaders that enables them to retain the loyal devotion of their followers, even when their predictions have been exploded? The answer was provided in one word by the sociologist Max Weber: charisma.

Charisma

Methinks I am a prophet new inspired.

William Shakespeare, *King Richard II*

Charisma is a Greek word meaning gift of divine origin. Weber (1947) described charisma as 'a certain quality of an individual personality by virtue of which he is set apart from ordinary men and treated as endowed with supernatural, superhuman, or at least specifically exceptional powers or qualities. These are such as are not accessible to the ordinary person, but are regarded as of divine origin ... and on the basis of them the individual concerned is treated as a leader ...'

It is not sufficient for a leader to *claim* charismatic powers. He has to be *perceived* as superhuman by those who are attracted to him as followers. 'Charisma', wrote Weber (1946), 'shall be understood to refer to an *extraordinary* quality of a person, regardless of whether this quality is actual, alleged, or presumed.' The leader may perform miracles, go into ecstatic trances, or speak with the voices of the dead, but these capacities do not in themselves constitute charisma, for charisma is not just a personal quality but also a social attribution.

As Weber developed the concept in the course of his life he came to distinguish two forms of charisma which were directly opposed to one another. These were: (1) genuine or primary charisma, and (2) institutional or secondary charisma. Genuine or primary charisma he described as an intense and subversive force which 'is opposed to all institutional routines, those of tradition and those subject to rational management' (Weber, 1946). It is a 'specifically revolutionary force' occurring at times of social crisis which 'rejects all external order' and compels 'the surrender of the faithful to the extraordinary and un-heard-of, to what is alien to all regulation and tradition and therefore is viewed as divine ...' (Dow, 1978).

Institutional or secondary charisma, on the other hand, is attributed to an individual, not because of his personal qualities, but by virtue of his office or institutional role. This is the charisma of the establishment, the charisma that underpins the status quo. It con-

4

fers an aura of power on those privileged to wear a king's crown, a cardinal's hat, or a judge's wig, or to carry a field marshal's baton. Genuine charisma by contrast has an ecstatic, Dionysian quality. It represents a state 'divested of morality' beyond reason and self-control which 'revolutionizes men from within' by releasing a 'life-force' completely antagonistic to the 'dreary construction of the iron cage' of tradition.

A non-charismatic teacher does not attract a following, however wise or profound his teaching, because he lacks this elemental force.[2] On the other hand, the Führer screaming on his podium, the berserk warrior covered in blood and gore, the shaman crying in an unearthly voice or convulsing in an epileptic seizure – these are irresistibly charismatic.

For Weber, the very essence of charismatic authority is implicit in Jesus's words 'It is written ... But I say unto you ...'. To his followers the charismatic leader is infallible. Like the Duce he is always right. Whatever he says, however mad it might seem to outsiders, it is right because he has said it. His legitimacy is absolute by virtue of his divine connection. And it is this power that confers on him the ability to attract disciples and found a cult.

Cults

Beware of false prophets, which come to you in sheep's clothing,
but inwardly are wolves.   *Matthew*, 7:15

The word cult comes from the Latin *cultus* = worship. A cult is a group of individuals, who were previously disaffected from the wider society in which they lived, and have come together to share a common belief system, within a tightly knit community, based on devotion to the teaching and personal influence of a charismatic leader, who is believed to possess divine powers.

Few outsiders can contemplate the beliefs espoused by cult members without having their credulity stretched to its limits. How can apparently normal people come to believe something that most of us consider mad or, as in the case of Jim Jones, David Koresh, or Charles Manson, evil and extremely dangerous? The adoption of such bizarre beliefs is no rare aberration for, despite the disasters of Jonestown

5

and Waco, charismatic figures continue to declare themselves, and there is never a shortage of people eager to flock to them, often in their thousands. There are estimated to be over 3,000 cults in the United States at the present time and about 500 in the United Kingdom. Throughout the world there are many thousands more. What is the attraction?

Because of their growing numbers and their sometimes disastrous consequences, cults, or 'new religious movements' have been intensively studied by anthropologists, sociologists and psychiatrists.[3] Their findings can be quickly summarized. They confirm that cults typically form round an inspired and charismatic leader, who claims to have experienced direct revelations in the form of voices, dreams, visions or signs, which give him divine authority to change the lives of his followers and lead them to some 'Promised Land'. Before entering a cult, potential initiates are characteristically found to be demoralized, alienated and depressed: they have the low self-esteem of outcasts. The pull that a cult exerts on people in this state of mind is that it provides them with a chance to 'belong'.

Once integrated within the cult they are transformed: they feel elated, sanctified, and supremely well. Through their cult leader they *know* that God is on their side and, by committing themselves to the group's mission, they are carrying out His divine will. All other goals and activities then sink into insignificance in the light of the leader's teaching and the members' commitment to the group's destiny.

Having found the secret of health and happiness, members then want to spread the message, and they are usually encouraged to do so by the ethos of the cult. Such proselytizing may gain some converts but generally it puts off more people than it attracts. For the self-righteous conviction of cult members, their illogical assumptions and their suspension of critical judgement typifies all 'true believers' in faiths which outside observers do not share.

Once they are committed to a cult, many members tend to become alienated from their family and from their community of origin. As a result, cults often stir up powerful antipathies in those who do not belong to them. The perception of outside threat, whether it is real or imaginary, intensifies group cohesion, for it feeds the natural paranoia of cult members, activating in-group/out-group dynamics. When these become overheated they can pave the way for violence and even

6

genocide. Paranoid hostility directed towards people outside the cult is a common characteristic, and practically all cult leaders develop a philosophy and practical means for dealing with 'the enemy'. This is apparent in the history of cults centred round such figures as Bhagwan Shree Rajneesh, Shoko Asahara and the Belgian obstetrician Luc Jouret, whose Order of the Golden Temple resulted in the deaths of 48 members in Switzerland and 5 more in Quebec in the autumn of 1994. It is also true of Bonnie Lu Trusdale Nettles and her partner, Marshall Herff Applewhite, who masterminded the suicide of 39 members of their Heaven's Gate cult in San Diego in March 1997, as well as of Jim Jones's 'People's Temple', David Koresh's 'Branch Davidians' and Charles Manson's 'Family'. Manson succeeded in convincing his disciples that he was Christ incarnate, and led them in the apparently senseless killing of ten people. In a brilliant investigation of charismatic leadership, Charles Lindholm (1990) describes how people like these inspire incredible loyalty in the followers who gather round them. Yet to others unaffected by their personalities they appear half mad, 'driven by violent rages and fears that would seem to make them repellent rather than attractive, while their messages look, from the perspective of the outsider, to be absurd mélanges of half-digested ideas, personal fantasies and paranoid delusions'. Moreover, the success of a cult in inducing commitment to its ideology appears to be directly proportional to the bizarreness of the belief system on which it is based.

The fact is that once a prophet has established his cult an unbridgeable gulf opens up between the perceptions of his followers and the rest of society: to his followers, he is a saint, the lamb of God; to the rest of society, he is a false prophet, a wolf in sheep's clothing, a demon of whom the most terrible things can be expected.

Gurus with feet of clay

Men never do evil so completely and cheerfully as when they do it from religious conviction.   Blaise Pascal

One form of charismatic leader who has received careful scrutiny in recent years is the *guru* (a Sanskrit term meaning both 'weighty' and 'one who brings light out of darkness'; in India it is used to designate a Hindu or Sikh religious teacher). In his invaluable book on the subject, *Feet of Clay* (1996), Anthony Storr characterizes gurus as people who believe they have been granted some special life-transforming insight, which typically follows a period of mental or physical illness (which has variously been described as a 'mid-life crisis', a 'creative illness' or 'dark night of the soul'). This *eureka* experience may emerge gradually or come like a thunderbolt out of the sky, in the manner of a religious conversion, a scientific discovery, or an intact delusional system of the type that occurs in schizophrenia. As a result, the guru becomes convinced that he has discovered 'the truth', and this conviction, as well as the passion with which he proclaims it, gives him the charisma which makes him attractive to potential followers.

Gurus, prophets and messiahs all have a great deal in common, as do the groups that gather round them. Anthony Storr, for example, draws attention to the parallels between Jim Jones and David Koresh. Both had been lonely, isolated children who were obsessed with Biblical studies; both became convinced that they had special powers and had been singled out by God for some great purpose; both became fluent, highly persuasive preachers who could harangue their listeners with an endless stream of words far into the night; both were unscrupulous sexually, ruthlessly exploiting their followers to satisfy their erotic demands, Jones with both sexes and Koresh with young children as well as with adults; both insisted on total acceptance of their teaching, would tolerate no argument and would inflict cruel punishments on those who offended against their rule; both were in the grip of paranoid anxieties which caused them to stockpile weapons to prepare for the armed attacks they were sure were coming; both hovered on the brink of insanity for much of their lives, and both ended up demonstrably mad.

Virtually imprisoning their followers, both Jones and Koresh posted armed guards on the perimeter of their enclosures whose job it was as much to keep members in as to keep intruders out. Yet surprisingly few wanted to leave, as interviewers of survivors from these cults have demonstrated. Only a minority defected and told horrifying tales of their experiences. The majority, who had previously been alienated from conventional society, felt themselves to be part of a new community to which they really belonged and where for the first time in their lives they felt accepted and valued. 'It appears that once a guru has convinced a follower of his Messianic status', comments Storr, 'his actual behaviour, as judged by ordinary human standards, becomes largely irrelevant. Belief in the guru, while it persists, entirely overrules rational judgement. Dedicated disciples are as impervious to reason as are infatuated lovers.'

Such facts are sharply at variance with our rational cultural expectations, permeated as they are by the philosophical assumptions of John Locke (1632-1704). Locke was the arch-empiricist, who launched a victorious assault on the doctrine, universally accepted at his time, that men have innate knowledge of certain truths. On the contrary, Locke maintained, we can account for all the ideas that pass through our minds on the basis of *experience*. Nature endows us, according to Locke, not with ideas or innate patterns of behaviour, but with certain *rights* – the right to life, to own our bodies, to enjoy the products of our labour and the right to liberty – as long as our actions do not infringe the natural rights of others. Society comes into existence in order to guarantee that people can enjoy their natural rights without having them infringed, and this forms the basis of the 'social contract'. It is the function of a constitutional government to enforce this contract.

Locke's view of 'natural rights', his endorsement of the rule of law, the function of the state as guarantor of these conditions and the rule of the majority, were ideas that shaped the American and French revolutions and provided the key concepts behind the development of liberal democracy. Because they are so embedded in our Western consciousness we accept them as self-evidently true. Yet they are hard to reconcile with the irrational realities of life in cults, where members willingly surrender their 'natural rights', submit to an absolutist and irrational regime, allowing themselves to be exploited, indoctrinated, abused and in some instances ultimately killed. This presents us with a paradox, for it seems that the kind of social contract entered into by members of a cult is less rational and less independent of innate predispositions than Locke's model would allow us to believe.

When Jones and Koresh told their followers they must prepare to die for their beliefs rather than submit to the forces of Antichrist that were massing against them, their followers obeyed them. As a result, over 900 people, including 260 children, died in Jonestown, Guyana on November 18th, 1978, on the instructions of Jim Jones; and on April 19th, 1993, 86 people, including 22 children, perished in the flames of Ranch Apocalypse, Waco, Texas, on the instructions of David Koresh. Having masterminded these apocalyptic disasters, both Jones and Koresh were found shot in the head. Before the end both had announced they were God: 'I come as God socialist', Jones proclaimed, and Koresh had taken to signing his letters Yahweh Koresh.

Such catastrophes are by no means confined to the United States of America. For example, 'Aum Supreme Truth' is a hugely rich and successful cult in Japan. In March, 1995, its leader, the half-blind seer Shoko Asahara, arranged for the release of sarin gas in the Tokyo subway system, killing 12 people and injuring nearly 6,000. In Thailand, the Sri-Ariya cult, whose members greet one another with Nazi salutes, is led by a guru who claims to be the master of the 'Millennium Kingdom'. In the same year as the Tokyo disaster, the Chinese authorities arrested 15 members of a doomsday cult called Bei Li Wang, while a former Russian policeman called Vissarion was reported to have declared himself to be Christ and to have gathered round him a group of intellectuals in Siberia.

In March 2000 news came of the appalling massacres of many hundreds of members of the Movement for the Restoration of the Ten Commandments of God in Uganda. World attention was focused on the cult following the horrific inferno of a makeshift church in the village of Kanungu of March 17th in which approximately 530 people died. This was initially seen as a mass suicide comparable to the Jonestown tragedy, but then it was found that a number of corpses had been mutilated and strangled. Mass graves were subsequently discovered in other parts of the region, and the total number of victims may never be known. Prior to the disaster, the cult had financed radio announcements appealing for new converts. These began in December 1999, declaring that the world would end on December 31st. Anyone wanting to go to Heaven must join the cult before the occurrence of Armageddon on that date. The leader of the cult, Joseph Kibwetere, a former Catholic priest, had been excommunicated for claiming to have visions of Jesus and the Virgin Mary. He shared leadership with an ex-prostitute called Credonia Mwerinde, who told followers towards the end of 1999: 'I've been receiving messages from God that the Virgin Mary is annoyed. People are sinning too much and God is going to end the world.' It emerged that Kibwetere had a long history of mental illness, with admissions to Butabika Psychiatric Hospital in Kampala. He had a condition in which he lost contact with reality, had delusions, heard voices and saw visions. His estranged wife, Theresa Kibwetere, immediately attracted media attention. She had born him 16 children and described him as 'a loving father and husband' with outstanding oratorical gifts. But, she said, 'he was a man who had eyes but led the blind into a ditch'.

Japan has provided particularly fertile soil for the growth of new religious movements. One of the world's largest cults is the Soka Gakkai which was founded in Japan in 1930 and now has 9 million members, with headquarters in major American cities. They worship a long-dead Buddhist monk, Nichiren. In the cultural confusion which followed Japan's defeat in World War II, with the disbanding of Shinto as the official state religion and the Emperor's renunciation of his divine status, hundreds of new religions emerged to fill the vacuum. Shoko Asahara (born Chizuo Matsumoto) was but one of the most notorious of these. Born in 1955, blind in the left eye and partially sighted in the right, he was a disturbed, difficult and violent child. He did poorly at school where he was an inveterate bully and, when he failed to get into Tokyo University, he turned to business and to God.

Meditating on a beach one day in 1986, he says he received a divine revelation. A voice told him: 'I have chosen you to lead God's army.' Shortly afterwards he was captivated by a historian who predicted that 'Armageddon' would come at the end of the twentieth century, and that the whole world would perish except for a godly race in Japan, whose great leader would soon emerge. These two experiences combined to produce an earthquake in Asahara's mind. He knew beyond all shadow of doubt that he had been 'chosen' to save the world.

Making full use of his outstanding entrepreneurial abilities, Asahara founded Aum Inc., which was to become a multi-million dollar concern marketing electronic equipment, amongst many other things. Aum is pronounced 'Ohm' and is a Hindu mantra encapsulating the ultimate truth of the universe. With Aum as a secure financial base, Shoko Asahara began spreading his message throughout the world.

The message that gurus preach is never entirely original. It is invariably a kaleidoscopic rearrangement of beliefs and doctrines already in existence. In Asahara's case, his theology was a weird amalgam of Hinduism and apocalyptic Christianity. Of the Hindu trinity of Brahma (the Creator), Vishnu (the Preserver) and Shiva (the Destroyer), it was inevitably the last with whom Asahara identified. Shiva is the four-armed deity, who lays waste the world with a cosmic dance and then recreates it in a violent cycle of death and rebirth. The Judeo-Christian concept of Armageddon, the ultimate catastrophic showdown between the forces of Good and Evil, fitted in very well with this scheme of things. Armageddon was to feature colourfully in Asahara's speeches (though, having difficulty in getting his tongue round the word, it usually came out as '*Harumagedon*'). The apocalyptic prophecies of the sixteenth-century French astrologer Nostrodamus provided a rich additive to this odd synchretic mix, since his work had been translated into Japanese in the 1970s and had proved extremely popular.

From any orthodox standpoint, this is bizarre theology, but it makes psychological sense, for the notions of death and rebirth, the struggle between light and darkness, creation and destruction, and the beginning and the end of all things, are themes which permeate the symbolism of practically all the religions devised by man. The notion of an apocalyptic showdown inaugurating a Golden Age of peace and tranquillity is by no means peculiar to those nurtured in the Judeo-Christian tradition. It is so widespread in its implications, so universal in its manifestations, that it would appear to constitute what C.G. Jung would have called an archetype of the collective unconscious, and what we might term a naturally recurring product of the evolved psyche (the phylogenetic psyche) of our species.

In their book *The Cult at the End of the World: The Incredible Story of Aum* David Kaplin and Andrew Marshall (1996) describe how this fourth son of a straw mat weaver proceeded to assemble a huge arsenal of chemical, biological and conventional weapons in preparation for *Harumagedon*. Dressed in flowing purple robes, Asahara lived a life of great luxury and, while imposing strict rules of chastity

12

on his members, indulged 'a libido of truly imperial proportions'. His private quarters were in a compound separated from the accommodation provided for his wife and children, and there he installed a bath large enough to accommodate ten people. In this he delighted in entertaining young ladies from the cult's 'Dance Department'.

At different times Asahara claimed to be both Buddha and Christ, as well as being a reincarnation of Imhotep, builder of Egyptian pyramids. He was gifted, he declared, with a 'Divine Ear' which enabled him to hear the voices of gods and humans, and also with the holy skill to compose 'astral music', which was performed at Aum meetings, often with the guru's off-key voice setting the tune and the tempo.

All this might have proved harmless enough had Asahara's charismatic appeal not drawn to him some of the best scientists in Japan. On his instruction they began producing the poison nerve gas sarin, as well as mustard gas, hallucinogens, barbiturates, TNT, anthrax bacilli, botulinus toxin, and the virus of Q-fever. A commando unit, the Soldiers of White Love, was to be armed with AK74s, while Aum scientists continued to research lasers, nuclear bombs, and other weapons of mass destruction. This was done under the nose of the Japanese police, who, fearing accusations of religious intolerance, sat by and did nothing until it was almost too late.

Fortunately, Aum's military lieutenants proved incompetent and several potentially lethal offensives were bungled. It was only after they had failed to gas deputees sitting in the Diet (the Japanese parliament) and members of the Japanese royal family, that Asahara determined to fulfil his prophecies of Armageddon by launching the deadly sarin attack in the Tokyo subway during the rush hour on March 20th 1995. Completely without remorse for the terrible suffering he had caused, Asahara declared that the dead should be grateful, for he had given them the opportunity to reach a higher spiritual plane. 'It is good', he said, 'that the victims lost their souls to this holy leader, and to Shiva'. When eventually arrested, Asahara had to be accommodated in a padded cell, and his insanity was not open to dispute. The leaders of his cult, at the time of writing, are all in prison, and one is under sentence of death.

Just as charismatic leaders mushroom in different parts of the contemporary world so they have been recorded throughout history, some playing a spiritual role like Jesus Christ, others adopting a belligerent military stance like Hong Xiuquan, leader of the Taiping Rebellion, in mid-nineteenth-century China. With an army of over a million men, this Chinese visionary carved out a huge fiefdom which stretched from Nanjing in the north to near Canton in the south. As a youth, he had come under the influence of Christian missionaries, and this must have determined the content of his visions: God appeared to him and informed him that he was the younger brother of Jesus Christ and was destined to establish a great kingdom on earth. His charismatic power was clearly impressive, for he quickly attracted a large army of devoted followers.

Hong's heavenly kingdom endured for over ten years. His rule was based on Biblical premises (though he rewrote parts of the Bible he didn't like, such as the story of Noah's drunkenness): men and women were strictly segregated, adultery was banned under threat of Draconian punishment, as was the consumption of alcohol and opium. As time passed Hong became less concerned with his politico-military role and increasingly devoted to the Almighty. When, on one occasion, news was brought to him of a British gunboat coming up the Yangtze, he wrote to the captain explaining that since Europeans had been worshipping God so much longer than the Chinese they must be better acquainted with His attributes. Accordingly, Hong requested that the captain should provide him with a physical description of God, with details of His height, His weight and especially the size of His abdomen.

As a result of Hong's bizarre eccentricities, several generals defected, the most important of them being Yang, who had been granted the title of 'Holy Ghost'. Aware of this internal disunity, the imperial forces surrounded Hong's capital, Nanjing, and the siege lasted for months. To console his starving subjects, Hong assured them that manna would come down from Heaven, and proceeded to eat weeds from his courtyard, as a result of which he died (Spence, 1996). It would be 100 years before another charismatic visionary arose to unite China, with the principles of his no less doctrinaire rule neatly set out in a Little Red Book.

Messiahs and the millennium

Art thou he that should come, or should we look for another?
Matthew, 11:3

Charismatic leaders have appeared throughout the history of Christendom, as Norman Cohn has described in his masterly account of messianic movements, *The Pursuit of the Millennium* (1970). These movements, which tended to arise at times of grave economic hardship and social unrest, were inspired by the visions of St John, recorded in the Book of Revelation. These predicted that Christ, after his Second Coming, would establish a messianic kingdom on earth and reign over it for a thousand years before the Last Judgement. The citizens of this kingdom would be Christian martyrs, who would be resurrected a thousand years before the general resurrection of the dead. From the earliest times, many Christians identified themselves with these martyrs, especially those suffering severe adversity, and expected the Second Coming in their lifetime.

As contemporary studies of new religious movements have repeatedly shown, they tend to attract most powerfully people who experience themselves as disaffected from the wider society in which they live. Nowhere was this more true than among the messianic cults that flourished among the rootless poor in Western Europe between the eleventh and sixteenth centuries. Cohn stresses, however, that the poor did not create these cults themselves: they invariably grew out of the millenarian fantasies of would-be prophets and messiahs. As a result of their charismatic influence, the natural desires of miserably hungry people to improve their lot were inflamed with fantasies of a world reborn into innocence through a final apocalyptic massacre. An essential component of these fantasies is the overwhelming presence of The Enemy, symbolized by the Beast or the Antichrist, that has to be defeated before Paradise can be regained. This embodiment of evil, conceived to be more demonic than human, was projected onto the prevailing power – Rome, the ruling Prince, the Church, the clergy, the rich, the Jews or the Pope himself. These must be exterminated, so that the Saints (the suffer-

Prophets, Cults and Madness

ing poor) can set up their Kingdom, a realm without suffering or sin. Then history will achieve its triumphant culmination.

This potent myth has not only intoxicated Christian messiahs and their followers for the last two thousand years[4] but has inspired the fantasies of political prophets like Hitler, Lenin and Karl Marx, as well as intellectuals like Francis Fukuyama with his belief in 'The End of History', which has been achieved with the triumph of Capitalism over the Communist Antichrist. It is this ancient, eschatological vision of an ultimate age of bliss, in which injustice, pain, disease, untimely death, violence, strife, want and hunger will be banished forevermore, that has unconsciously guided our scientific, technological and political aspirations, as well as our religious ideals, throughout the millennium which has now come to an end. As Cohn's monumental study demonstrates, the social conditions which engendered outbreaks of revolutionary millennialism were remarkably uniform: 'The areas in which the age-old prophecies about the Last Days took on a new, revolutionary meaning and a new, explosive force were in the areas which were becoming seriously over-populated and were involved in a process of rapid economic and social change.'

Between the eleventh and thirteenth centuries a large area of Europe extending from the Somme to the Rhine became sufficiently peaceful and well governed for commerce to flourish and the population to expand. But gradually, here and in neighbouring regions, the land was increasingly called upon to carry a population too large for the traditional agricultural system to support. As a result, many peasants migrated eastwards to colonize lands previously occupied by the Slavs; but others stayed behind to form a rural proletariat, barely subsisting on the margins of society in a state of chronic insecurity. These formed 'the most impulsive and unstable elements in medieval society', maintains Cohn. 'And one way in which they attempted to deal with their common plight was to form a salvationist group under a messianic leader.' Cohn recounts the histories of many holy men and prophets thrown up by these forces at this time and centuries earlier: from the freelance preacher of Bourges, reported by the Bishop of Tours in 591, who claimed supernatural gifts of healing and set himself up as Christ in the Cévennes, achieving such fame that the Bishop of Le Puy had him hacked to pieces, to

16

1. Charismatic Leaders and Their Cults

Tanchelm of Antwerp, a wandering preacher active from 1112, who proclaimed he possessed the Holy Spirit and was the Son of God, and reigned over a band of devoted followers with all the sovereign conviction of a messianic king.

With the misery and social disorder of the fourteenth and fifteenth centuries, brought on by war, plague and famine, messiahs and their followers appeared in ever growing numbers to throng the streets and countryside of Europe. To this huge vat of religious ferment was added one more explosive ingredient, the Crusades. If messiahs mobilized the eschatalogical fantasies of the disorientated and the oppressed, the Crusades employed them to overcome the foreign Beast, the infidel, to displace him from the Promised Land. The Jews suffered from this identification as much as the Saracens: their destruction, it was believed, would inaugurate the first stage of the great battle of Armageddon and would result in the final elimination of the Prince of Evil himself. Accordingly, Emmerich, Count of Leiningen, had visions sent by God that inspired the massacres of Jews in cities along the Rhine in the early years of the twelfth century. This demonology was to persist well into the century just ended to inspire another charismatic prophet to fulfil similar genocidal fantasies in the apocalyptic holocaust of Auschwitz.

But it would be wrong to assume that such events have been confined to Christendom and its conflicts with other races and other beliefs. All over the world in practically all places and times charismatic leaders have arisen, cults have formed round them, and conflicts, often bloody, provoked with their neighbours. The emotionally charged fantasy of an apocalyptic struggle, and the establishment of an egalitarian community in some utopian paradise or promised land is so universal in its occurrence among human populations everywhere on the planet that it must be regarded as some kind of 'archetype' of enormous power and salience.

This presents us with a puzzle of staggering dimensions. How on earth are we to explain the ubiquitous occurrence of so bizarre and often catastrophic a phenomenon? How is it that, in conditions of hardship, an apparently mad visionary can persuade normal men and women collectively to take leave of their senses?

17

The ecology of group splitting

And before him shall be gathered all nations: and he shall separate them one from another, as a shepherd divideth his sheep from the goats: And he shall set his sheep on his right hand, but the goats on the left.   *Matthew*, 25:32-3

In trying to find explanations for the extraordinary facts of cult formation and charismatic leadership, we shall start from the position that any universally human characteristic must have a long evolutionary history, and must have evolved because of its *adaptive* value. Because it contributed to the 'fitness' (the capacity to survive long and successfully enough to reproduce) of individuals possessing it, the characteristic flourished rather than disappeared. How can the apparently mad behaviour of messiahs and their followers possibly have contributed to their *fitness*? And why did such behaviour evolve in the first place? What adaptive functions could it perform? More precisely, what adaptive functions did it perform in the social and environmental conditions prevailing during our hunter-gatherer past? For it was then that its adaptiveness would have been established, and the propensity to indulge in such behaviour would have been fixed in the human genome.

Human groups, like all groups of social animals, possess an inherent dynamic to thrive and multiply until they reach a critical size at which the resources at their disposal are no longer adequate for their needs.[5] At this point they become unstable and split.[6] When the split occurs, the group divides into two opposing factions, and all the mechanisms which previously served to promote group solidarity are put into reverse so as to drive the two subgroups apart.[7] At this point, the issue of leadership becomes crucial for survival, because the leader has to inspire the departing group with its sense of mission and purpose, its need to unite against all odds, its belief that it can win through and find its own 'promised land'. Such a leader would evidently benefit from the sort of charisma traditionally granted by divine will and maintained through direct communion with the gods. Could it be that when he is called upon to fulfil this exalted role the charismatic prophet comes into his own? This fissive process, repeated again and again wherever human groups have taken up residence, would have had an adaptive function in spreading out human communities over the surface of the planet in a quest for new resources.

It is difficult, if not impossible, to know what our forebears may have gone through as a hunter-gatherer band grew beyond its critical size of 100 to 150 members, and suffered the social tensions, the personal rivalries and conflicts, which paved the way for the eventual split. How would the decision to separate be taken? Who would leave and who would stay? Would there be a rational political decision, or would half the community suddenly get up and leave, like starlings abruptly setting off on their migration south? Would there be a preliminary polarization into two potential units, like an amoeba preparing to divide and reproduce itself? How much verbal and physical hostility would be generated between them? Would the subgroup that remained behind be in possession of the principle resources, and would the disaffected subgroup leave because these were denied them? How would they plan their departure? How would they know where to go and what to do when they got there? Could they possibly have risked the separation without a leader to inspire and guide them?

Answers to some of these questions may be gleaned from contemporary studies of disaffected groups which separate from their host community and set off in quest of some promised land, as well as anthropological studies of pre-industrial peoples in a similar situation. These studies suggest that having a charismatic leader may be indispensable to the survival of such groups. So far so good. But if this is true, why do these crucially important figures have to be mad? Or are they mad? Are they, like Hamlet, but mad north-north-west, and when the wind is southerly do they know a hawk from a handsaw? And what of their followers? Do they have to abandon their reason in order to enter a cult? As psychiatrists these impress us as highly significant questions, for the attempt to answer them must take us deep into the realm of insanity.

19

2

Thin Partitions

Extraordinary Abilities and Madness

Great wits are sure to madness near alli'd
And thin partitions do their bounds divide
                                        John Dryden

Since classical times it has been believed that the psychic partitions
between genius and madness are thin indeed. Of his contemporaries
and predecessors, Aristotle observed that few became eminent in
philosophy, politics or poetry without manifesting a marked tendency
to melancholia; while Seneca, tutor to the future Emperor Nero (who
subsequently ordered him to commit suicide) declared that no outstanding genius ever existed without a touch of madness. Over a
century before publication of Dryden's poem, Shakespeare wrote,
'The lunatic, the lover, and the poet / Are of imagination all compact'
(a view that Freud espoused when he described the state of being in
love as a kind of madness, 'the normal prototype of the psychoses').

   Closer to our own times, Thomas Babington Macaulay remarked
that 'perhaps no person can be a poet, or can even enjoy poetry,
without a certain unsoundness of mind.' Philistines, on the other
hand, have usually congratulated themselves on their healthy normality: as that most stolidly Teutonic of Kings, George I, observed, 'I
hate all Boets and Bainters!' By way of contrast, the Romantic
Movement generated the stereotype of the 'mad genius' which was to
dominate artistic and intellectual life throughout the nineteenth
century and to persist into the twentieth, finding particular expression in the Dada movement and André Breton's surrealist manifesto:
'Dictée de la pensée en l'absence de toute controle.' There was no
shortage of eminent philosophers, psychologists and psychiatrists
willing to endorse such views. In his classic *The Man of Genius* (1891)

21

Cesare Lombroso affirmed the equation of genius with madness, while Friedrich Nietzsche, himself destined to go mad with tertiary syphilis, wrote that 'it seems impossible to be an artist without being diseased', and maintained that ecstatic insanity permitted 'a collective release of all the symbolic powers.'

The eminent British psychiatrist, Henry Maudsley, clearly believed genius and insanity to be related: 'To forbid the marriage of a person sprung from an insanely disposed family might be to deprive the world of a singular genius or talent, and so be an irreparable injury to the race of men ... If, then, one man of genius were produced at the cost of one thousand or fifty thousand insane persons, the result might be a compensation for the terrible cost' (quoted by Crow, 1995). Support for such views has come from the finding that the relatives of schizophrenic patients are more creative than members of the general population (Karlsson, 1972).

The kind of outstanding abilities generally considered to be related to madness would thus seem to be those possessed by artists, musicians and writers. As Simonton concluded in his study of *Greatness* (1997)[1], 'Creators exhibit more psychopathology than average persons, but less than true psychotics. They seem to possess just the right amount of weirdness. They are strange enough to come up with odd ideas, and to pursue those ideas no matter what the rest of the world says. Yet creators are not so outlandish that they lose all contact with reality. They are always hovering on the brink of madness. Dryden's phrase "thin Partitions" seems an apt metaphor.'

So much for creative artists. But what of those with outstanding *spiritual* gifts, the mystics, saints, prophets, and gurus? Here the links are even more striking and more difficult to overlook. William James, the authority who wrote *The Varieties of Religious Experience*, remarked that 'borderline insanity, crankiness, insane temperament, loss of mental balance', and so on, when combined with 'a superior quality of intellect' increased the likelihood that an individual 'will make his mark and affect his age' than if his temperament were less disturbed. That such individuals are particularly likely to affect the religious life of their age was echoed by Maudsley, who asked, 'What right have we to believe God is under any obligation to do this work by means of complete minds only? He may find an incomplete mind a more suitable instrument for a particular purpose.'

2. Thin Partitions

That the partition between religious experiences and psychotic experiences is indeed thin has been so frequently commented upon by anthropologists, sociologists, psychologists and historians that it is difficult not to believe that the two sets of experiences must in some very profound sense be related. Before we attempt to enter this mysterious and frightening border zone, a certain amount of definition and clinical description will be necessary.

True madness

To define true madness, what is't, but to be nothing else but mad.   William Shakespeare, Polonius in *Hamlet*

Until the late nineteenth century, most people, physicians included, would have agreed with Polonius's answer to his own question. But then, thanks to the efforts of French psychiatrists like J.P. Falret (1794-1870) and German psychiatrists like Emil Kraepelin (1855-1926), it became apparent that there were different forms of psychosis (madness), which could be broadly differentiated into *organic* psychoses (those forms of madness that had a physical cause, like senile dementia, or severe forms of mental disturbance caused by temporal lobe epilepsy or drugs) and the *functional* psychoses (those forms of madness which possessed no known physical cause, like manic-depressive psychosis and schizophrenia). It is the group of functional psychoses that must hold our attention, for it is patients with these conditions whom charismatic prophets and messiahs most closely resemble.

Mood disorders ('mania' and 'depression') are exaggerations of the universal human capacity for elation and despair. Psychiatry classifies these moods as illness when they are judged to be extreme, of long duration, disproportionate to the circumstances, and found to be unresponsive to advice or outside influence. Mood disorders may be moderate or severe, and it is in the severe forms that hallucinations (perceptions occurring in the absence of appropriate stimuli) and delusions (beliefs judged by others to be false) may occur, and warrant the diagnosis of 'psychosis'. Delusions, if they do occur, tend to be compatible with the exaggerated mood. Thus in severely depressed patients, feelings of guilt and worthlessness can be exaggerated into the absolute conviction that they are financially ruined, that they have committed the unforgivable sin, or that their bowels are riddled with cancer. Conversely, in the extreme euphoria of mania people tend to develop delusions of grandeur, convinced that they possess limitless resources or that they have a religious mission to save the world from some apocalyptic disaster.

Mood disorders tend to follow an episodic course and, although some patients may have only one episode of mania or depression in their lifetime, others may have recurrent episodes of either or both, alternating between times when they are manic and times when they are depressed (so-called 'bipolar disorder'). As we shall see, some prophets, like 'Mother Earth' the earth goddess of Trinidad, and Sabbatai Sevi, the seventeenth-century rabbi who converted to Islam, may possibly belong to this group.

But the majority of prophets display few signs of bipolar disorder. On the contrary, their behaviour would seem to be more compatible with the signs and symptoms of the other form of functional psychosis, schizophrenia.

What is schizophrenia?

If you speak to God it's prayer; if God speaks to you, it's schizophrenia.
                                                        Thomas Szasz

The term schizophrenia was introduced during the first decade of the twentieth century by Eugen Bleuler (1857-1939), Jung's chief at the Burghölzli Hospital in Zurich. It is derived from the Greek *schizein* = to split and *phrēn* = diaphragm. This terminology has given rise to popular misconceptions, such as the belief that schizophrenia is identical with split or dual personality of the Jekyll and Hyde variety, which it is not. In fact, Bleuler introduced the term because he considered the primary feature of schizophrenia to be a fundamental split between thinking and emotional functions, both of which were impaired, resulting in a grossly disordered relationship to the external world. Although Bleuler acknowledged that delusions and hallucinations were extremely common in schizophrenia, he considered them to be secondary to the primary split.

A century later the condition is viewed somewhat differently.

24

Nowadays no single symptom such as hearing voices, having bizarre delusions, or displaying extreme apathy or agitation, is considered to be clearly diagnostic of schizophrenia. On the contrary, the diagnosis is based on recognition of a constellation of signs and symptoms together with a history of difficulty in holding down a job and relating to people socially.

The characteristic symptoms are broadly grouped into 'positive' and 'negative' categories. The positive symptoms represent an excess or distortion of normal functions, whereas the negative symptoms reflect a diminution or loss of these functions. Positive symptoms include distortions of thinking (delusions), perception (hallucinations), language (disorganized speech), and behaviour (varying from odd, bizarre, eccentric behaviour to grossly disorganized behaviour). Negative symptoms include restrictions in the range and intensity of emotional expression, in the fluency of thought and speech, and in loss of drive and will power.

It is not necessary for all these symptoms to be present for the diagnosis to be made. The Diagnostic and Statistical Manual of the American Psychiatric Association (generally referred to as DSM-IV, which is becoming a kind of international psychiatric Bible) provides a 'shopping list' of criteria from which the diagnosis can be made. These are summarized in the end notes.[2]

A schizophrenic genius

Paul, thou art beside thyself; much learning doth make thee mad.   *The Acts of the Apostles*, 26:24

In some individuals the partitions between genius and madness become so thin as to disappear altogether. One of the most fascinating studies yet published is a *Beautiful Mind: A Biography of John Forbes Nash Jr* by Sylvia Nasar (1998). It concerns a man who for 32 years of his life was both a mathematical genius and schizophrenic.

Nash was awarded a Nobel Prize for his insight into the dynamics of human conflict and co-operation which proved to be of crucial significance for 'game theory'. He had been famous among mathematicians for several decades prior to winning his award for the 'Nash equilibrium' or 'Nash bargaining solution' which was to provide a basic paradigm for social science and biology. Nash defined equilibrium as a situation in which each player adopts a strategy which cannot be improved upon, provided all other players adopt the best strategies available to them. 'Like many great scientific ideas', Sylvia Nasar comments, 'from Newton's theory of gravitation to Darwin's theory of natural selection, Nash's idea seemed initially too simple to be truly interesting, too narrow to be widely applicable, and, later on, so obvious that its discovery by *someone* was deemed all but inevitable' (p. 98). Nash's insight transformed the relatively young science of economics, much as Mendel's work had transformed our understanding of the principles of genetics.

Like many other outstanding scientists or philosophers, such as René Descartes, Immanuel Kant, Isaac Newton, Albert Einstein and Ludwig Wittgenstein, Nash had the kind of socially withdrawn, emotionally detached, and eccentric personality that psychiatrists diagnose as 'schizoid' or 'schizotypal'.[3]

Nash's contemporaries found him immensely strange: they described him as 'aloof', 'haughty', 'without affect', 'detached', 'spooky', 'isolated' and 'queer'. Although accepting that he was decidedly odd, his colleagues did not consider him to be mad – until one day in January 1959 when, aged 30 and about to be made a full professor at MIT, he slouched into the common room carrying a copy *The New York Times* and remarked, to no one in particular, that 'the story in the upper left hand corner of the front page contained an encrypted message from inhabitants of another galaxy, but only he could decipher it' (p. 16).

When he was hospitalized soon after this incident, his psychiatrists agreed that he was suffering from schizophrenia. 'The bizarre and elaborate character of Nash's beliefs, which were simultaneously grandiose and persecutory, his tense, suspicious, guarded behaviour, the relative incoherence of his speech, the blankness of his facial expressions, and the extreme detachment of his voice, the reserve which bordered at times on muteness – all pointed toward schizophrenia' (pp. 258-9).

The median age of onset for the first schizophrenic episode is in the early to mid-twenties for men and in the late twenties for women. The onset may be sudden, but the majority of people display a slow and gradual development of a variety of symptoms before the onset of the first psychotic episode. This was true of Nash. Since childhood, he had been a strange, solitary, introverted boy, whose lack of friends and complete disinterest in childish pursuits were a source of worry to his parents. He was an insatiable bookworm who hero-worshipped solitary thinkers like Newton and Nietzsche, and developed a passion for computers ('thinking machines'), science fiction and the idea that there could be supernatural aliens in outer space who had learned to disregard all emotions.

It is still not fully understood why schizophrenia should attack one person rather than another, but after two centuries of research into the condition (something very like it was first described in 1806), it looks as if it is the result of stressful life events acting on an inherited predisposition. After his recovery, Nash himself attributed the onset of his illness to a failed attempt, which he made in 1957, to solve certain contradictions in quantum theory, and this seems to have taken a severe toll on his self-esteem. Another precipitating factor could have been his arrest in Santa Monica on a charge of gross indecency in a men's public lavatory, which resulted in his discharge from the staff of the Rand Corporation in 1954. Although he subsequently married, Nash, like some other schizoid men of genius – for example, Newton and Descartes – formed erotic attachments to young men who were unable to reciprocate his feelings. These experiences increased his sense of isolation and may have contributed to his eventual psychosis.

In the majority of cases, schizophrenia is a condition which persists. Nash's illness lasted, with the usual pattern of relapses and remissions, until 1990. During this period he was admitted to hospital on a number of occasions and treated with insulin coma therapy, electro-convulsive therapy, and anti-psychotic drugs. When not in hospital, during the 1970s and '80s, he haunted the mathematics faculty at Princeton University, studying Biblical texts and scribbling cryptic messages on blackboards. These intrigued and puzzled students, who knew they were the products of a genius who had 'flipped'. They called him 'the Phantom'. A typical blackboard inscription was: 'Mao Tse-Tung's bar mitzvah was 13 years, 13 months and 13 days after Brezhnev's circumcision.'

When not in Princeton, Nash travelled: usually to Europe with a view to establishing himself as a 'citizen of the world' and setting up

27

a 'world government'. To this end he sought to renounce his American citizenship. Nasar comments: 'In the overwrought, hyperpatriotic atmosphere of the America he was leaving behind, Nash was choosing the "path of most resistance", and one that captured his radical sense of alienation. Such "extreme contrariness" aimed at cultural norms has long been a hallmark of a developing schizophrenic consciousness. In ancestor-worshipping Japan the target may be the family, in catholic Spain the Church. Motivated as much by antagonism to his former existence as a by an urge for self-expression, Nash particularly desired to supersede the old laws that had governed his existence and, quite literally, to substitute his own laws, and to escape once and for all, from the jurisdiction under which he had once lived' (p. 271). This is a particularly interesting observation, for this 'anti' tendency is one of the most salient, and culturally significant traits of charismatic prophets.

Throughout his illness, and to some extent after his recovery, Nash heard voices, which he described as being 'like telepathic phone calls' from private individuals. Despite the fact that these could be irritating, as when he recognized them as the voices of 'mathematicians opposed to my ideas', he seems in some way to have depended on them and even to have enjoyed their company. When asked at an out-patient consultation why he had stopped taking his anti-psychotic medication, he replied, 'If I take the drugs I stop hearing the voices.'

Despite the widespread use of anti-psychotic drugs during the last half of the twentieth century, the long-term outlook for patients with schizophrenia has remained relatively unchanged. About 40 to 60 per cent remain chronically ill and never recover, 20 to 30 per cent continue to have moderate symptoms and are socially and professionally incapacitated, while 20 to 30 per cent recover sufficiently to lead marginally normal lives. Nash is unusual in achieving an apparently complete recovery after more than 30 years of severe incapacity, in which 'negative' symptoms of emotional blunting, impoverished fluency and loss of willpower were as apparent as the 'positive' symptoms of auditory hallucinations, delusional thinking ('I am the left foot of God on earth') and crazy behaviour. Given the usual course of the condition, Nasar is right to stress the probability that Nash's marked clinical improvement was a remission rather than a cure.

Nash himself described the illness as gradually 'tapering off' in the 1970s and '80s. He seems to have remained well up to the publication of Nasar's book in 1998, although he admitted to close colleagues that he was still plagued by paranoid thoughts and hallucinated voices, even if these were much less troublesome than in the past. But it was not easy to keep on an even keel, and Nash likened his struggle to keep sane to that of a fat man dieting: it required constant vigilance to police his thoughts and to weed out paranoid ideas before they took too firm a hold on him – in the same way as a fat man would have to make a determined effort to avoid fats or sweets if he wanted to lose weight and stay thin. Nash denied that his remission had anything to do with the treatment he had received: 'I emerged from irrational thinking', he said in 1996, 'ultimately without medicine other than the natural hormonal changes of ageing' (p. 353).

However, there is one contributory factor which may have been of great therapeutic significance. Through the compassionate generosity of the Princeton University authorities, despite his bizarre and grossly incapacitating illness, Nash was retained as a member of the mathematics faculty through the 1970s and '80s. After his recovery, Nash himself said: 'I have been sheltered here and thus avoided homelessness'. At Princeton, Nash's madness was contained: 'It is obvious that, for Nash, Princeton functioned as a therapeutic community. It was quiet and safe; its lecture halls, libraries and dining halls were open to him; its members were for the most part respectful; human contact was available but not intrusive.' His eventual recovery may also have been sustained by the worldwide recognition his mathematical genius received when he was awarded the Nobel Prize in 1994.

As Nasar suggests, a predisposition to schizophrenia was probably integral to Nash's genius as a mathematician. 'When he focused on some new puzzle, he saw dimensions that people who really knew the subject (he never did) initially dismissed as naive or wrong-headed. Even as a student, his indifference to others' scepticism, doubt and ridicule, was awesome' (p. 12). When recovering from a psychotic episode, Nash was once asked by a visitor how he, 'a man devoted to reason and logical proof' could believe that extraterrestrials were sending him messages. 'How could you,' asked the visitor, 'believe that you are being recruited by aliens from outer space to save the world?' Nash replied: 'Because the ideas I had about supernatural beings came to me the same way as my mathematical ideas did. So I took them seriously' (p. 11).

*

This is precisely the way in which charismatic prophets receive the 'call' to save their people, and become convinced of their 'mission'. A crucial question which must concern us, therefore, is whether the strange belief systems, visions, heard voices, and eccentric behaviour of prophets and messiahs warrant their classification as schizophrenics. If they are not schizophrenic, how can we explain the very obvious similarities they display with psychiatric patients who are?

The problem is more complex, and far more interesting, than it might at first appear, and its resolution could yield the answer to a more fundamental question which has puzzled psychiatrists since Kraepelin, namely, *why does schizophrenia exist at all*? On the face of it, it shouldn't. The potential to develop the disorder should have disappeared from the human gene pool many generations ago. Indeed, the odds are so loaded against its evolution that it is remarkable that it came into existence in the first place. Yet, it flourishes as one of the great scourges of humanity, afflicting approximately one in every hundred human beings in the course of their lifetime in every corner of the world.

This is an extraordinary statistic that it is extremely difficult to explain. We know for a fact that some gene or genes contribute to vulnerability to the disorder. Schizophrenia is more common in the families of schizophrenic patients than it is in the population at large. For example, of the second-degree relatives (grandchildren, nephews, nieces) of a known schizophrenic, 3 to 5 per cent run a risk of developing the psychosis; for siblings the risk is 10 to 15 per cent; and for the children of two schizophrenic parents 37 to 45 per cent. Twin studies give the clearest indication that a genetic factor is at work, for if one twin of an identical pair is schizophrenic, there is a 45 to 50 per cent chance of the other twin becoming schizophrenic.

Studies of adopted children brought up away from their biological parents from an early age lend impressive weight to the importance of genetic influences. A pioneer study by Heston (1966) compared two groups of fostered children. The mothers of one group were schizophrenic, while those of the other had no psychiatric diagnosis. None of the latter group developed schizophrenia, but 17 per cent of the former did. Moreover, they also showed a higher incidence of other disorders, especially personality disorders. Another interesting finding was that in members of the former group, who had schizophrenic mothers but were themselves free of psychopathology, a greater number took up artistic or creative professions. In the last thirty years, a considerable amount of confirmatory evidence has been gathered in a number of developed countries. In the case of John Forbes Nash Jr, the genetic configuration responsible for his mathematical genius and schizophrenic illness was transmitted to one of his two sons, John Charles Nash, who was himself a highly gifted mathematician and also developed schizophrenia.

So there can be no doubt that genes play a crucial role. Yet we also know that schizophrenics have a much lower fertility rate than normal. Nash was an exception in this regard. How then does schizophrenia survive? How can it possibly be that far from having been selected out of the human gene pool, this severely disadvantageous condition now accounts for 60 million people (roughly equivalent to the population of the British Isles) in the world today. Or is it so disadvantageous as it would seem?

An advantageous predisposition

We want a few mad people now. See where the sane ones have landed us!   G.B. Shaw *Saint Joan*, scene 1

Despite all appearances to the contrary, there must be some selective advantage in the genetic predisposition to schizophrenia, if not in the schizophrenic disorder itself, otherwise it would no longer be with us.

The genetic predisposition for a certain trait or characteristic is known as the *genotype* for that trait. The trait itself, when it is expressed or developed in the living individual, is called the *phenotype* of that trait. The form that the phenotype takes may be rigidly determined by the genotype, as it is for such traits as eye or hair colour or the development of teeth. This fact is demonstrated by identical twins: they always have eyes and hair of the same colour and their teeth are exactly alike. Many phenotypes are, however, less rigidly determined by the genotype, and traits of this less rigidly determined kind are said to display '(phenotypic) plasticity': the development of such traits can be influenced by environmental factors.

Let's assume, for example, your son has inherited your genotype for broad shoulders. When he grows up, this genetic predisposition will in all probability be expressed in shoulders (the phenotype) which are broader than normal. But exactly how broad they are will depend on such factors as what kind of diet he has had in the course of growing up, whether he is sporty, goes to the gym lifting weights, takes steroids, and so on. Unlike eye colour, therefore, shoulder width displays some degree of 'phenotypic plasticity' in the sense that the phenotype is not the rigid and absolute fulfilment of the genotype.

Could this be true of the genetic predisposition to schizophrenia? Could it be that this genotype displays phenotypic plasticity in individuals possessing it? If so, this could mean that this predisposition might express itself in a way that, depending on different life events, is either *disadvantageous* (i.e. results in the development of schizophrenia) or *advantageous* (i.e. results in the individual becoming, for example, a prophet, a messiah or a guru)?

This would seem to be a distinct possibility, since the schizophrenic genotype certainly does not display phenotypic rigidity. If it did, everybody with the genotype would become schizophrenic, but they don't. As already noted, identical twins possess identical genotypes. Yet if one of these twins becomes schizophrenic, on average only in about 50 per cent of cases does the other twin develop schizophrenia. Thus other factors must be involved in determining whether or not the genotype is expressed in the schizophrenic phenotype.

It is therefore theoretically possible that certain life events could switch the individual carrying the genetic predisposition into a career either as a schizophrenic patient or a charismatic prophet. If this is so, what is there about the role of prophet that could make the inclination to become one selectively advantageous? It is this crucial issue that we must now address.

2. Thin Partitions

Psychosis or religious experience?

A sane person is one whose fiction is supported by the society. He has manipulated the society to support his fiction. An insane man is one whose fiction is supported by nobody; he is alone so you have to put him in the madhouse.

Bhagwan Shree Rajneesh

A strange thing happened to a 43-year-old office manager as she drove to work one wet autumn morning in Oxfordshire. She had just stopped at some traffic lights when suddenly a loud voice said, 'Sara, this is Jesus! When are you coming to work for me?'

Her first thought was that her brother must have hidden in the back of the car and was having her on. But when she turned round to see, there was no one there. She turned back to attend to the traffic lights. 'He must have put a tape in the car', she thought. Then the voice spoke to her again. This time, she says, 'I knew beyond any shadow of doubt who it was ...'

For Sara this marked the beginning of a long series of divine communications. They gave her detailed instructions and, she says, granted her paranormal abilities in such realms as telepathy, clairvoyance, synchronicity, healing, and communication with the dead. At first she found this all very disturbing and she became 'terrified of going mad'.

Eventually she consulted her vicar. 'He thought I was having a religious wobbler at first and said "Don't give up your management career." But he gradually realized that it wasn't, it was something solid, not a schizophrenic breakdown ... I was behaving rationally, coping with my job, making decisions, talking to my husband about the fact that I needed to leave work ... Making sensible arrangements about changing my life, and because I wasn't showing any phobias, paranoias or whatever.'

Both Sara and her vicar concluded that her experiences were genuine and fully compatible with Christian doctrine. If they were delusional and hallucinatory, their consequences were wholly positive, both for herself and for others. She went on to live a fulfilling, altruistic life as a counsellor and spiritual director to Anglican priests.

33

Speaking of her relationship to the Divine, she concluded, 'It has always enhanced my life; it's brought a great deal to other people and it is benign; it is co-operative; it is loving; it helps me see the beauty of nature; ... begin to grasp something about ultimate reality and the way the universe is ... If I'm mad, so be it, but this is the most real thing I've ever known.'

Reporting this case from the records of the Alister Hardy Research Centre in Oxford, Mike Jackson and K.W.M. Fulford (1997) comment that it would be interesting to know how Sara's experiences would have developed, and what would have become of her mental state, had she not had the good fortune to receive such a validating response from her priest. This is a most important point, and we shall return to it.

What are we to make of Sara's story? Did she have a psychotic episode or should we regard it as a normal, if somewhat unusual, spiritual experience? The question is one of practical (clinical) as well as theoretical interest. When these episodes began, Sara says that she was 'terrified of going mad'. What if instead of consulting a priest she had gone to a psychiatrist? Suspecting the onset of an acute psychosis, the psychiatrist might have started her on a course of anti-psychotic drugs and even admitted her to hospital, thus aborting what proved to be a wholly beneficial experience and treating her as a psychiatric patient. As Jackson and Fulford point out, the very *similarities* between spiritual and pathological psychotic experiences demand an account of the *differences* between them. But is such differentiation possible? Though hearing what sounds to be an external voice addressing the subject is common among schizophrenics, a diagnosis of schizophrenia depends, as we have seen, on recognizing a constellation of signs and symptoms combined with a history of impaired social or occupational functioning. In addition to the so-called 'positive symptoms' (delusions, hallucinations, disorganized speech and bizarre behaviour), 'negative symptoms' (reduced intensity of emotional expression, impoverishment of thought and speech, and a reluctance to engage in productive activities), are also apparent.

Fortunately, Sara exhibited no such negative symptomatology and far from being impaired, her social and occupational usefulness was enhanced. Moreover, before her first experience of being addressed by Jesus, she had been depressed following the discovery that she

34

was unable to have children and was in a state of confusion about what she should do with her life. What a busy, hard-pressed psychiatrist might have diagnosed and treated as an acute psychotic illness, in fact proved to be a highly effective means of solving her problems.[4]

Whether or not an unusual experience should be considered 'spiritual' or 'pathological' can therefore be extremely difficult to decide, for it depends not only on the nature of the experience but on its social consequences for the subject. It is the judgement of others which decides whether a sensory experience or a strongly held belief is to be regarded as a result of divine inspiration, or as a hallucination or delusion to be diagnosed as a sign of madness.[5]

Delusions

Convictions are more dangerous enemies of the truth than lies.
Nietzsche

A delusion is defined by the psychiatric textbooks as a false belief. But this definition is dependent on the criterion of falsity and is relative to the community in which the judgement of falsity is made. A more satisfactory definition is that a delusion is a belief which the social group as a whole does not share. If you go to church on a Sunday morning and, surrounded by a congregation of Christians, you say you believe that Jesus Christ was the son of God, no alarmed eyes will swivel in your direction. Should you, on the other hand, declare *yourself* to be the son of God, come to redeem the earth, the response will be rather different.

People are categorized as 'mentally ill' when they cannot persuade others of the truth of their beliefs. Some psychiatrists, such as R.D. Laing and Thomas Szasz, have stressed the importance of social consensus in judging someone to be mad – an opinion which the subject by no means always shares. Recalling his admission to Bethlem Royal Hospital in the seventeenth century, the playwright Nathaniel Lee declared, 'They called me mad, and I called them mad, and damn them, they outvoted me!'

Delusions are a form of intuitive hypothesis-formation. The hypothesis is accepted by the individual who had formed it not because of evidential proof but because it feels so right that it produces a state of absolute *conviction*. The characteristics conventionally attributed to delusions in British and North American textbooks have been summarized by Mullen (1979) and, despite some recent caveats, they still stand. They are as follows:

– They are held with absolute conviction

– They are experienced as self-evident truths usually of great personal significance

– They are not amenable to reason or modifiable by experience.

– Their content is often fantastic or at best inherently unlikely.

– The beliefs are not shared by those of a common social or cultural background.

Though the majority of psychiatrists would accept the practical value of this description, some have quibbled that psychiatric texts fail to specify how degrees of conviction (absoluteness) and degrees of incorrigibility ('not amenable to reason') are to be assessed. Others have argued that false beliefs are common enough in the community at large and that if having a false belief were a sufficient condition for a diagnosis of delusional insanity then most of us would have to be classified as mad. Opinion polls in the United States have established that over 25 per cent of Americans believe in witches, about 50 per cent believe in ghosts, the devil and the literal truth of the Book of Genesis, nearly 90 per cent believe in the Resurrection of Christ, and 96 per cent believe in God. Clearly there must be some criterion by which a belief can be established as so deviant as to be regarded as delusional.

As Philippa Garety and David Hemsley (1997) have observed the problem of establishing a criterion of deviance is the difficulty of choosing the 'right' group as the reference class. This is particularly true when judging the beliefs of people who start or join cults. To the good Cornish People of St Just, Holy John was self evidently 'maze', as they say in those parts. But, to his followers, he was hypernaturally sane. And his belief that Lyonesse was going to emerge from the Atlantic was not delusory but true. It was only when the miraculous eruption failed to obey the timetable John had set for it that his followers began to think that he could have been mistaken, and to wonder whether he might even be mad.

Looking at the issue from the non-psychiatric standpoint, we might ask under what circumstances the utterances of a madman will be accepted by his contemporaries as valid. Evidently, what he says must connect in some way with the needs and perceptions of the group at the time. As we saw in the last chapter, periods of crisis are particularly fertile. When the group is desperate it is more willing to give credence to extraordinary solutions which, at more usual times, it would dismiss as mad. Many historical instances demonstrate this truth. In the 1660s, for example, Solomon Eccles wandered round London half naked with a brazier of fire on his head, proclaiming the imminent destruction of the city. He was ridiculed as a madman until London was devastated first by the Plague and then by the Fire in quick succession. Then he became a celebrity. However, as London was rebuilt, Eccles continued to preach the identical message, and was once more relegated to the lunatic fringe in popular esteem (Littlewood, 1984).

Bryan Wilson (1975) sums it up well in his book *Noble Savages: The Primitive Origins of Charisma*: 'If a man runs naked down the street proclaiming that he alone can save others from impending doom, and if he immediately wins a following, then he is a charismatic leader; a social relationship has come into being. If he does not win a following, then he is simply a lunatic ...'

Hallucinations

And it came to pass, that, as I made my journey, and was come nigh unto Damascus about noon, suddenly there shone from heaven a great light round about me. And I fell unto the ground, and heard a voice saying unto me, Saul, Saul, why persecutest thou me? And I answered, Who art thou, Lord? And he said unto me, I am Jesus of Nazareth, whom thou persecutest. And they that were with me saw indeed the light, and were afraid; *but they heard not the voice of him that spake to me*. And I said, What shall I do, Lord? And the Lord said unto me, Arise, and go into Damascus; and there it shall be told thee of all things which are appointed for thee to do.

The Acts of the Apostles, 22:6-10 (italics added)

Hallucinations are defined as sensory perceptions in the absence of external stimuli. The auditory hallucinations so common in schizophrenia are experienced as actual voices: they are externalized and heard as if they came from *outside*, not manufactured inside the head. The voices heard by schizophrenics may speak to them personally: they are often bossy, admonitory, dictatorial, critical or even abusive, like a cross, nagging parent (which, in terms of the patient's personal history, is a possible source of them) or they may be cajoling, encouraging, and supportive. Equally, the voices may be attributed to an overheard conversation between third parties, their comments usually taken as referring to the patient. Some patients also report hearing their thoughts spoken aloud (so-called *echo de pensée*) and this can go along with the development of a delusion that these thoughts are being broadcast to the world.

Like delusions, hallucinations are resistant to correction when the absence of an external source is demonstrated to the person who is experiencing them. When during a clinical interview a female patient explained that she was at that very moment being harassed by a man's voice making improper suggestions, it was pointed out to her that there was no one in the room but her doctor, and she agreed that the voice was not coming from him. 'Where then is it coming from?' he asked her. She looked straight at the telephone on his desk and, nodding meaningfully, she said: 'He must have got your number!' But if she appreciated the *double entendre*, she didn't laugh. In schizophrenia the capacity for such laughter is lost. The subjective impression of the man's voice was so vividly clear that she *knew* that his voice *must* be real.

Ordinarily one checks up on an unusual, unexpected or inexplicable perception. We seek further perceptual information to establish the nature of what it is that we 'thought' we saw, heard, or felt. As he contemplates the murder of Duncan, Macbeth has a vivid hallucination of a dagger, its handle towards his hand. He tries to take hold of it, but grasps nothing but thin air. He asks it, 'Art thou not, fatal vision, sensible to feeling as to sight? Or art thou but a dagger of the mind, a false creation, proceeding from the heat-oppressed brain?' Had Macbeth been schizophrenic, it would not have occurred to him to ask such questions.

A clinical distinction has to be made, therefore, between subjects who accept their hallucinations as real and those who realize they are imaginary. For example, exhausted mariners on watch commonly report 'seeing' ships escorting them and 'hearing' their foghorns, while knowing for a fact that there are no other ships in the vicinity. Explorers like Richard Byrd and Sir Ernest Shackleton reported having hallucinations under lonely, isolated conditions. Hallucinations which are recognized for what they are by the people experiencing them are called 'pseudohallucinations', but they are uncharacteristic of prophets and schizophrenic patients, who generally consider their visions and voices to be real.

One highly significant characteristic of hallucinations and delusions is that they are mutually reinforcing. The prophet's 'voices', composed from elements of his unconscious mind, provide him with an inner reference group with which to test and confirm his convictions. Voices carry tremendous force when, as in the case of Joan of Arc, they are believed to be direct expressions of the Will of God. They are of particular importance to the prophet when he is in a state of isolated withdrawal before any followers have gathered round him. Even for the schizotype it is difficult, without at least one close confidant, to maintain an intact belief system in opposition to the majority view. In the absence of outer companions, voices may compensate by providing the necessary support.

Although our primary concern is to find explanations for the 'ultimate' cause of schizophrenia (i.e. the biological reason for its existence), we should not overlook the important contributions of researchers who have attempted to find 'proximal' (i.e. neurological and biochemical) causes for the condition.[6] For example, Frith (1992, 1994) has suggested that schizophrenic delusions and hallucinations are due to deficient self-monitoring. When we think, speak, or make some movement, there are 'corollary discharges' in the central nervous system that inform us that these thoughts, words, and actions are, in fact, our own. When we move our eyes, for instance, a perceived object shifts its position on the retina, yet, subjectively, we experience the object as remaining in the same place. If, however, the eye muscles are experimentally paralysed with curare, an attempt to shift the gaze results in a subjective sense of the room spinning round. In schizophrenia, Frith argues, there is a central nervous abnormality which prevents these corollary discharges from getting through to their appropriate receptors, so that our subliminal speech is heard in the form of hallucinatory voices, and our actions appear to be directed from outside. Such a failure in self-monitoring could well be a component of the spiritual awakening and 'Damascene shift' characteristic of the prophet. His new ideas and beliefs seem to come from outside and are attributed to the direct intervention of God.

An adaptive response: the meaningful delusion

The delusional formation, which we take to be the pathological product, is in reality an attempt at recovery, a process of reconstruction.   Sigmund Freud

The evolutionary approach to a psychiatric symptom, such as a delusion, is not to consider it first and foremost as an affliction or 'illness', but as an adaptive response to challenges arising from the environment. One researcher who has considered delusions from this standpoint is Glenn Roberts (1991).

Roberts discerns a sequence of three phases in the development of a delusion. In the first phase, the individual is subject to some deeply perplexing experience produced by one or more of a number of recognized 'predisposing factors', for example, job insecurity, emotionally stressful personal relationships, fears of hostile neighbours, etc. A delusion begins to form during the second phase as the individual tries to make sense of what is happening. 'The attribution of meaning to this experience', writes Roberts, 'brings relief, for there is a basic need to make sense of one's condition, and the worse the conditions are the greater is this need.' In the third phase the delusion is elaborated and built into a stable belief system, and the condition becomes 'chronic'.

That the new belief system becomes lastingly established is due to the mental and emotional relief as well as the security that it brings. As a result, the individual very understandably clings to it, defends it with stubborn determination, and is vigilant in protecting it from erosion. Moreover, so satisfying do delusional systems become that clinically psychotic people can firmly reject the notion that they are mad, having achieved the conviction of actually *knowing* the truth – a truth which has played a decisive role in curing the sufferings of their pre-psychotic state. In this manner, they enter a final phase which Roberts calls 'pseudo-sanity'. This is accompanied by a subjective perception of having attained insight and comprehension. But, from the clinical standpoint, individuals who have achieved this happy state have become psychotic.

So the achievement of what to the patient is an entirely satisfactory explanation of his circumstances, can be seen as both a victory and a defeat. At one level it is adaptive, in that it seeks to promote survival of the self through the construction of a fundamentally altered view of reality. But the down side is the social price that the 'successfully' deluded subject pays in the form of psychotic isolation – unless he can find others who are prepared to share his newly created beliefs.

The development of hallucinations may pass through a similar sequence as delusions and possess the same adaptive function. Here again, a protective factor against their leading to psychotic isolation could be the presence of people willing to accept the value of their content – as we saw in the case of Sara, whose experiences were endorsed by her vicar.

But even when deluded individuals have no community to share their beliefs they seem to be better off than 'recovered' schizophrenics who have been cured of their delusions. The chronically deluded patients in Roberts's study were found to have a very high level of perceived meaning and purpose in life and low levels of depression and suicidal inclination, in contrast to a comparable group of chronic schizophrenic patients in remission. How much better would they have fared, one wonders, had they been surrounded by a group of adoring followers who enthusiastically endorsed their delusions as representing ultimate and absolute truth.

Only one of Roberts's deluded patients recovered during the course of his study, and this was a man who had previously developed an elaborate delusional system centred on believing in himself as the Messiah. He said: 'I liked to imagine it because I felt so useless without it ... I still feel inadequate now – it's as though I don't know anything. I always felt everything I said was worthless, but as Jesus everything I said was important – it came from God ... [But subsequently] I just wanted to hide away, I don't feel able to cope with people ... I always feel lonely, I don't know what to say.' In the potentially fertile field of cult formation this was a wasted opportunity, a sad instance of messianic seed falling on stony ground.

For John Nash it was the same story. Having felt himself privy to cosmic, even divine, insights, his recovery of rational thinking, which his wife and colleagues greeted as a tremendous improvement, was experienced by him as a personal impoverishment. After receiving his Nobel Prize, he wrote that 'rational thought imposes a limit on a person's concept of his relation to the cosmos' and reported that his periods of remission from acute psychotic episodes were not for him welcome returns to health and normality but 'enforced interludes of rationality' (Nasar, 1998, p. 295).

Though Roberts's description of the phases of delusion formation may fit many cases, it must be acknowledged that in numerous instances the process is extremely sudden and occurs in a flash. In our own culture, the best known example of this is the sudden, dramatic conversion of St Paul on the road to Damascus. Many people have reported similar experiences and, as we have noted, practically all prophets and messiahs claim to have had them. The phenomenon is invariably reported to have possessed a hugely impressive quality which the religious philosopher Rudolf Otto (1917) described as *numinous* – a term he used to designate the sense of awe and wonder engendered by the presence of the sacred.

The onset of a religious delusion is experienced almost like a sudden 'attack' as if one has been overwhelmed by some tremendous outside force. Immediately, everything assumes a heightened sense of importance, and is accompanied by an intoxicating sense that one has been granted awareness of an eternal truth possessing enormous power. One *knows* oneself to be the instrument of some suprahuman energy, that one has been called to perform a special mission that it would be a sinful dereliction to deny. It is not surprising that in these circumstances one should feel impelled to proclaim oneself, to proselytize, and to preach. One's destiny is then determined by the people one encounters and whether or not they have 'ears to hear'.

Was Jesus mad?

Many of them said, 'He has a demon, he is mad, why listen to him?'   *John*, 10:20

For Western civilization the prototype of the charismatic leader who founded a cult which, through the lottery of history, became a world religion is Jesus of Nazareth. The accounts of his life which have come down to us in the Gospels portray him as a sane man with special gifts as a healer, orator and religious teacher. However, on one occasion, according to St Matthew, a conversation occurred which had such a powerful effect on Jesus that it transformed Jesus's conception of his role, completely changing his behaviour and his teaching. It was to shape the course of history for the next two thousand years.

During a discussion in which his disciples irritate him by misunderstanding his teaching and speculating whether he could be one of the old prophets come again, Peter has a sudden insight, and exclaims: *'Thou art the Christ, the son of the living God.'* This instantly triggers a state of high excitement in Jesus, who declares that Peter has received a revelation direct from God. He makes a pun on Peter's name, and decrees that he shall be the founder of his Church.

Henceforth, Jesus is convinced of his own divinity, and his followers accept this as fact. Like other 'dying gods' before him – Osiris, Dionysus and numerous others – he prophesies that he will be killed and buried, but will rise again and return to earth within the lifetime of those present to establish his kingdom on earth. He also adapts the ancient tribal ceremony of 'eating the god' by blessing bread and wine, telling the disciples that it is his body and his blood and that they must eat it and drink it in memory of him.

On his arrival in Jerusalem he is arrested as a troublemaker for creating a riot by driving the money lenders out of the temple and reviling the priests and elders in outrageous terms. He offers no resistance to the authorities who detain him because he accepts that it is his destiny to be executed and to rise again, though he says that if he wanted to escape he could summon twelve million angels to his aid. His total conviction as to his identity, his role, and his mission, sustains him through the most appalling torments of mockery, scourging and crucifixion. It is only after many hours of agony and thirst on the cross that he dies with the cry, 'My God, why hast thou forsaken me?'

The story is so familiar to us, repeated for generations in schools, chapels and churches, and so gloriously celebrated in the artistic and architectural achievements of our culture, that it does not stretch our incredulity as much as it might had we grown up in a quite different society. But if we attempt to stand outside the cultural indoctrination we have received, Jesus and his followers look very much like any other charismatic leader with his cult, and it is legitimate to enquire whether Jesus was schizophrenic.

On the face of it, his sudden declaration that he was God made flesh, that his body and blood were miraculous food for his disciples to consume in order to guarantee their salvation, that his ritual torture and assassination were necessary preliminaries to his resurrection and Second Coming among falling stars and heavenly trumpets, is not the discourse of a man with his feet set firmly on the ground of empirical reality. Yet he said many wise things as well, and the image of the man that emerges from the Gospel according to St Luke has won the hearts and minds of many reared outside the Christian tradition.

Some have argued that before the Renaissance and the Enlightenment, when belief in spirits and outside supernatural influences was general, the pronouncements of prophets would have inspired less incredulity, and their message would have seemed less bizarre or 'cognitively dissonant', in such societies than they do in our own. Indeed, prophetic experience and utterance is expected in such communities. It is therefore plausible to argue that the same charismatic teacher in the grip of a delusional system may be revered as a prophet in his own time or land and classified as a schizophrenic in ours.

One such authority is Edward F. Foulks (1977), who has suggested that, although schizophrenia endows sufferers with no advantages in contemporary social conditions, it may have done in the ancestral environment, when the experience of being subject to outside influences was accepted as entirely valid. To support this view Foulks points to the similar histories that are typical of both schizophrenics and prophets. Like people destined to become schizophrenic, future prophets begin to manifest in adolescence certain psychological and behavioural characteristics which set them apart from other people – a tendency to introversion and a liking for solitude, absent-mindedness, a propensity towards dreams and visions, and a somewhat nervous, excitable or unpredictable temperament. Moreover, a patient with the acute 'reactive' type of schizophrenia resembles a prophet undergoing a sudden 'epiphanic realization', an 'awakening' – often characterized by hallucinations and the emergence of what an impartial observer might plausibly regard as a delusional belief

44

system. On the basis of this argument, Jesus could be seen as a schizophrenic whom history has celebrated as an instrument of the Divine Will and has not dismissed him as a madman in view of the time at which he lived and because of the abiding devotion of his faithful followers.

However, there is a flaw in Foulks's argument. While some prophets both in industrial and pre-industrial societies clearly satisfy the criteria for a diagnosis of schizophrenia, a great many do not. All may indeed experience hallucinations and undergo a radical revolution in their beliefs but these in themselves are not diagnostic of schizophrenia. With the very evident exception of crazy characters like 'the saintly madmen of Bengal', whom we shall meet in a later chapter, few prophets display the 'negative' symptoms so characteristic of the condition – the emotional blunting, the poverty of speech and expression, the lack of drive and willpower, the apathetic loss of all sense of purpose or direction. On the contrary, as careful and detailed studies of contemporary prophets have shown, they possess 'extraordinary energy', are extremely generous with their time and the attention they give to their followers, and are incorrigibly fluent and loquacious (Oakes, 1997). This appears to have been as true of Jesus as it was of his more recent exemplars, and these qualities are the complete obverse of those one would look for in making a diagnosis of schizophrenia.

Moreover, in all pre-industrial societies where the occurrence of psychosis has been surveyed, it is found that the concept of insanity does indeed exist. Everywhere it seems, people make a distinction between the madman and the prophet, and it is not true that in some cultures the insane are rewarded and assigned special roles, such as shaman, prophet, or medicine man. One Eskimo made the distinction very neatly: 'When the shaman is healing he is out of his mind,' he said, 'but he is not *crazy*.' Naturally, there are some shamans or prophets who are mad, but the same can be said about psychiatrists. It is not a necessary condition for the job.

To take advantage of abnormal states of mind in the manner of a shaman or a prophet demands that he should be capable of making realistic appraisals of the needs of the people around him and the effects that his abnormal behaviour is having on them (Torrey, 1980).

It is this that Jesus, and other charismatic figures like him, was particularly good at and that schizophrenics conspicuously fail to do.

How then can we account for the similarities which exist between the prophetic and schizophrenic conditions? Are they purely coincidental? Do they have nothing in common at all? Judged from an evolutionary standpoint, this seems unlikely. That prophets share some of the 'positive' symptomatology of schizophrenia suggests that some similar propensity is at work. Prophets are not like everyone else. They are everywhere regarded as special. But equally they are not, on the whole, schizophrenic. It would seem reasonable to suppose that they reside on some continuum between schizophrenia and normality. This conclusion would imply that if the prophet is not entirely normal, and is not schizophrenic either, there could exist some other psychiatric category in which he might, without suffering the fate of Procrustes, be fitted.

3

Spacing Out

A Natural History of the Prophet

I will raise them up a Prophet from among their brethren, like
unto thee, and will put my words into his mouth: and he shall
speak unto them all that I command him.

Deuteronomy, 18:18

People with spacing disorders all have a major characteristic in
common: they have difficulty forming and maintaining personal
relationships and in functioning appropriately in their social group.
They tend to deal with these social difficulties by adopting a strategy
of withdrawal. Withdrawal effectively removes them from the social
arena and puts them in an alternative space of their own making.

This alternative, private space may have a geographical location
(such as a hermitage, a desert island, a cave, a monastic cell, or the
secure ward of a psychiatric unit) or it may have a psychological
location – a 'walled citadel' so to speak – within themselves. It is true
to say, therefore, that people with these disorders have crossed the
social boundary which contains all other members of their group, and
have moved into 'outer' (or 'inner') space. An alternative strategy
used by many is to 'space out' through the use of drugs and, in this
sense, drug addiction may be looked upon as a spacing disorder. But
what is of greater interest for our inquiry is the form of spacing out
adopted by prophets and their cults. These individuals may, of course,
use drugs, but usually they find such behaviour unnecessary for they
are sufficiently intoxicated by the apocalyptic vision of their guru and
their shared dedication to his cause.

A fundamental attribute of the human mind, when confronted by
an assortment of facts, is its tendency to split things into opposites.
Thus, in addition to viewing human populations in terms of their

willingness to affiliate on the one hand and compete on the other (Empedocles' love and strife), we may also understand them in terms of their tendency either to concentrate within a confined area or to spread out over a large one.

Social gregariousness was first systematically investigated by Sir Francis Galton (1822-1911). He concluded that patterns of gregariousness evolved through natural selection for the reason that individuals who lived in groups would be less at risk from predators than those who lived in solitude. But there were critical limits of degree. Too close gregariousness would result in overcrowding and destructive disputes over territory and mates, while groups becoming too widely scattered would not provide adequate defence. This balance between *affiliation* which is too close and *isolation* which is too great is one that individuals and all groups continuously strive to maintain.

A fundamental tension between individuality and relatedness seems to have persisted throughout the course of evolution. Many observers have noted the emergence of individual personality types specializing in one or other of these directions. C.G. Jung's distinction between introverted and extraverted psychological types is probably the best known and most widely accepted of these. When exaggerated, these orientations can result in psychiatric disorders which can be broadly classified as 'spacing' and 'linking' disorders. For example, *fear of closeness* in introverted types may turn into 'spacing disorders' (such as schizoid, schizotypal, and paranoid personality disorders, as well as schizophrenia), while *fear of distancing* (loss, isolation, rejection and abandonment), in extraverted types can lead to 'linking disorders' (such as depression, anxiety and obsessive compulsive disorders). Linking disorders affect vulnerable people who still experience themselves as committed members of their social group but who suffer from a subjective prediction that they will fail in competing for those two invaluable social resources: love and esteem (Stevens and Price, 2000). This tension between opposing tendencies towards linking and spacing was of particular interest to the late R.D. Laing (1960), who held it responsible for the induction of psychosis – the fear of being 'engulfed' driving the individual over the borderline into psychotic isolation.

Probably a continuum exists between those who are reasonably adjusted to their status as members of their group and those who, for whatever reason, feel compelled to withdraw from it. (Along this continuum lie individuals whose relative degree of withdrawal can result in them being diagnosed as having borderline, paranoid, schizoid or schizotypal personalities.) At the extreme end of the spacing continuum lie those who become frankly schizophrenic. Prophets, gurus, and charismatic leaders are highly represented among these spacing personality types. Although a few of them may fit precisely into one diagnostic category, the majority show traits which, from time to time, may fit any or all of them.

On the borderline

Almost by definition, charismatic leaders are unpredictable, for they are bound by neither tradition nor rules; they are not answerable to other human beings.   Eileen Barker

The *borderline* concept has had a vexed and turbulent history. It first arose in psychoanalytic circles in the United States, where it was argued that borderline disorders represented a halfway stage in the disintegration of the personality in the course of its decline into schizophrenia. Such diagnostic terms as 'pseudoneurotic schizophrenia', and 'borderline schizophrenia' were used to describe people who were emotionally unstable and unpredictable and displayed a poor sense of identity. They tended to indulge in a rich and somewhat bizarre fantasy life, and to make use of the ego-defence mechanism known as 'splitting', whereby contrary feelings, such as love and hate, could be sustained for the same person. While many were lonely and depressed, others managed to form personal relationships, though these characteristically tended to be of a dependent or dominant rather than a reciprocal nature. Usually they were more socially and sexually active than schizophrenics, though their work and educational records tended to be similarly poor. Moreover, some were observed to have occasional, if brief, episodes of psychosis, and many displayed other schizophrenia-like characteristics such as an inability to experience pleasure, the display of eccentric behaviour, and odd or bizarre patterns of thought.

It was difficult to decide whether such patients were to be classified as neurotic or psychotic. Broadly speaking, neurosis is the term applied to a group of psychiatric disorders which, however severe, do not involve hallucinations, delusions, or loss of insight; while psychosis covers those severe disorders in which hallucinations and delusions do occur in people with relatively poor insight into their condition. It thus seemed that they lived in a no man's land between the two conditions.

The English psychologist Peter Chadwick (1992) has given a graphic account of his own journey from the borderline to the schizophrenic state. He says he reached a critical point where he felt himself to be in touch with 'a presence' – 'an awe-inspiring force, which existed, now, as if behind a thin membrane. Any sense of ego or identity was gone, I was a *vehicle*, a channel, my existence was "vehicular". Psychosis this was not, at least not yet. For example, there was no Messiah delusion: "A Christ could be said to *accompany* the world, but not a Borderliner," I penned. But there was none the less a sense of unearthly knowledge and of joy that pervaded me at this time – objectivity and ecstasy were now fused. My religiosity, such as it was, magnified a thousandfold. The Lord's Prayer resonated and thundered through my mind. I felt I had been given a spiritual mission of the utmost importance. I could "see to infinity", I had reached a zone where "the life system" was strangely making contact, through me, with "the not-of-this-life system" – as indeed maybe it was.'

When someone develops a psychiatric disorder, what determines whether they become neurotic, psychotic or 'borderline'? And if they are driven over the borderline, what determines the form that the psychosis takes? The answer that psychiatrists invariably give is that combinations of factors are involved, including genetics, early conditioning, traumatic events and the character structure of the individual. The evolutionary psychiatrist Brant Wenegrat (1984) has suggested that a psychosis is in many ways like a fever. Just as fever assumes different forms according to the underlying disease process (in, for example, malaria, lobar pneumonia, or tuberculosis), so psychosis assumes different forms according to the psychopathology of the individual. Thus the term 'borderline personality disorder' has come to be applied to people whose abnormal personalities combine features of both neurotic and psychotic symptomatology, without being clearly assignable to either category.

The schizotypal personality – with a touch of paranoia

He that is not with me is against me.   *Matthew*, 12:30

Refinement of the borderline concept came with the work of Spitzer and his colleagues (1979), who conducted a nationwide survey of the diagnostic practices of American psychiatrists in their use of the term 'borderline personality disorder'. On the basis of this survey they felt they could distinguish two major forms of usage. One emphasized schizophrenia-like characteristics, such as eccentric behaviour, odd beliefs, and disordered thought patterns, which they classified as 'schizotypal personality disorder'. The other stressed signs of emotional instability, such as impulsiveness, hostility, and self injury, which they categorized as 'borderline personality disorder'. In our view, the distinction between these two disorders is determined by the fact that a person with a borderline disorder is still operating within the boundaries of the group, whereas someone with schizotypal disorder is crossing the border and may even have crossed beyond it.

Both disorders are conspicuous among prophets. The majority exhibit signs of schizotypal disorder, particularly in their inability to form close reciprocal relationships, their proneness to unusual perceptual experiences, their odd beliefs, thought patterns and speech, their eccentric behaviour and appearance, their suspiciousness and tendency to paranoid ideas. Those who do not involve themselves in founding a cult survive by persisting in a strategy of detachment – namely, detachment from the need for emotional support, and detachment from the need for status. It is as if the outer world ceases to be of much account for them and the inner world comes to supplant it. In this way they may avoid crossing the brink of psychosis. For someone with a schizotypal personality, the borderline is a tightrope, along which he walks with relative impunity, by dint of keeping himself very much to himself – unless he founds a cult.

In addition, many charismatic leaders display paranoid traits, in

51

that they suspect, without sufficient basis, that others are hostile to them and exploiting, harming or otherwise deceiving them. They read hidden meanings (usually threatening to their status) into innocent remarks or benign events, and perceive attacks on their reputation that are not apparent to others. They are consequently quick to take exception and to react with anger or rage. Paranoid people experience themselves as existing in a permanent state of siege and may compensate for this by entertaining fantasies of exercising exceptional power and rank, which, when implemented in reality, can provide them with the necessary energy and determination to establish and rule a cult. When they succeed, they readily develop a negative stereotype of the wider social group. Such attitudes, if persisted in and affirmed by loyal followers, can tip the schizotypal leader over the brink into insanity, and this, it seems, is what happened to Jim Jones, David Koresh and Shoko Asahara. Although the existence of disciples can apparently protect many prophets from becoming mad, there are clear instances when the reverse is the case, and this seems to be particularly true when the prophet's paranoid delusions infect the whole community and bring them collectively into conflict with the surrounding society. The most dangerous prophets are those whose schizotypal personality is seasoned with a powerful dose of paranoia.[1]

The distinction that psychiatry makes between schizotypal and schizoid personality disorders would effectively exclude the majority of charismatic leaders from the latter category. Schizoid personalities are marked by a more rigid pattern of detachment from social relationships, a more restricted range of emotional expression, and more dedicated determination to pursue solitary activities. In keeping with their aloof detachment and emotional frostiness, they appear quite indifferent to the praise or criticism of others. Their primary need in life is to be left alone to get on with their inner preoccupations, which, if they are gifted, can result in scientific or philosophical discoveries of epoch-making importance. Isaac Newton, René Descartes and Albert Einstein are examples of this type. Schizoid personalities can be intellectual virtuosi, but their extreme detachment means they lack the craving for adulation so characteristic of the majority of charismatic leaders. To the purely schizoid type, the demands of emotionally and ideologically hungry followers would be utterly intolerable.

The schizotypal Narcissus

Nobody understands me!   Charles Manson

It is the craving for adulation which has caused some authorities to stress the narcissistic qualities of prophets rather than their very evident schizotypal traits. Interest in the narcissistic personality was stimulated in the 1970s by the American psychoanalyst Heinz Kohut (1971, 1977), whose opaque writings on the subject are so difficult to digest that one is grateful to A.M. Seigel (1996) for providing a coherent account of them. The most striking features of people with narcissistic personality disorder are the grandiose sense of self-importance, an insatiable hunger for admiration, and a regular indulgence in fantasies of unlimited success, power, brilliance, beauty, or ideal love. Narcissists tend to believe they are unique and 'special', and they have a strong 'sense of entitlement', in that they entertain unreasonable expectations of especially favourable treatment from others and an automatic compliance with their wishes. Their need for approval renders them extremely vulnerable to criticism, which can cause them painful feelings of humiliation and inferiority, as well as driving them to respond with rage and vindictiveness. Being acutely aware of their own needs, they commonly demand special favours without feeling obliged to give anything in return. Not unexpectedly, they are bad at forming deep and lasting relationships because others experience them as exploitative, demanding, and arrogant. As a consequence, if they become leaders, they relate to their followers from a position of authority: they are élitist, anti-democratic, and domineering.

Although Kohut fails to adopt an evolutionary perspective, and does not acknowledge the contribution of schizotypy to charismatic leadership, he has drawn attention to the importance of parental *mirroring* in the development of both narcissistic and charismatic personalities. By 'mirroring' he refers to the way in which parents feed back to the child delight and pride in its activities. Strong parental approval enables the child to form a self-concept as being

53

valued in the eyes of others. As Freud memorably wrote when recollecting his own childhood, 'He who has been the undisputed darling of his mother retains throughout life that victorious feeling, that confidence in ultimate success, which not seldom brings actual success with it.' Paul Gilbert (1989) has suggested that in eliciting positive mirroring from the parents, the child learns to control the attention of others – acquiring the capacity to attract positive attention to the self through the display of talent, unusual abilities, or physical appeal. Thus, the parents are the first bestowers of status and what Gilbert calls 'social attention holding power', and it is as if narcissistic personalities have become arrested at this stage of development. Other people are treated as if they were parent figures whose function is to provide a constant and unending bonanza of love, admiration, and praise.

Exhibitionism, which is characteristic of the narcissist, as well as many prophets and gurus, is also a normal constituent of peer group relationships in childhood. The function of parents is not just to enhance self-value but to give a child the confidence to be assertive, to show off, and to take a lead in peer group interactions. Successful passage through this stage leads to the capacity to be socially effective in later adult life.

Narcissistic disorders arise from damage to the emerging self-image at these early stages of development. Parents can, for example, reflect to their children an inflated view of their beauty and accomplishments with the result that their self-esteem receives a series of blows when tested in the harsh market-place of peer relations. Damaged individuals compensate by trying to maintain self-esteem through fantasies of power and success while trying to hold in check their feelings of inferiority. Driven by the desire for status and approval, they entertain the painful expectation that others will humiliate rather than praise them, because they do not possess the qualities that others value.

Since their exaggerated need for praise and approval is seldom adequately met, they tend to switch to an assertive, authoritarian mode, to satisfy their emotional hunger by manipulating and controlling others. The anxiety from which people with narcissistic disorder are trying to escape is the fear of being found out, humiliated and demoted. Their profoundly self-centred feelings of entitlement mean that they are usually poor reciprocators and, when they sense they can get away with it, are prone to adopt a 'free-rider' strategy in their dealings with others. This is apparent in those cult leaders who use trickery, lies, and special pleading to acquire the demonstrations of love, attention, and reverence which they could never receive from the world outside.

The prophetic career

I have heard of thee by the hearing of the ear: but now mine eye seeth thee.   *Job*, 42:5

One authority who has applied Kohutian insights to the psychology of prophets is Len Oakes (1997). His book *Prophetic Charisma: The Psychology of Revolutionary Personalities* is based on interviews he carried out with fifteen charismatic prophets and almost two hundred of their followers. At the time of writing, three of his prophets were in jail for major criminal offences. In addition, Oakes studied the biographies of such prophets as Jim Jones, Bhagwan Shree Rajneesh, L. Ron Hubbard, Chuck Dederich, Werner Erhard, Fritz Perls, David 'Moses' Berg, Katheryn Kuhlman, Father Divine and J.H. Noyes. Occasionally he drew on material from the lives of charismatic political leaders such as Adolf Hitler, Winston Churchill and Mahondas Gandhi. Numerically, successful male charismatic leaders prevail over female. Oakes intended to study female charismatics but they proved difficult to find. Other authorities have reached a similar conclusion (Willner, 1984; Zablocki, 1980).

On the basis of this extensive investigation, Oakes detected what he describes as the 'natural history of the charismatic prophet', which he sees as passing through five stages: (1) early narcissism, (2) incubation, (3) awakening, (4) mission and (5) decline or fall.

(1) *Early narcissism*: All the examples Oakes studied gave a history of care-taking from an excessively devoted parent-figure. In every case, Oakes believes, this relationship provided the child with an inappropriate defence against reality, trapping him in an infantile mode of adjustment which distorted his subsequent social development. As a result, the future prophet feels driven to recreate the dynamics of this 'early narcissistic relationship' through the uncriti-

cal, unqualified devotion of followers. The adoption of a 'divine' role, through a personal identification with the archetype of the Divine Child, becomes a means to this end.

(2) *Incubation*: Perplexed by the indifference shown to him by others, the emerging narcissistic adult comes to the conclusion that there must be something 'very special' about him and something 'very wrong' with the world. This realization goes along with a sense of not belonging to any group, the construction of a personal 'myth of calling', and the acquisition of the ideology and practical skills appropriate to his future career as a prophet.

(3) *Awakening*: This occurs with the mystical experience, divine revelation ('hierophantic realization') which is the pivotal event in the biography of every charismatic prophet. The word prophet comes from the Greek *pro* = for and *phētēs* = speaker. Thus a prophet is one who speaks for someone, namely God. God's intervention solves the major problems of his life by bringing about a radical reassessment of himself in relation to the world. Henceforth, the prophet assumes the mantle of God's messenger.

(4) *Mission*: Convinced of the supreme importance of his divinely ordained role, the prophet sets out to recruit disciples. It is necessary for him to possess and display extraordinary qualities at this stage. The passion with which he asserts his conviction that he is the Saviour who can lead his followers to the Promised Land must be so powerful as to fascinate his listeners and arouse faith, hope and love in their hearts. In Oakes's view, he needs to impress them with the suprahuman aura of the mystic – 'a creative freedom, turbulence of thought, and a wildness of mood' together with 'novel perceptions and experiences' (all qualities which we can recognize as characteristic of schizotypal rather than narcissistic personalities).

(5) *Decline or fall*: 'From Jesus to Jonestown, the most consistent thing about prophets has been their failure', declares Oakes. The motive for the prophet's success – the need to satisfy the emotional hunger of 'his narcissistically closed world' – contains the seeds of its own destruction. The remorseless pressure of having to sustain the divine role, the failure to consult, delegate, or befriend, the lack of genuine empathy, and the unrealistic estimates of his own abilities, virtually doom him from the start.

In assessing their fate, Oakes makes a useful distinction between two types of of cult leader: the messiah and the prophet, the latter being possessed of greater charisma that the former. The messiah tends to be realistic in his dealings with society, seldom comes into conflict with the law and accepts the decline of his influence and power. The charismatic prophet, by contrast, rejects society, often gets into major legal difficulties (he may end up being jailed or crucified) and tends to hang on to power as long as he can. This corresponds closely to Max Weber's concept of genuine or primary charisma.

In terms of our group-splitting hypothesis, it is the highly charismatic prophet who defects with his followers from the traditional group while the messiah continues to function within it. 'The charismatic type is trying to express something that is fundamentally opposed to *any* order,' comments Oakes, 'something primitive, nascent and unrestrained. This leads charismatics into conflict with convention frequently and disastrously.' As a result, under contemporary social conditions charismatic cults have a high failure rate whereas messianic cults stand a somewhat better chance of survival, since their leader may take care to put a properly structured administration in place before he or she dies. Examples of such organizations are those set up by Mme Blavatsky, founder of the Theosophical Society, Mrs Baker Eddy, founder of the Church of Christ Scientist, Phineas Quimby, the metaphysical healer and founder of New Thought, Kathryn Kuhlman, Father Divine, founder of the Peace Mission, Ann Lee, founder of the Shakers, Prabhupada Bhaktivedanta, founder of the International Society for Krishna Consciousness (the Hare Krishnas), Joseph Smith, founder of the Mormons and Mohammed, the Prophet of Islam. It is noteworthy that women are much more numerous among messianic leaders (and are more likely to bequeath viable communes of belief and practice) than they are among charismatic prophets.

The Bhagwan

Shoes and minds to be left here.
Notice outside the Bhagwan's Lecture Hall

One of the many charismatic prophets who illustrates the stages described by Oakes is Bhagwan Shree Rajneesh (1931-90). He had been brought up in a small town in Madhya Pradesh by adoring grandparents. So graceful and captivating a child was he that his grandfather swore he must have been a king in a previous life, and called him 'Raja' (hence 'Rajneesh').

When Rajneesh was only 7, his grandfather died, and this tragedy was to affect him for the rest of his life. His grandfather was, he said, the only person he ever really loved, and he was so traumatized by his grandfather's loss that he had never been able to form a close attachment to any other human being: 'Aloneness became my nature', Rajneesh recalled. 'His death freed me forever from all relationships. His death became for me the death of all attachments. Thereafter I could not establish a bond of relationship with anyone ... Afterwards I came to feel that this close observation of death at a tender age became a blessing in disguise for me. If such a death had occurred at a later stage, perhaps I would have found other substitutes for my grandfather. If I had become interested in the other I would have lost the opportunity to journey towards the self. I became a sort of stranger to others. Generally it is at this stage that we become related to the other – when we are admitted into society. That is the age when we are initiated, so to speak, by the society which wants to absorb us. But I have never been initiated into society. I entered as an individual and I have remained aloof and separate like an island' (Laxmi, 1980, pp. 12-13).

His parents assumed responsibility for his upbringing, but he was a difficult, solitary, yet rebellious child. Though undeniably bright, he was constantly in disciplinary trouble at school, leading other children into mischief, and getting himself branded as a habitual liar. He was, however, a voracious reader, and became knowledgeable in the tenets of Eastern religion and Western philosophy. On graduating from high school in 1951, he entered Hitkarini College in Jabalpur, but proved so argumentative, and so arrogantly dismissive of his teachers, that he was compelled to leave. He then seems to have had a 'creative illness' of the type we shall examine later in this chapter. He stopped eating, suffered from terrible headaches, and lost all confidence in himself. Convinced that he was mentally ill, his parents took him to an Ayurvedic practitioner, who sensibly advised them that Rajneesh was suffering an important personal crisis from which he would eventually recover.

And so it proved to be. Rajneesh could date the moment of his recovery as occurring on 21st March 1953, when he became 'mad with blissfulness'. He described this as his 'enlightenment': 'everything became luminous, alive and beautiful.' As a result of this 'awakening', Rajneesh proceeded to acquire the necessary qualifications to become an assistant professor in philosophy at the university that originally rejected him as a student. He was a charismatic lecturer and began travelling around India speaking to large audiences, who were both fascinated and appalled by him. Though he was capable of saying wise and interesting things, he also caused deep offence by outraging conventional opinion, as when he attacked Mother Theresa as a fraud, accused Mahatma Gandhi of being a sexual pervert, and himself used sexually explicit and scatological language.

His teaching, based on his encyclopaedic reading and on what he claimed he had learnt in previous incarnations, was a mélange of Buddhism, Hinduism, Christianity and Mohammedism, and he presented it so attractively that it drew disciples (*sannyasins*) to him. In 1971 he gave himself the title *Bhagwan*, which means 'blessed one' or 'incarnation of God'. Storr thinks there is little doubt that Rajneesh believed in his own divinity, for like other prophets in that state of mind, he considered his hair and nail clippings to be sacred relics to be presented to his faithful *sannyasins* in specially made little boxes.[2] This could also be seen as a manifestation of his narcissism – as was his concern that every photograph of himself should be carefully posed and lit so as to bring out his best features.

Throughout the 1970s his fame spread and people came from all over the world to join the ashram he set up in Poona. From 1974 onwards about 6,000 followers would be in residence at any one time and about 30,000 visitors came every year. This was big business: it made a profit of up to $200,000 a month, and Rajneesh began to grow rich. In 1981 he moved to the United States, in order to evade Indian taxes, and bought the second largest ranch in Oregon (over 64,000 acres) for nearly $6 million. Here he set up a new ashram, Rajneeshpuram. Of the 2,500 *sannyasins* who took up permanent residence there (and the further 2,000 who came on protracted visits), the majority were white, middle-class, college educated and in their late 20s or early 30s. Rajneesh taught that it was not possible to be both poor and religious, and unashamedly proclaimed himself to be a rich man's guru.

The very success of Rajneeshpuram had two disastrous consequences: it brought the community into conflict with the local population and led to the rapid mental and physical deterioration of the Bhagwan himself. Like many other prophets, he became corrupted by wealth, power, self-indulgence and greed. Dosing himself on Valium and inhalations of nitrous oxide, he increasingly devoted his time to watching trashy videos, collecting Rolls Royces, platinum watches, and – as paranoia began to get the better of him – assault rifles and automatic carbines. Because of his growing incapacity, day-to-day management of the ashram was taken over by one of his closest and most trusted *sannyasins*, the sinister and egregious Sheela. Sheela not only assumed the powers of an absolute dictator, but shared the Bhagwan's growing paranoia to the point where their relationship could be considered a form of *folie à deux* (a relation where a psychotic individual convincces a non-psychotic companion to share his or her beliefs). In a manner reminiscent of Jim Jones in Guyana, and in anticipation of David Koresh in Texas, the security of the ranch was tightened and the stockpile of lethal weapons increased. A special Rajneeshpuram police force was created, residents were forbidden to leave the ranch, telephones were tapped and rooms bugged so as to detect potential traitors within the commune. Residents who proved restive were given powerful sedatives in their food. When a local election threatened to return candidates hostile to the ashram's building plans, Sheela and her henchmen caused a salmonella outbreak in the general population by deliberately infecting food in salad bars and restaurants. For these and other crimes, Sheela was arrested and after a much-publicized trial sentenced to a long term in jail. Rajneesh was able to do a deal with the US authorities and escaped to India. 'He ended, as he had begun,' comments Storr (1996), 'isolated, narcissistic and unable to relate to anyone on equal terms at any ordinary human level.' When the time came to abdicate from his responsibislities as Bhagwan of Rajneeshpuram, he seemed almost thankful: 'I am so relieved that I don't have to pretend to be enlightened any more,' he told his bodyguard, Hugh Milne. 'Poor Krishnamurti – he still has to pretend.'

3. Spacing Out

Is narcissism enough?

Just imagine you believe someone is Jesus Christ. He can tell you anything. If you argue, you go to Hell. He's the Son of God. Who wants to fight against God?
Marc Breault, a disciple of David Koresh

Oakes's description of the charismatic prophets in his investigative study, as well as his analysis of the 'natural history' of their career, provides valuable information and some penetrating insights. But his attempt to explain their most salient characteristics in terms of Kohut's psychology of narcissism fails because it leaves out too much. Like Freud and Melanie Klein, Kohut was quite prepared to attribute to infants and young children his own ideas or fantasies about what they were actually experiencing. Because he was so heavily committed to constructing a theoretical edifice entirely on the basis of these imaginative projections, he overlooked the central role of evolution in providing the innate structures on which the human personality develops.

In Kohut's view, the entire life cycle of the individual is organized by a programme laid down in 'the nuclear self' during infancy. As a result, what Oakes accurately describes as 'the fundamentally different, seemingly alien psychology' of prophets is entirely attributed to the 'magical mind-set they retain from childhood'. This ignores the possibility that the fundamental difference apparent in prophets could be the expression of a genetic predisposition. In fact, many of the descriptive features which Oakes would like us to see as illustrative of disordered narcissism are more compatible with several other diagnoses (including hypomanic, schizotypal, paranoid, and anti-social personality disorders). Thus he singles out for our attention the grandiose self-confidence of charismatic leaders, 'sustained by a faith in themselves and their god that verges on the deranged', their 'delusions of omnipotence and refusal to compromise or hear criticisms', their absolute 'fixation on a *revolutionary vision*' (Oakes's italics), their capacity 'to immerse themselves in their ideals so totally', their paranormal, almost clairvoyant insights into the minds and hearts of those around them, tempered by a self-contained autonomy that seems to need little or nothing from others, their committed, all-or-nothing quality which drives them in the direction of two options: 'success through strength or destruction through defeat, suicide or psychosis. Such leaders may be quite paranoid ...' Paraphrasing Kohut, he says that because of their grandiosity and lack of self-doubt prophets seldom seek therapy – unless forced to do so 'because of having been compromised by various fraudulent or sexually perverse behaviours'. In this way he subsumes abnormal traits characteristic of spacing and anti-social disorders under the portmanteau of disordered narcissism which both he and Kohut consider to be the fundamental characteristic of charismatic leaders.

The most valuable aspect of Oakes's study is the attention he draws to the role of *early* narcissism in the creation of the prophet – the Kohutian notion that parental worship during infancy and early childhood creates an exaggerated need for expressions of love and devotion which persists into adulthood. Charismatic leaders are not merely narcissistic personalities, nor can they be entirely accounted for in terms of a genetic loading for schizotypy. It is undeniable that a great many of them display paranoid and schizotypal traits, but Oakes's findings lead us to suspect that, to feel driven to become a successful leader of a cult, may well require an early parental input of exaggerated love to inflate self-esteem to the point where the guru feels justified in demanding his followers' devoted attention. To possess schizotypal genes is, like patriotism, not enough: they must also experience over-idealization in childhood. This is a hypothesis that needs to be tested.

In many cases, there is also an anti-social ('free-riding') admixture. This seems particularly true of prophets as opposed to messiahs. Prophets are much more likely to indulge in anti-social behaviour, are prone to lie, be manipulative, and break the law. As we have noted, a number end up in jail. The key to the prophet's success is his accessibility to unconscious processes, to the borderline or liminal state. This makes him compellingly attractive to his followers, for it seems to them that he must have a hot line to God.

So far, our approach to charisma has been constrained by a need to find an evolutionary explanation for schizophrenia. It is important that we should not pathologize charisma in the process. Charisma is a vital aspect of the human condition: it is creatively innovative, for it is opposed to convention and received wisdom. Charisma provides

62

an essential catalyst to the reaction between that which has been and that which is in the process of becoming. The need for members of the younger generation to establish their identity, social position, economic status and geographical space creates both the need for the charismatic leader and the desire to follow him. The same process is apparent in the revitalization of oudated traditions. Heresy is charisma's boisterous child, its role being to challenge the deadening effects of orthodoxy.

Prophets can be understood as 'possessed' by an ancient archetype which is at once coercive and seductive. Those who declare themselves to be Jesus are essentially giving His name to the charismatic figure – the archetype of the hero-saviour – that has taken hold of their own psychology. The potent force of this archetype is seen not only in its ubiquity but in its historical implications for the religious life of practically every community known to anthropology. All religions begin as cults and are founded on the basis of charismatic leadership. It is a process as old as our human capacity for speech.

Creative illness

It was necessary for me to pass through the purgatorial fires of horrifying psychosis before I could set foot on my promised land of creative activity.   Anton Boisen

One charismatic leader who, being a psychologist of genius, threw much light on the 'borderline' condition, was the Swiss psychiatrist, Carl Gustav Jung (1875-1961). A controversial yet major contribution made by him to twentieth-century thought was his theory of archetypes operating as components of the human 'collective unconscious'. This theory was far ahead of its time and, as a consequence, was rejected by most academic psychologists and social scientists for the reason that it ran counter to the prevailing social science model which held that all psychological and social phenomena were culture-dependent and owed little or nothing to innate propensities. Moreover, many detected more than a whiff of mysticism about the notion of a 'collective unconscious', with the result that the idea never really caught on, except among Jungian analysts, their patients, and élite groups of writers, artists, and musicians. The truth is, however, that

Jung's conception of the human psyche as being made up of arche-typal building blocks provided by our evolutionary history is ex-tremely close to the contemporary understanding of evolutionary psychologists that the psyche is composed of 'modules' put there by natural selection (Stevens, 1999).

'I have chosen the term "collective"', wrote Jung, 'because this part of the unconscious is not individual but universal; in contrast to the personal psyche, it has contents and modes of behaviour that are more or less the same everywhere and in all individuals' (Jung, 1959). He related this 'common psychic substrate of a suprapersonal nature' to the structure of the brain: 'Every man is born with a brain that is profoundly differentiated, and this makes him capable of very various mental functions, which are neither ontogenetically developed nor acquired ... This particular circumstance explains, for example, the remarkable analogies presented by the unconscious in the most remotely separated races and peoples' (Jung, 1953).

That few evolutionary psychologists have acknowledged Jung's priority in this theoretical area is at least in part due to their concern with different kinds of data. Whereas evolutionary psychology has focused on objective and observable patterns of behaviour, Jung, being a profoundly introverted person, was all his life preoccupied with 'subjective manifestations of innate psychic propensities' as they appeared in dreams, visions, myths, religions, legends and folk tales. The near-psychotic breakdown Jung experienced during the years following the severance of his relationship with Sigmund Freud in 1912 was to have a profound influence over the course of the rest of his life. This has been described and analysed by himself and many others (Jung, 1963; Ellenberger, 1970; Stevens, 1999). For him it was precisely the kind of crisis which we shall come to see as one of the most salient characteristics of the charismatic leader. Henri Ellen-berger called it a 'creative illness' and has detected it in the personal history of such gurus as Freud, Theodor Fechner, Friedrich Nietzsche and Rudolf Steiner, as well as Jung. It is a relatively uncommon condition whose onset usually occurs after a long period of intense intellectual work. The main symptoms are exhaustion, depression and irritability, and can present the picture of a severe neurosis and, sometimes, a psychosis.

During the illness the sufferer remains preoccupied with the problem that absorbed his attention before the onset. He feels isolated and develops the conviction that no one can help him. He is driven as a result to find ways of healing himself. Not infrequently, these attempts seem to increase his suffering, and the illness can last as long as 3 or 4 years. Recovery occurs spontaneously, is associated with feelings of euphoria and is followed by a transformation of the personality. The subject emerges believing that he has gained access to a new spiritual truth which it is his duty to share with the world. Examples of the 'illness' are to be found among Siberian and Alaskan shamans, among mystics of all religions and among certain creative writers, philosophers and artists.

Indeed, there are significant parallels between what goes on in a creative illness and the normal processes underlying all forms of creativity, as described by Graham Wallas (1926), Anthony Storr (1972) and others.[3] There are four stages: (1) *preparation*: this involves concentration and *immersion* in the problem or data under consideration; (2) *consolidation* and *incubation* of the information gathered and integrating it with relevant memory storehouses which are not readily accessible to consciousness; (3) *illumination*: this is the *eureka* experience of Archimedes as he jumped out of his bath, and it comes, appropriately enough, after a variable period of immersion and consolidation: suddenly the focal material is reorganized, a new insight bursts through, the problem is solved and the whole issue is viewed in a new and transforming light; and (4) *verification*, when the new insight which comes at the moment of illumination is put to the test, its implications worked through and its value assessed.

Interestingly enough, creative thinkers commonly compare the moment when a new insight hits them (stage 3, *illumination*) with a flash of lightning. When, for example, Kekulé had his dream which effectively solved the problem of the molecular structure of benzene which had preoccupied him for months, he reported: 'As though from a flash of lightning I awoke. I occupied the rest of the night working out the consequences of the [benzene ring] hypothesis' (de Becker, 1968, p. 84). Similarly, Karl Gauss reported that the solutions to mathematical problems came to him after long hours of preoccupation like 'a sudden flash of lightning' (Hadamard, 1945, p. 15). The similarity between this creative process and the onset of a schizophrenic delusion – or a sudden religious conversion of the type reported by St Paul – is so evident as to require little comment. Something like it must also occur in the mind of the prophet when he suddenly perceives the solution to his own plight and to that of his people. The withdrawal from all outer contacts in order to focus exclusively on an inner, mental problem is probably much easier for an introverted person than for an extravert. And whether or not such withdrawal demands that an individual should suffer a 'creative illness' will depend on the nature and importance of the problem as much as on the characteristics of the thinker.

It must be of interest to the cultural historian of the twentieth century that both Freudian psychoanalysis and Jungian analytical psychology owe their theories, practices and origins to the creative illness of their founders. In the course of their personal crises each underwent the perilous journey of the hero, with its hallmarks of isolation, initiation and return. (Having undergone his superhuman ordeal, the mythic hero re-emerges as a man transformed, possessed of great wisdom and the power to bestow benefits on his fellow men and women.) Such experiences result in a profound intuition that carries the visionary into the realm of the sacred, which is inaccessible to those engaged in the profane matters of hunting and gathering, getting and spending. Properly understood, the mental suffering involved can transcend the usual life-maiming experience of a psychiatric breakdown because it brings insight, vision and understanding. This is particularly so when the visionary, on returning from his ordeal, finds sympathetic listeners willing to attribute significance to the tale he has to tell.

4

Splitting and Revitalization

A Natural History of the Cult

The nation's hoop is broken and scattered. There is no centre
any longer and the sacred tree is dead.   Black Elk

Some of the most tragic casualties of the great material progress
which has marked the course of the twentieth century have been
those indigenous cultures that have shattered under the impact of
Western expansionism. Many have disintegrated beyond repair and
have been swept away in the avalanche of history. But some have
managed to rescue themselves in the nick of time, revitalized their
basic customs, mores and beliefs, and have re-established the roots
of their cultural identity. In many cases this resuscitation has coincided with the emergence of a 'hero-saviour' figure bearing unmistak-
able schizotypal characteristics.

When crisis strikes, the presence of schizotypal traits in every
community appears to be of adaptive advantage, both for the hero
who assumes the mantle of charismatic leadership and for the members of his group. When disintegration in society proceeds
synchronously with disintegration in the schizotypal personality, he
becomes the Christ-like leader who takes on the sufferings of his
people. By healing himself (through a radical revisioning of his own
beliefs) he succeeds in healing them. As he undergoes his inner crisis,
the prophet may actually cross the uncertain threshold which sepa-
rates schizotypy from acute schizophrenia: but, as long as he
succeeds in communicating his message, his visionary experience
will have adaptive consequences for himself and for his group. Anthony Wallace (1956) has recorded several examples illustrating this
point, and we will examine one of them.

The Old Way of Handsome Lake

There is not the least use preaching to anyone unless you chance to catch them ill.

Sydney Smith

In the spring of 1799 a 54-year-old chieftain of the Seneca tribe lay on his bed dying of drink and despair. He was called Handsome Lake, and his condition precisely reflected that of his people. Only a generation previously the Seneca had been the most powerful nation of the League of the Iroquois, ruling all the tribes inhabiting the present States of Ohio, New York, Pennsylvania and New Jersey, and for nearly sixty years they had been able, by pursuing a shrewd policy of armed neutrality, to hold the balance of power in North America between England and France. But since 1775 things had been going badly wrong for them. Abandoning their neutrality, they made the fatal error of siding with the British in their struggle to suppress the American Revolutionaries. This brought down on them the wrath of General Sullivan's hit-and-run invaders who devastated their villages and burned their orchards and cornfields. Their fate was sealed when, ditched by the British at the end of the Revolutionary War, they signed away vast tracts of land to the American authorities, and were forced into small reservations, isolated from one another by the influx of white settlers. Deprived of the comfortable houses, fields and mellow orchards that Sullivan's men had sacked, they were unable to continue their traditional life as hunters, warriors, and forest statesmen. Hungry, demoralized and miserable, they turned to brawling, to witchcraft, and to drink.

It was in the midst of this cultural catastrophe that in June 1799 Handsome Lake had the first of a series of visions that were to transform not only his own life but the lives of the Seneca people and the whole Iroquois nation. Three angels appeared to him from Heaven and explained that his illness, like the malaise of his people, was due to drink and to witchcraft. The cure was to abandon these evil ways.

Instructing his brother, Cornplanter, to assemble the people, Handsome Lake arose from his deathbed, and described his vision. Other visions followed, and they told him he must tour the reservations preaching to the tribes of the Iroquois. The most dramatic of

68

these visions occurred on August 8th 1799 when he fell into a trance at 7 o'clock in the morning and did not wake until 3 in the afternoon. During this time he lay as if dead: perceptible respiration stopped and his extremities were cold up to the knees and elbows. Shortly after his recovery, Handsome Lake was visited by a Quaker missionary who wrote down the details of the visions he said he had experienced during his trance. He had been taken on a tour of Heaven and Hell. A supernatural Guide had warned him that an Evil Spirit was promoting the traffic of liquor amongst the Seneca and that it was essential to keep away from all 'frolicks and dancing' at which liquor was used. He was given a number of specific recommendations: not only must there be no more dancing and drinking, but no more card playing or witchcraft, no more adultery, no more wife-beating or mistreatment of children, and no more selling off of Iroquois lands.

Inevitably some of his visions were apocalyptic in character: the world would be destroyed in a great holocaust; the wicked would be given the fire torture in Hell, while the good would go to Heaven. In the meantime, the Seneca must learn English, build frame houses, take to the horse and the plough, and begin to rear cattle. They were to return to the 'Old Way' of religion: some of the ancient rituals were to be abandoned, some modified, and others were to be kept and strictly observed.

The effect of Handsome Lake's teaching astounded white settlers. Practically the whole Seneca nation became teetotal. The men, who had despised farming as woman's work, took to the plough, built fences, amassed herds of cattle and pigs, and built substantial homes. Within ten years, Wallace tells us, the Seneca transformed themselves from a frontier slum society to a vigorous and enterprising nation. This achievement was directly attributable to Handsome Lake's visions and to the teaching he based on them.

After his death in 1815, his disciples gathered at Tonawanda in the State of New York and put together what they could remember of the prophet's visions, sayings and actions. This became the Gospel of the 'Old Way of Handsome Lake' as the new religion was called, and within a generation it was institutionalized and established as a 'pagan' church. At the time of Wallace's report in 1956, the 'Old Way' still had many followers on Iroquois reservations.

The spread of Western imperialism and capitalism throughout the world has meant that many indigenous peoples have suffered a fate similar to that of the Iroquois, and numerous examples of nativist and revitalist movements led by charismatic prophets have been gathered by missionaries and anthropologists during the last 200 years.[1] That most of the 'cargo cults' of Melanesia proved abortive was not due to a lack of prophets but because the cargoes they prophesied invariably failed to materialize, though Palieau's movement on Manus, started by a mystic called Wapi (whose voices told him to advise his people to abandon all their possessions in anticipation of the millennium), resulted in economic reorganization, new political institutions and efficient town planning (Mead, 1961).

Pre-eminently an anthropologist of religion, Anthony Wallace understood the significance of charismatic leaders and charismatic groups, not as indispensable to group splitting, but as essential for cultural revitalization. He introduced the term 'revitalization movement', to embrace all messianic, charismatic, nativistic, millenarian, cargo and revolutionary cults. A revitalization movement develops when members of a society perceive their culture to have become unsatisfactory and in need of renewal so as to produce a better one. What is it in their culture (and in themselves) that they seek to revitalize? Wallace's answer is: the *mazeway*.

Revitalizing the mazeway

Religions are kept alive by heresies, which are really sudden explosions of faith. Dead religions do not produce them.

Gerald Brenan

Wallace conceived human society as a kind of living organism ruled by homeostasis, the self-regulatory principle whose function is to keep all the dynamic components of an organism in a state of balance. The components of this organism are people, and each one of them must of necessity formulate a mental image (*Gestalt*) of the culture in which he or she lives. It is this image that Wallace calls 'the mazeway'. He coined this term because it best summed up for him the highly complex model formulated by each individual of himself or herself living in the context of society as a whole: 'The mazeway is

70

nature, society, culture, personality, and body image, as seen by one person', he wrote.

Thus the mazeway is Wallace's crucial concept,[2] for it is the mazeway that revitalization movements revitalize. When individuals group together in a collaborative effort to change the mazeway they are committing themselves to a 'revitalization movement'. Different cultures are subject to different stresses and accordingly each advocates a different kind of change in the mazeway so that a different form of revitalization movement emerges. For example, 'nativistic movements', which characteristically arise among subject colonial peoples, emphasize the need to eliminate alien nationals, alien customs and alien values from the mazeway and to replace them with native ones. 'Cargo cults', on the other hand, stress the need to incorporate alien values, customs, wealth and technological expertise into the mazeway: this, they believe, will be achieved when a special ship or aeroplane arrives bearing its cargo.[3] 'Millenarian movements' predict a mazeway change as part of an apocalyptic world transformation produced by divine intervention; whereas 'messianic movements' perceive the necessary change in the mazeway as being brought about by a hero-saviour who is the incarnation of God. However, these various subgroups do not represent mutually exclusive categories: a revitalization movement may be nativistic, millenarian and messianic all at once.

Revitalization movements are ubiquitous and so prevalent throughout history that Wallace asserts that few human beings have ever lived without being exposed to their influence. 'Both Christianity and Mohammedanism, and possibly Buddhism as well, originated in revitalization movements,' he declares. 'Most denominational and sectarian groups and orders budded or split off after failure to revitalize a traditional institution.'

Absolutely central to the whole process of cultural revitalization is the charismatic leader. The reformulation of the mazeway that the new prophet will propose depends on 'a restructuring of elements and subsystems which have already attained currency in the society' and which are already known to him. Their resynthesis into an ideological package which seems to possess an internally consistent structure is abrupt and dramatic, a moment of insight that is experienced as a revelation. This reformulation of the mazeway, Wallace

71

repeatedly asserts, seldom if ever grows directly out of group deliberations but occurs in its initial form in the mind of a single person.

This sudden reformulation of the mazeway in the leader, so crucial for the destiny of his group, has such evident parallels in the phenomena of religious conversion and the onset of an intact, incorrigible psychotic delusion that many writers have expressed difficulty in attempting to differentiate between them. In many respects William James's classic definition of religious conversion as 'the process, gradual or sudden, by which a self hitherto divided, and consciously wrong, inferior and unhappy, becomes unified and consciously right, superior and happy' would seem very close to Anthony Wallace's description of mazeway resynthesis.

Mazeway resynthesis is what happens in the prophet; conversion, if the prophet succeeds in communicating his mission, is what happens in his followers. Excitement induced in the potential convert by the charismatic speaker, the ecstatic hopes engendered by his vision, augmented by the hysterical enthusiasm of the crowd, can produce an assortment of dissociative behaviours such as rolling on the ground, weeping and 'speaking in tongues'. Following conversion, individuals may subscribe completely to the beliefs and codes to which they have been exposed. But, as Wallace points out, the behaviour of converts changes not because of deep, inner, radical resynthesis, but because of a passive acceptance of a new set of doctrines under the influence of *suggestion*. If removed from the reinforcing symbols of the new belief system, it is quite possible for them to relapse into their old ways – something that would seldom happen to the prophet, whose mazeway has been profoundly and lastingly resynthesized as a consequence of his mystical and numinous experiences. The importance of the new symbols and rituals that the prophet ordains lies in their ability to sustain converts in their devotion to the new cause.

Again and again we are brought to the observation that collective conversion led by individual mazeway resynthesis makes possible the profound cultural transformation of whole populations. From Akhnaton's attempt to establish a new monotheistic religion in ancient Egypt, the charismatic origins of Christianity, Buddhism and Mohammedanism, the Protestant Reformation under the influence of such charismatic leaders as Luther, Calvin and Zwingli, to the

American, French, Fascist, Nazi and Communist revolutions of more recent times, these mechanisms of cultural change have operated continent by continent, throughout history and pre-history in all human societies that have ever existed. It is difficult to avoid the conclusion that genetic factors must be operative in all human populations which are responsible for coordinating the characteristic behaviour of charismatic leaders and their groups.

Though the content of the leader's teaching, and the type of charismatic group forming round him, may vary from place to place and from time to time, the basic structures involved are seemingly invariable. Both before and since the conquest of South America, for instance, the indigenous people have periodically set off on migrations for 'the Land Without Evil', where a Utopian way of life (and, since the conquest, a land free of Spaniards and Portuguese) would be found. Revivalist movements such as the Ghost Dance occurred regularly among North American Indians during the eighteenth and nineteenth centuries, while South Africa has witnessed the growth of numerous small, enthusiastic sects which have broken free from the missionary organizations. And during the last 150 years 'cargo cults' have arisen among the peoples of New Guinea and Melanesia. Despite this diversity, the origin and history of such groups conform to the hallowed archetypal pattern.

A natural history of the cult

Behold, how good and how pleasant it is for brethren to dwell together in unity.   Psalm 133:1

Whither thou goest, I will go; and where thou lodgest, I will lodge: thy people shall be my people, and thy God my God.
Ruth, 1:16

Anthony Wallace (1956) described the sequence of stages characteristic of the revitalization process in groups. In doing so he again asserted his firm belief that genotypal structures must be involved which are independent of local differences. The stages he described are as follows:

steady state
↓
individual stress
↓
cultural distortion
↓
revitalization
↓
new steady state

With his 'steady state' concept Wallace would appear to be groping towards some such idea as the theory of 'flexible mutualism' developed by the American evolutionary psychiatrist, Brant Wenegrat (1989), which holds that natural selection has specifically adapted human beings to stable group life. This adaptation is linked to a number of predispositions such as the tendency to classify other people either as in-group members (to whom one directs 'affiliative behaviour') or as strangers (of whom we are wary and towards whom we may become actively hostile). To feel alienated from one's in-group results in unhappiness and insecurity and in a powerful need to find a new stable group with which to become affiliated. Once such a group has been found, there is an innate imperative to learn and endorse the group's consensual beliefs, even if this demands that one should ignore or override one's personal understanding and experience. The disposition to 'flexible mutualism', declares Wenegrat, is 'powerful and intractable' and 'cannot be washed away'. It is the feeling of alienation that religious sects and cults have always served to heal.

Because Wallace was not concerned with why charismatic leadership and cult formation evolved and what functions they perform he does not discuss the phenomena involved in group splitting, for example, when a hunter–gatherer community outgrows its resources. His analysis does, however, throw light on the possible processes involved. For example, the period of 'individual stress', which disrupts the previously prevailing 'steady state' of the culture, Wallace relates to such factors as 'climatic, floral and faunal change; military defeat; political subordination; extreme pressure toward acculturation resulting in internal cultural conflict; economic dis-

74

tress; epidemics; and so on.' It is not hard to imagine that individual stresses set up in strife-torn hunter–gatherer communities about to split would be of a similar order of intensity. As a result of such stressful events, 'a point is reached at which some alternative way must be considered.' This may itself increase levels of individual distress because it gives rise to fears that the alternative way may be even less effective than the original. 'In other words', says Wallace, 'it poses the threat of mazeway disintegration.'

People differ in the strategies they adopt to meet this threat: some choose a conservative policy of learning to tolerate high levels of chronic stress without attempting to change their mazeway; others take a more liberal line, endeavouring to reduce stress levels by trying out limited mazeway changes in their personal lives; still others indulge in essentially regressive responses, becoming apathetic, or alcoholic, disregarding kinship responsibilities and sexual mores, indulging in intragroup violence, and so on, as we found in the case of the Seneca Indians before Handsome Lake had his visions. This marks the period of 'cultural distortion' and, when regressive patterns are adopted by a substantial number, it gives rise to feelings of collective guilt, fears of offending the gods and the ancestral spirits, and terror of the consequences of breaking taboos. It is at this point that the need for revitalization is felt as a collective need and that a leader perceived as capable of fulfilling it is likely to arise. If this fails to happen the population is in grave danger of extinction – through increasing death rates, decreasing birth rates, factional disputes, territorial dispossessions, military defeat, 'ethnic cleansing', and genocide.

At such moments of crisis the schizotypal leader comes into his own. Whether he will succeed in his mission depends on his eloquence as a preacher, his possession of striking physical attributes, the awe inspired by his message (numinosity) and the degree to which it is tuned to the times. Indispensable to this personal and cultural transmutation are the dreams, visions, voices, and visitations the prophet experiences at this time. The dreams of prophets are 'big dreams' – or 'culture pattern dreams' as the anthropologists call them. They possess enormous power, being as capable of transforming society as the dreamer himself. His personality undergoes radical alteration, he becomes active, purposeful, and supremely

75

confident. Old habits like alcoholism are dropped and old illnesses cured.

Content analysis of the typical dreams and visions of prophets at these critical times contain a number of familiar elements: these include the overwhelming presence of some supernatural figure or power, images of world destruction (the apocalypse, the flood), and Utopian images of a new and ideal state. The underlying theme is invariably that of death and rebirth: the old way of life is dead; the new way of life is about to come into existence. Inspired by his new mazeway the prophet feels driven to tell others what has been revealed to him and to fulfil his messianic obligations.

Though Wallace does not focus on the issues of conflict inside the group and group splitting, he nevertheless acknowledges that a revitalization movement, being a revolutionary organization, will inevitably encounter resistance either from a powerful faction within the society or from agents belonging to a dominant foreign or alien power. The response of the movement to such opposition will vary from the use of diplomatic and political initiatives to the mobilization of physical force. 'In instances where organized hostility to the movement develops, a crystalization of counter-hostility against unbelievers frequently occurs, and emphasis shifts from cultivation of the ideal to combat against the unbeliever.' If this occurs it involves projection of Jung's 'shadow' archetype (the archetype of evil) onto the opposition, with the accompanying possibility of 'pseudospeciation' (Erikson, 1984), warfare, ethnic cleansing, and genocide. We shall return to these issues in Chapter 7.

Provided the majority or a controlling portion of the population embraces the new religion and its injunctions (and provided the prevailing environmental conditions are propitious), a highly significant social revitalization occurs, with a marked reduction in the ills with which individuals were collectively afflicted, and the society embarks enthusiastically on some organized programme of group action. The new belief system then becomes routinized and established as normal in the various religious, political, social and economic institutions and customs of the group. The 'new steady state' is then inaugurated.

The stages described by Wallace are those passed through by a successful revitalization movement. However, the process may be aborted at an early stage, and in most instances it probably is. As the historic record of prophets demonstrates, many are called, but few carry their gospel to fruition.

Group splitting and the principle of opposites

Without contraries there is no progression.   William Blake

In discussing the ecology of group splitting we suggested that the foraging groups in which our ancestors lived split when they reached a critical size at which their range could no longer support their numbers. When the split occurred, the group divided into two opposing factions, and all the mechanisms that previously promoted group solidarity went into reverse so as to drive the two subgroups apart. At that point the issue of leadership became crucial for survival, because the leader had to inspire the departing group with its sense of mission and purpose, and its need to unite in a shared belief so that it had the guidance and the will to win through and find its own 'promised land'.

Because there are so few hunter–gatherer communities left in the world inhabiting the kind of environment our ancestors frequented, it is difficult to study this divisive process at first hand. One population that has been studied by that intrepid anthropologist, Napoleon A. Chagnon, is the Yanomamo of Venezuela (Chagnon, 1980). Although the Yanomamo are a horticultural people who cultivate gardens in clearings in the tropical forest, their population density is extremely low (less than one person per square mile) and in this they resemble hunter–gatherers rather than horticulturalists in other parts of the world. Warfare and group fissioning is endemic among the Yanomamo, though the resource that Yanomamo men fight over is not land but women. Vast expanses of tropical forest surround Yanomamo villages, so that, when conflict becomes intolerable among groups living on the periphery of the population (consisting of some 15,000 people), they can migrate outwards. Intense conflicts between males occur because of the absolute shortage of females in Yanomamo communities, probably because of preferential female infanticide at birth and because relative neglect of little girls results in higher female infant mortality.

The Yanomamo live in about 150 widely scattered villages, which range in size from approximately 30 people at one extreme to 300 at the other. Chagnon, who mapped a number of these villages and carried out a detailed census of their members, discovered that his findings rapidly became obsolete because village groups quarrelled among themselves and split up so frequently. He believes this process was exacerbated as the population continued to grow at the rate of 2 to 3 per cent a year. The most stable communities he found among the smaller villages, where incest taboos and kinship obligations were strong and sexual trysting frowned upon, with the result that a relatively high level of trust prevailed between the males. But as the village grew in size, the group dynamics changed in the manner we would predict: 'tensions within the group mount, internal friction and fighting increase, and bitter arguments are chronic', Chagnon reported. 'The major source of the conflict is sex and seduction: younger men frequently attempt to seduce the wives of older men, and seize every opportunity to approach the women when their husbands are not around. Men who go on several-day hunting trips, for example, keep their ears sharp when they return to pick up any telltale gossip that suggests infidelity on the part of their wives, and often beat them soundly if there appears to be substance in the rumors. The wronged husband usually challenges the suspected lover to a club-fight as well. Such fights rapidly spread to involve large numbers of the village men, who take sides with close kin.'

On the basis of an analysis of his field data, Chagnon concluded that closeness of kinship, measured genealogically, was a highly significant variable in predicting whether or not a village community would split. 'As villages grow over time, members of the same lineage grow progressively less related to one another in each generation and become one another's competitors for wives.' In these circumstances group splitting and migration call less for the emergence of a charismatic leader than the assertion of close-kin solidarity and distant-kin hostility. As a result, there is no mazeway resynthesis, no restructuring of reality, no Damascene shift: the departing group moves off in search of a new location with its traditional belief system intact.

It appears, therefore, that in relation to belief and ideology, group splitting and population dispersal can occur in two different ways. When, as among the Yanomamo, the dispersing portion of the community carries away with it the same belief system as its forefathers, we may call this *homopistic dispersal* (from the Greek, *homo* = the same, and *pistis* = belief). In this kind of group splitting and dispersal the charismatic leader is redundant. In the formation of cults, on the other hand, the charismatic leader is indispensable. He gathers round himself a group of believers in whom he inculcates a set of unique beliefs which are at variance with those of the parent group. It is this clash of beliefs that gives rise to conflict within the group, splitting, and dispersal. We may call this *heteropistic dispersal* (from the Greek *hetero* = other, and *pistis* = belief). It is the divergent belief systems, rather than sexual rivalries, which split the group in two and drive the new groups apart.

Of the two kinds of splitting, heteropistic fissioning is the one that applies to our study. It invariably brings into operation the dynamic principle of antithesis (enantiodromia), whereby a set of attitudes, if persisted in, eventually becomes transformed into its opposite. It is as if a psychic pendulum is at work in human affairs, and all forms of innovation, whether personal or cultural, may be understood as an expression of this dynamic. Examples can be gleaned from anthropological records of field studies on all five continents and the major islands between them. They range through the gamut of what Feuerstein (1990) calls 'crazy adepts of Tibetan Buddhism, the eccentric teachers of Ch'an (Zen), the Holy fools of Christianity and Islam, the *avadhutas* and *bauls* of Hinduism, and the tricksters and religious clowns of tribal traditions'.

In order to teach what are spiritual truths to them, all such 'masters' embrace unconventional means: 'Every tradition has its own version of the charismatic teacher, but in all of them he is recognizably the same figure, whether he be a Hindu *guru*, a Sufi *shaykh*, a Tibetan *lama*, a Zen *roshi* or a Hasidic *zaddik*.' The contemporary success of charismatic leaders in Western societies, the proliferation of cults, and psychiatric interest in them, can be explained very largely in terms of their compensatory function and their willing collusion with the principle of opposites. It is their 'antinomian' (Greek, *anti* = against; *nomos* = the law) character that renders cults so attractive to disaffected people – particularly young people – because they advocate values directly opposed to the rugged individualism and democratic value system prevalent in Euro-American countries. This is one reason why specifically Eastern spiritual traditions have proved so attractive, as in the success of such cults as the Hare Krishnas (Jacobson, 1998) and the Rajneeshees (Milne, 1986).

Describing his own infiltration of the Hare Krishna movement, William Shaw (1994) writes: 'The denial of the Western values the devotees grew up with becomes a spiritual mission. In the Hare Krishnas, you learn Sanskrit, you deny Darwinian evolution, you prostrate your unworthy body on the floor, and instead of glorifying the body beautiful, you regard it as a bag of rotting meat. Women cover their bodies from head to toe to avoid arousing lust. Possessions are kept to a minimum'. Shaw describes how acts of self-abasement and servitude to Krishna and the temple seniors are part of the daily life of the temple. 'For the Westerner the fear of this submission becomes part of the attraction', writes Shaw. 'It turns Western liberality on its head.' As a consequence, everything Indian in the Hare Krishna movement acquires a degree of sanctity. 'Many disciples not only adopt the clothes, but adopt the sort of odd body language too. Spurning the plastic spoons offered, they scoop up their *prasadam* with their fingers, and thank the servers with palms pressed together. Some even acquire twitchy pseudo-Indian neck movements.'

A very evident contrast exists between the consensual world view (which celebrates the triumph of Mammon and scientific materialism) and the esoteric world view endorsed by the cults and their leaders (which is essentially spiritual). As Feuerstein (1990) puts it: 'The esoteric perspective represents a definition of reality that is diametrically opposed to the one by which most people live in our post-modern world.'

However, the adoption of antithetical beliefs and the advocacy of antinomian practices, is by no means confined to contemporary cult leaders in the West: it was ever thus. In the 1660s, for example, Sabbatai Sevi, a devout young rabbi living in the Ottoman Empire, began to behave in a shocking manner as the result of divine revelations evoked by fasting, purifying rituals and all-night prayer. Instead of maintaining the Law of God as any good rabbi should, he preached the need to break it. According to one Kabbalistic tradition, the only way to redeem evil is for the Messiah to emerge who will incorporate that evil in himself. Consequently, Sabbatai offered up a new prayer: 'Praised be Thee O Lord who permits the forbidden' (i.e. the opposite of what the Law permits).

80

Not surprisingly, he was expelled by his local rabbinate. But he was undaunted. Inflamed with an overwhelming conviction of his mission, he gathered round him a fanatical group of followers, who experienced mass visions, fell into states of ecstasy, and proclaimed Sabbatai as the Messiah. True to form he invented new ceremonies which negated the traditional ones and turned days of ritual mourning into days of rejoicing. In defiance of God's Holy Commandments, he advocated free love, married a prostitute, and encouraged nudity and incest. If the messianic age could only be ushered in by sin (i.e. behaviour contrary to the Law) then Sabbatai and his followers must become sinful virtuosi. Eventually, he was arrested and, under pain of death, he converted to Islam. Thereupon most of his followers deserted him, though a few remained loyal, justifying his apostasy as the ultimate messianic sacrifice.

Significantly, the psychic pendulum was no less active in Sabbatai's psyche, for, whatever else there may have been in his psychology, he was evidently manic-depressive. He was subject to frequent episodes of depressive withdrawal and apathy of the type that Jewish mystics called *yourinda* ('lowness', remoteness from God) and which Sabbatai's followers labelled 'The Hiding of the Face'. These alternated with periods of 'illumination', when he refused to eat or sleep, and displayed infectious elation and enthusiasm of the kind the mystics termed *aliyah* ('highness', closeness to God). Sabbatai's followers accepted his extreme mood swings as indices of his holiness and emulated them as normative behaviour for the elect. As the anthropological psychiatrist Roland Littlewood (1984) comments: 'It is likely that the jokes and tricks and inversions of normal behaviour make an individual with periodic manic-depressive psychosis a particularly well-placed person to modify traditional modes of belief and behaviour through antinomian acts.'

Mother Earth of Trinidad

I am the Cunt, the Source of all Life.   Mother Earth

Another striking instance of 'antinomian' beliefs and practices is provided by the Trinidadian, Mother Earth (Jeanette Baptiste), and her followers, the 'Earth People'. In a still predominantly devout

81

country familiar with the Rastafari movement and the millennial beliefs of the Shouter Baptists, most Trinidadians nevertheless pronounced themselves shocked and puzzled by Mother Earth and her People. Not only did they come into 'Town' naked and shouting obscenities but Mother Earth openly proclaimed herself to be both the Devil incarnate and the Mother of Africa and India.

All this began in 1975 when, having given birth to twins, Jeanette Baptiste received a number of revelations from which she discovered with absolute certainty that the Judeo-Christian doctrine of God the Father as Creator of All Things was completely untrue. The world was in fact the creation of the Primordial Mother as manifested in Nature and the Earth. The first people She created were in Africa and India and they were black. But She also gave birth to a Son, who re-entered Her womb so as to acquire the secret of procreation and produce a new race of people who were white. Called the 'Race of the Son' they were really the Race of Death. Not only did they enslave the blacks but they had exploited them mercilessly ever since.

Contrary themes pervaded every aspect of Jeanette's teaching: the Way of the Son was at all points contrasted with the Way of the Mother, to the detriment of the former. His Way was the way of power, technology, science, schools, factories, computers, waged labour and clothes. Her Way was the way of love, the nurture of land and animals, affectionate human relationships, simple age-old customs, and nudity. Hitherto, the Mother had put up with the Son and His appalling behaviour out of love for Him, but Her patience was running out, and sometime in the future She was going to bring His Rule to an end with an apocalyptic catastrophe. Then the world would be returned to its original state of nature under the benign rule of the Mother.

In preparation for this transformation, Mother Earth had to adopt a position completely opposed to that of traditional Judeo-Christianity. To uphold Life and Nature against the murderous threat posed by God the Father and the Son, She must be the Devil, committed to the overthrow of churches, schools, prisons, governments, banks, corporations, traditional morals and fashionable opinions. Since God was 'Right' and ruled in Heaven, She espoused the 'Left' and ruled on

Earth. The use of obscenities became a religious duty, because they were the words of Nature.

Jeanette did not make the mistake of predicting when the final apocalypse would come, but she said it would be in her own life-time. Then Paradise would be regained with the usual consequences: time would cease, all diseases would be healed and all nations speak with one tongue. The Son would return to His Planet, the Planet Sun, which had until then been hidden by fire placed there by the Mother.

In common with most other charismatic leaders, both Mother Earth and Sabbatai Sevi belonged to a people who suffered dominion by an alien culture, where the 'Us' and 'Them' mentality prevailed – black v. white, Jew v. Gentile. Littlewood describes those attracted to the Earth People as coming from the young male proletariat for whom the disappearance of the agricultural economy and its associated way of life had been particularly traumatic.

Up to the time that Littlewood's paper was published (1984), Mother Earth had twice been admitted to a mental hospital in Port of Spain with a diagnosis of manic-depressive psychosis, for which she was treated with anti-psychotic drugs. Jeanette believed herself to be only a partial incarnation of the Mother, but that She would fully enter into her at the End. The Earth People seem to have equated Jeanette's episodes of hypomania with the Mother's strong incarnation in Jeanette and her intercurrent episodes of depression with the Mother's withdrawal. As a consequence, these episodes did not diminish their faith in her or her message: 'If she mad, then we mad', they said.

Archetypes and the prophet

> The Hero can be Poet, Prophet, King, Priest or what you will, according to the kind of world he finds himself born into.
>
> Thomas Carlyle

Of the archetypal figures investigated by Jung and his followers, those most deeply related to the psychology of prophets are the 'hero–saviour' (Campbell, 1990), the 'trickster' (Henderson, 1967), the 'priest–shaman' (Eliade, 1964), and the 'Great Mother', in both her 'Good' and 'Terrible' aspects (Neumann, 1955). That these represent 'archetypal roles' may be deduced from the fact that they are apparent in the myths and folk tales, as well as the institutional roles and behaviours, of human communities across the planet. In the Jungian view, they are to be conceived as inherent possibilities in all human beings, their potential being encoded in the psyche of the species. Their active expression in the personal psychology and social behaviour of an individual depends on his or her genes, early life experiences, and the prevailing social conditions. The awesome power of charismatic leaders may be understood as due to the ready access they enjoy to these archetypal potentials. Prophets are border-line characters whose personality renders them uncanny and numi-nous (awesome) to potential followers because their bizarre convictions enable them to be dramatically subversive of the estab-lished order. That they become the living embodiments of legendary figures celebrated in the mythic history of their culture consolidates in the minds of their followers the belief that they must be in direct communion with the gods, ancestors and spirits, inhabiting that mysterious region on the other side of reality, the realm of the sacred.

Jung spoke of an archetype as being 'constellated' in the psyche. By this he meant that it was activated so powerfully in the life and behaviour of a susceptible individual that he or she could be said to have become 'possessed' by the archetype in question. Perhaps the commonest example is the very evident 'possession' by the Great Mother archetype undergone by a woman as she passes through pregnancy and parturition to give care and nurture to her child throughout its earliest years. Another form of archetyal possession experienced by most people at some time in the course of their lives is that appropriately described as 'falling in love' – so powerful is the attraction exercised by the beloved that it can indeed be equated with the force of gravity.

Of the prophets we have considered so far, the archetype which the males have evidently constellated and been 'possessed' by both in themselves and their followers, is the hero–saviour; while our one female example constellated the archetype of the Great Mother. Other examples are difficult to find, but they do exist. For example, Catherine Théot (1716-94) claimed to be the Mother of God. No less a person than Robespierre was impressed by her, and it is said that he saved her from the guillotine. She predicted that her death would be followed by some frightful cataclysm. Her followers were not surprised, therefore, when on the very day that she died in prison, the great powder magazine at Grenelle exploded. They were all of the opinion that she would rise again.

In England, Joanna Southcott (1750-1824) received a Divine Command to join the Methodists in 1791. She claimed she had visions of the coming millennium and the destruction of Satan, and declared herself to be the 'Bride of the Lamb' and the 'Woman Clothed with the Sun' described in the Book of Revelation. When she was 64, and still a virgin, she convinced her followers that she was about to 'bring forth the man child who was to rule all nations with a rod of iron' (*Revelation*, 12:5). Before she could do so, she died. Her funeral was delayed for several days while her followers waited for the miraculous birth, but nothing happened. Nevertheless, Southcottians persisted well into the nineteenth century.

Those women prophets who identify with the mother archetype have little difficulty in fulfilling the maternal longings of their followers. The Indian charismatic, Mother Meera, has attracted devotees since the age of 18. It has been her practice to give *darshan* four times a week. She does little and says nothing. Followers kneel before her and she gazes into their eyes, claiming to guide and teach them through silence. One devotee who wrote a book about her was the Oxford graduate and member of All Souls College, Andrew Harvey (1991). He subsequently defected on account of Mother Meera's disapproval of his homosexuality. In an interview published in *The Times* (5 April 2000) he said: 'She saw herself as the Divine Mother. In retrospect it seems like craziness ... When I met Mother Meera, I wasn't brainwashed so much as hypnotised by my own need for a divine feminine presence, which I projected on to her.'

More frequently encountered than women charismatic prophets, are female children who claim to have had visions of the Virgin Mary. As with the 'awakenings' of prophets, these have tended to occur at times of social crisis. Perhaps the most famous of them occurred at Fatima, 80 miles to the north of Lisbon, in the Spring of 1917, when the Virgin appeared to a shepherd girl: she bemoaned the Great War, the religious persecution of the ruling anti-clerical regime and the hunger brought on by high prices and food shortages. She asked for prayers to restore peace to the world. A similar apparition visited a girl at Marpingen in 1876, also at a time of agricultural depression and religious persecution. In the twentieth century apparitions of the Virgin reached epidemic proportions, and they invariably coincided with difficult conditions (Weber, 1999). Many such encounters were investigated by Karl Rahmer, who commented: 'In turbulent times the minds of men are agitated not only by events, but by the search for interpretation and promise for the future.'

Two other female archetypes described by Jungians are the Amazon, or Martial Maid, and the Medium, or Priestess (Wolff, 1956). The most famous woman to embody the archetype of the 'Martial Maid' was, of course, Joan of Arc (1412-31), whose voices gave her the necessary charisma, despite her gender and the times in which she lived, to lead the French Army to victory against the English at Orléans, only to be captured by the Burgundians, who sold her to the enemy. She was convicted of witchcraft and heresy by a tribunal of French ecclesiastics[4] sympathetic to the English, and burnt at the stake in Rouen on May 30th 1431. She was canonized in 1920.

Another example of this archetypal embodiment was Boudicca (Latin name Boadicea), Queen of the Iceni, a native British tribe, whose warlike mission was no less bloody and personally disastrous than Joan's. In 60 AD, the Romans annexed the territory of the Iceni, scourged Boudicca and raped her daughters. Such was the power of her personality, that Boudicca was able to raise the whole of South East England in revolt, and burned Londinium (London), Verulamium (St Albans) and Camolodunum (Colchester). However, when the Romans under Suetonius Paulinus counter-attacked in force, Boudicca's army was annihilated and, in despair, she poisoned herself.

Across the Atlantic, a 'Martial Maid' appeared on the North West Coast area in the mid-nineteenth century, when an Indian woman adopted the attire and weapons of a male warrior, and became the principal leader of her tribe, being called the 'Manlike Woman'. Since she was young, female, and delicately made, her successful military exploits were attributed to supernatural agencies. In such an exclusively masculine world as that of the warrior, a woman has to be endowed with enormous charisma to achieve the status of a warlord.

By contrast, many women throughout history have embodied the archetype of the 'Medium'. These are the wise women and female

86

shamans of preliterate societies, the priestesses and oracles of classical times (the most famous being the Pythoness at Delphi), the female saints and mystics of Christian hagiography, and the mediums and clairvoyants of more recent times. Though undoubtedly charismatic, such women have in the past seldom become leaders of cults. Only with the beginnings of female emancipation in the nineteenth century, did women like Mrs Baker Eddy (Dakin, 1929) and Madame Blavatsky[5] begin to emerge to establish charismatic institutions carrying on their work after their death. Women of this 'mediumistic' type tend to be messiahs rather than charismatic prophets.

One kind of male charismatic we have not yet examined is the mad saint, crazy adept, or spiritual clown who appears to be the embodiment of the 'trickster' archetype. One of the best descriptions of this archetype has been given not by a Jungian but by an authority on Hindu metaphysics. In the course of his book on holy madness, Georg Feuerstein (1990) describes holy madmen as 'crazy-wise teachers' and as 'eccentrics who use their eccentricity to communicate an alternative vision to that which governs ordinary life.' They are, he says, 'masters of inversion, proficient breakers of taboos, and lovers of surprise, contradiction, and ambiguity. They share these skills and penchants with the traditional figures of the trickster and the clown.'

At this point he stops to describe this figure: 'The trickster, who is usually male, belongs to the realm of tribal religion and mythology. He is either a god or a superhuman hero. He is a being who is very clever but unprincipled, delighting in the irrational … They are out to best their adversaries and spare no cunning to achieve their goal. As part of their duplicity, they often pretend to be stupid.' He is, moreover, depicted as 'having a voracious sexual appetite, which is often indicated by a huge penis'. [This is sometimes transposed into a grotesquely long phallic arm as in the Greek trickster, Karangyozi.] 'His character is a juxtaposition of carnality and spirituality. More than any other mythological figure, the trickster celebrates bodily existence, which includes all the many functions that civilization seeks to suppress or control. After the moment of creation, the Winnebago trickster Wakdjunkaga scattered all creatures across the earth by means of an enormous fart. His flatulence was thus essential to life on earth.'

As Feuerstein rightly points out, trickster stories are extremely common and people very obviously delight in them: 'The stories have an archetypal appeal', he says, 'They hold the listener spellbound, and even the modern reader is fascinated.' They are an imaginative way of escaping the social and moral constraints brought into existence through the necessity to sustain cultural order against the ever present possibilities of chaos. Here again we find parallels with Weber's description of the genuine charismatic leader.

In our own culture the most easily recognizable example of the trickster archetype is the clown. The word 'clown' first appeared in the second half of the sixteenth century (it meant 'clod' or 'clot'). Again, female examples are rare. Standing on the threshold between reason and nonsense, wisdom and ignorance, idiocy and saintliness, he is the quintessential insider/outsider, living in a liminal reality all his own. 'All clowns are great risk-takers,' comments Feuerstein, 'their way is that of the hero whose courage knows no bounds. This aspect of buffoonery is also shared by the adept–teacher who, for the sake of the enlightenment of others, is willing to go out on a limb.' As with prophets, gurus, and saints, the great clown has a curiously permeable psyche, possessing a wafer-thin membrane between conscious and unconscious processes.

In the Hindu tradition the *avadhutas* provide striking examples of charismatic individuals who have withdrawn from all social commitment. The *avadhuta* (a Sanskrit word meaning 'he who has cast off ') has no home, wife, children, job or social responsibility. Many of those described by Feuerstein were clearly schizotypal if not completely schizophrenic, displaying the negative as well as the positive symptoms of the condition. They often go about naked and do not bother to clean or feed themselves. One revered example was the modern sage, Swami Samarth of Akkalkot, a village in Maharashtra, who had to be looked after by his devotees: they fed and bathed him and had to tolerate his often disturbed and unpredictable behaviour. As his biographer records, 'Nobody could ever dare flout Sri Swami Samarth's wishes even though they would sometimes appear whimsical and eccentric .... and [he] was completely unpredictable in his behaviour. Sometimes he was so free that one could approach him and talk freely as to a mother, but at other times he seemed unapproachable and stern. Sometimes he himself talked freely and sweetly; at others, he would keep silent, uttering not a word for several days at a stretch' (Karandikar, 1978; quoted by Feuerstein).

The holy fool not only renounces the hero–saviour role for the trickster but may even cross the gender divide to identify with the archetype of the Great Mother. The nineteenth-century Indian saint, Sri Ramakrishna, who possessed some of the characteristics of an *avadhuta* began worshipping his own genitals as representing the *linga* of Shiva, then would dress as a woman, identifying with the Great Mother, whose presence he saw manifest in all things. Though a *Brahmin*, he would take food from untouchables and would offer ritually prepared food to a cat, saying, 'Won't You take it, Mother?' He did this, says his biographer, 'because the old and familiar universe was disintegrating before his eyes' (quoted by Feuerstein, p. 27).

The popularity of Tarapith in West Bengal as a centre of pilgrimage owes less to its famous temple and cremation grounds than to the astonishing celebrity of its once-resident holy madman, Bama Khepa (Morinis, 1985). Bama is derived from the Sanskrit word meaning 'left' and refers to the antinomian conduct of the mad saint as opposed to the 'right-handed' rituals of orthodox Hinduism. The 'left-handed' path exemplified by Bama Khepa led him into practices wholly unthinkable to the conventional Hindu. These involved eating meat and fish, drinking wine, meditating in the cremation ground squatting on a corpse, and indulging in ritual sexual intercourse.

The second part of Bama Khepa's name confirms his generally accepted madness (Khepa means 'madman'). As Morinis describes him, 'he could, for no apparent reason begin to weep uncontrollably, then just as quickly break into wild laughter. He would wander naked through the village talking to himself, sometimes frothing at the mouth. He could become suddenly and unpredictably violent.' He is said to have throttled a man who asked him to cure his tuberculosis, and his treatment of another humble acolyte wanting a cure for a hernia was a swift kick in the belly.

Bama Khepa's devotion was centred on Ma Tara, a version of the Great Mother Goddess in her 'Terrible' destructive aspect. She is depicted with a countenance dripping blood, wearing a garland of severed heads or skulls, and carrying a bloody sword. Tara is conventionally worshipped by her devotees in an attitude of self-demeaning supplication. In accordance with his role as holy madman, however, Bama Khepa did the opposite, shocking the faithful by consuming the deity's ritually prepared food, and allowing dogs to eat food from his plate. On one occasion he publicly urinated on her image, crying out: 'I do not accept your idol-image, whose face is made of metal; I do not accept your garland of skulls, made of metal, I only accept the formless Tara.'

To Western eyes, the 'god-intoxicated saints of Bengal' are just as mad as their unholy counterparts in psychiatric clinics. How do Bengalis distinguish between them? The answer must lie in the culture-specific mind state recognized through hundreds of years of Bengali history of the god-intoxicated madman with saintly powers. In all probability they are no less mad than patients with schizophrenia, but Bengali religious practices provide them with a saintly role into which they become assimilated. They thus escape the stigma of madness and are revered as saints.

Moreover, the paradigm of God-intoxication provides both a rationalization and a justification for the negative symptoms as well as the positive symptoms of schizophrenia. Their nakedness, lack of personal hygiene and fondness for excrement are recognized as mad, but classified as being symptomatic not of illness but of achieving an intimate relationship to the God or Goddess. For example, Bama Khepa's gross blasphemy of urinating on the statue of Ma Tara was interpreted by the faithful as the wise action of a holy madman. Did it not draw attention to the fact that the deity transcends her metal representation as an idol, which is no better than a latrine?

Consequently, the culturally sanctioned concept of saintly madness may be seen as providing what amounts to a form of 'community care' in that it presents the psychotic with a socially valued role in a community which sets great store by all forms of religious practice as well as the altered states of consciousness that such practices may induce. Nevertheless, most cultures make a distinction between madness and saintliness.

4. *Splitting and Revitalization*

Cultural division

I come not to send peace, but a sword.

Jesus Christ (*Matthew*, 10:34)

Though anthropologists of the stature of Victor Turner, Napoleon Chagnon and Robin Fox have openly declared their willingness to apply a Darwinian approach to human social behaviour, few sociologists and psychiatrists have followed their example. One exception is Brant Wenegrat, whose concept of 'flexible mutualism' (1989) we have already mentioned. 'Flexible mutualism', he argued, is an evolved strategy 'hard-wired' into the species, causing us as individuals to form stable groups within which we may co-operate for our long-term mutual benefit. This may be understood as an attempt to give Locke's 'social contract' a root in human biology. Of the few psychiatrists who have adopted a similar approach, Mansell Pattison and Robert Ness (1989) argue that the human propensity to form what anthropologists term a 'commune' is 'a reflection of fundamental biosocial components of the human organism, not simply culturally patterned modes of living'. They stress the importance of religion as providing 'the cosmological glue that binds the fabric of social relations within the commune'. And the commune, they maintain, finds its fullest social expression in the intimate, small religious cult.

In seeking to establish the essence of these close-knit social entities, Pattison and Ness declare that, in the cult, 'we find a full rejection and withdrawal from the dominant ethos, an attempt to create a new social universe ...' This statement accurately summarizes the point we have been making throughout this chapter, and it carries our argument a stage further.

In our formulation so far we have observed that the charismatic prophet is thrown up by his group when it passes through the preliminary crisis heralding its impending split and dispersal – as if he were a piece of precious flotsam brought ashore by a tempestuous tide. We can now see that this falls short of the truth, for it attributes too passive a role to the prophet. Far from being produced by divisions within the group, the prophet engages himself actively in promoting them. By undergoing his personal revelation and then preaching it within the group, he generates what we may term the 'unacceptable opposite' which his disaffected followers endorse and proceed to flaunt in the face of the establishment – the elders in control of the parent group – thus effectively alienating himself and his followers from it.

It is this critical factor that anthropological and psychiatric authorities of the cult phenomenon have hitherto failed to recognize. Though they have accurately described the mutual hostility that invariably develops between members of a cult and the surrounding community, they have viewed it as merely a cultural misfortune – as a reason for advertising the perils of cult membership, discouraging young people from joining cults, or even for forcibly abducting them once they have joined. Lacking an evolutionary understanding of cult formation, these authorities have failed to recognize that the *achievement of alienation* at this stage, between the new group and the parent group, is the charismatic leader's primary function.

While he is revered as a saint, a holy lamb of God by his devotees, he is perceived by the rest of the community as a ravening wolf. That is his role. It is his *raison d'être* to appear to the host society as a 'false prophet', a 'wolf in sheep's clothing', for the profound sense of alienation produced by his preaching is the necessary precondition for the group to split. The process resembles what goes on in a unicellular organism, such as an amoeba, when it reproduces itself by cell division – the process that biologists call *mitosis*. For mitosis to occur the cell nucleus has to split and polarize to opposite ends of the cell, driven there by an active repulsion that develops between the components of the two halves. When this process is complete, the whole cell divides into two parts which then go their separate ways to live out their life span.

In much the same way, the ideological conflict which the prophet generates between the two halves of a human community provides the active repulsion without which they could not separate. His charismatic leadership and revitalized (if heterodox) belief system then provides his band of followers with a renewed nucleus round which to built its separate identity. Re-energized with a triumphant sense of righteous self-sufficiency, they are then ready to move off in quest of their promised land.

5

Leaders and Led

The Revolutionary Relationship

I shall light a candle of understanding in thine heart, which
shall not be put out.   *2 Esdras*, 14:25

The passionate bonds formed between charismatic leaders and their
followers have long challenged the minds of those who have sought
to explain them.[1] As one might expect, there has been no shortage of
published insights and observations, or of ingenious descriptive terminologies. Emile Durkheim (1965) understood such phenomena as
the consequence of 'collective effervescence' emanating from a vola-
tile populace; Gustave Le Bon (1952) described the 'inspired leader'
as one recruited from 'the ranks of those morbidly nervous, excitable,
half-deranged persons who are bordering on madness', who dragged
his followers into his psychosis; while Weber (1946) designated him
an 'epileptic', Nietzsche a 'superman', and Eliade (1964) a 'technician
of the sacred'.

Many authorities are agreed that one of the most awesome things
about such leaders is their *shamanic* quality. The Tungus noun
saman means 'one who is excited, moved, raised.' As a verb, it means
'to know in an ecstatic manner.' Ethological studies of shamans in
Siberia, Africa and North America reveal them, as we have already
noted, to be close to the borderline but not over it (they are schizotypal, not schizophrenic). As with all charismatic leaders, their
influence arises from the uncanny, hypnotic power of their personalities, the force of their rapidly shifting emotions, the bizarre manner
of their speech, their capacity to enter a state of dissociation and to
leave it at will, and their apparent ability to put themselves in close
touch with the unconscious and to articulate its contents, in a way

93

that convinces their followers that they are divinely inspired (Eliade, 1964).

Central to the charismatic experience is the ecstatic merger of leader and led in a form of *participation mystique* which assumes religious intensity. The inspired figure is always one who stands apart, completely focused on his inner vision. This sets him on a level above that of ordinary humanity. It means that he speaks with the conviction of 'higher authority', which puts the followers in awe of him. They adore him and long to place themselves under his influence, for he can heal their fears of separation by giving them direction and welcoming them into the arms of a charismatic group. With time, this union, even in the most secular charismatic movement, assumes an unmistakably religious form, as the new group is bound together by its faith and rituals. One of the most devastating upheavals in European history was due to a charismatic movement of this kind.

Hitler and the Third Reich

Fascism is a religion; the twentieth century will be known in history as the century of Fascism ... I should be pleased, I suppose, that Hitler has carried out a revolution along our lines. But they are Germans, so they will end by ruining our ideas.

Benito Mussolini, on the accession of Hitler to power

We have argued that the social conditions from which charismatic leaders characteristically arise are similar to those which would have prevailed in an ancestral group that had outgrown its available resources – deprivation, mutual suspicion and hostility, lack of cohesion, the decay of traditional authority, and desperation intensifying to a sense of severe crisis. All this induces paranoia and feelings of wounded narcissism among the alienated individuals of the disaffected group and renders them susceptible to the 'borderline' utterances of the charismatic. Having undergone a mazeway resynthesis, he presents them with a new vision and a new goal. In Germany all these circumstances were in place for the advent of Adolf Hitler as Reich Chancellor in 1933 – the social fragmentation and internal hostility following the defeat in the First World War, rocketing inflation followed by the great depression of 1929, millions out of work and on the breadline, government locked between the numerous parties of the left and the right, the sense of being victims of 'encirclement' by hostile neighbours, and of being 'stabbed in the back by the traitors of 1918' (Hiden and Farquarson, 1988). A society in this chaotic state is ripe for domination by a schizotypal personality who is able to reflect its misery and to empower it with a vision of salvation.

A truly prophetic letter was written by General Ludendorff to President Hindenburg when the latter appointed Hitler as Chancellor: 'By your nomination of Hitler as Chancellor of the Reich, you have delivered our fatherland to one of the greatest demagogues of all time. I solemnly prophesy that this unholy man will throw the Reich into a precipice and bring our nation into unspeakable misery. Future generations will curse you in your grave for your deed.' For Hitler, the providential moment that decided his career came one day in the autumn of 1919 after he had given a particularly successful lecture to soldiers still seething with discontent over Germany's capitulation the year before. Suddenly a tremendous realization struck him, as he recalled in *Mein Kampf*: 'I could speak.' Hitler's biographer, Joachim Fest (1974) commented: 'That moment signified – if any specific moment did – the breakthrough to himself, the "hammer stroke" of fate, that shattered the shell of everyday life.'

Hitler was unquestionably a charismatic leader in Weber's sense of being an extraordinary individual who appears at a time of social crisis and compelling need for political and social change. Hitler certainly saw himself as a messianic leader whom Providence had chosen for the purpose of exalting Germany above all other nations so as to free the world from the 'poison' of international Jewry. At every stage of his career he felt the guiding hand of Providence and had sublime faith in his intuitions, which, he was certain, were divinely inspired: 'I go the way that Providence dictates with the assurance of a sleepwalker', Hitler declared. His extraordinary political and military successes up to 1942, often achieved in flat contradiction to the advice of his generals, confirmed this for him, as did his apparently miraculous escapes from death, which occurred with increasing frequency. His initial triumphs, combined with his charisma, persuaded the majority of Germans to believe in his Providential mission, and to persist in this belief even when he began to suffer massive defeats. Such was the strength of their devotion that they remained loyal to the end. The Third Reich did not fall because of internal dissensions but because of the overwhelming power of the Allied Forces massed against it. As is generally the case with movements following a cultic pattern, insiders saw their Führer as a Messiah, while outsiders saw him not as a saviour but as a devil.

But was the Nazi Party a cult? Strictly speaking it was not, though in its earliest years it resembled one and it did expand rapidly into a form of secular religion: Nazism had its Messiah, its Holy Book (*Mein Kampf*), its cross (the swastika), its religious processions (the Nuremberg Rally), its rituals (the Beer Hall Putsch Remembrance Parade), its anointed élite (the SS), its hymn (the *Horst Wessel Lied*), excommunication and death for heretics (the concentration camps), its devils (the Jews), its millennial promise (the Thousand Year Reich), and its Promised Land (the East).

Was Hitler a schizotypal personality? A considerable literature has been generated round the subject of Hitler's psychopathology. Most authorities agree that he suffered from a number of psychiatric symptoms, such as hypochondria, bacteriophobia and syphilophobia associated with excessive bathing and handwashing, as well as paranoid ideas. Most agree that he did not display signs of any major psychotic disorder; but there is disagreement concerning his personality type. Many have variously detected in him characteristic features of borderline, narcissistic, hysterical and anti-social personality disorders, but few if any have examined the possibility that Hitler had a schizotypal personality disorder.

In an extensive review of the literature, Fritz Redlich (1998) casts doubt on the value of attempts to force a psychiatric diagnosis on Hitler, preferring 'precise and subtle description' to inaccurate generalizations, though he acknowledges that 'with some pushing and shoving Hitler could be fit into the Procrustes bed' of borderline personality disorder as defined by DSM-IV. Redlich also gives muted support for the case advanced by Bromberg and Small (1983) that Hitler's personality combined borderline with narcissistic features.

Diagnoses in psychiatry are never mutually exclusive, particularly when it comes to diagnosing personality disorders. We agree that Hitler displayed certain narcissistic, borderline, hysterical and anti-social personality traits, but we will argue that the core character-

istics most characteristic of Hitler's personality indicate that he did
indeed have a schizotypal personality disorder.

As mentioned above, diagnosis of schizotypal personality disorder
can be established if five or more of the following features are
present: ideas of reference; odd beliefs or magical thinking; unusual
perceptual experiences; odd thinking and speech; suspiciousness or
paranoid ideas; inappropriate or constricted affect; behaviour or
appearance that is odd; lack of close friends or confidants other than
first-degree relatives; and excessive social anxiety associated with
paranoid fears rather than negative judgements about the self. Careful examination of the extensive records which exist of Hitler's
behaviour make it clear that, with the possible exception of ideas of
reference, he satisfies all of these criteria, and not merely five of
them.

Examples of Hitler's 'odd beliefs or magical thinking' abound in his
'table talk', the turgid monologues which he inflicted each night on
his bored and exhausted entourage. Thus he believed he could read
other peoples' thoughts and exert magical control over them and that
he had a sixth sense that protected him from danger. For example,
having made a speech at the Party Beer-Cellar in Munich just before
the outbreak of the Second World War, something suddenly prompted
him to leave, instead of staying on to chat with the Party faithful as
was his custom. Within minutes of his departure a bomb exploded,
killing eight of the old comrades and injuring scores of others. He
seems to have experienced no such premonition in March 1943 when
a bomb was placed on the plane in which he flew back to Berlin from
the Eastern front, but the bomb failed to detonate. A further attempt
to assassinate him at an exhibition a few days later also failed
because, once again, he decided on impulse to leave early. 'Who says
I am not under the special protection of God?' he exclaimed. An
example of his magical thinking is his frequently repeated declaration that he and Germany were mystically merged: 'I know that
everything that you are, you are through me, and everything that I
am, I am through you alone!'

Of the 'unusual perceptual experiences' reported by Hitler, he
acknowledged that he heard voices like those which inspired Joan of
Arc: they told him to rescue the Fatherland from the Jews. He also
claimed that he had a vision of Wotan, the old German war god,

pointing to the East above the heads of the cheering Viennese crowds at the time of the Austrian Anschluss.

Hitler's 'odd thinking and speech' is apparent not only in his monologues and writings, but also in his broadcast speeches. In particular he revealed the schizotypal penchant for the use of idiosyncratic language and neologisms. This often went along with that other hallmark of schizotypy, behaviour that is 'odd, eccentric, or peculiar'. For example, the Swedish businessman, Birger Dahlerus who acted as a go-between for the German and British governments immediately prior to the outbreak of war in 1939, recorded a meeting which took place on August 26th:

[Suddenly, says Dahlerus, Hitler stopped in the middle of the room and stood there staring.] His voice was blurred and his behaviour that of a completely abnormal person. He spoke in staccato phrases and it was clear that his thoughts were concentrated on the tasks which awaited him in the case of war. 'If there should be war,' he said, 'then I will build U-boats, build U-boats, U-boats.' His voice became more indistinct and finally one could not follow him at all. Then he pulled himself together, raised his voice as though addressing a large audience and shrieked: 'I will build airplanes, build airplanes, airplanes, build airplanes, airplanes and will destroy my enemies.' [Dahlerus says that Hitler seemed more like a phantom from a Swedish saga than a real person. Hitler continued to speak as if he were in a trance:] 'War does not frighten me, encirclement of Germany is an impossibility, my people admire and follow me faithfully. If privations lie ahead I shall be the first to starve and set my people a good example. I will spur them to superhuman efforts'. His eyes were glassy, his voice unnatural as he went on: 'If there should be no butter I shall be the first to stop eating butter, eating butter. My German people will loyally and gladly do the same.' He paused, his glance wandered and he said 'If the enemy can hold out for several years, I, with my willpower over the German people, can hold out one year longer. Thereby I know that I am superior to all the others.'

At a subsequent meeting, Dahlerus reports that Hitler became even more excited and began waving his arms and shouting in his face: ' "If England wants to fight for a year, I shall fight for a year, if England wants to fight for two years, I shall fight two years ..." He paused then yelled, his voice rising to a shrill scream and his arms milling wildly: "If England wants to fight for three years, I shall fight for three years ..." The movements of his body now followed those of his arms and when he finally bellowed "and if necessary I will fight for ten years", brandished his fist and bent down so it nearly touched the floor.' (Quoted by Redlich, 1998). The 'inappropriate affect' which struck Dahlerus as so bizarre at a diplomatic conference is yet a further schizotypal characteristic.

Many have commented on Hitler's eyes, especially on their hypnotizing power, and how, when he turned them on you, they seemed to bore into your soul. His eyes also had an uncanny capacity to reflect the emotions which coursed through him, and this could have an oddly unsettling effect. The British Ambassador to Berlin, Sir Eric Phipps, who was regarded in Foreign Office circles as something of a wit, had a long interview with Hitler on June 30th 1934: 'Whilst I spoke he eyed me hungrily like a tiger', reported Phipps, 'I derived the distinct impression that had my nationality and status been different I should have formed part of his evening meal' (Jaroch, 2000).

Observers also spoke of Hitler's 'terrible uninhibited garrulousness', the rambling, incoherent, and uncontrolled pressure of speech, and the difficulty they experienced in following his line of argument. Examples of his neologisms abound: he spoke of 'syphilization' (*Syphilisierung*), the 'mammonification' of the human mating instinct, and the 'Jewification' of spiritual life. He also had a tendency to turn nouns into adjectives and adverbs, such as 'Manchesterly' (*Manchesterlich*), and 'lemonade-y' (*limonadig*)'. His capacity for wild metaphor was legendary: having massacred the SA leadership he declared to the Reichstag, 'I have given the order to shoot the main culprits and have given further orders to burn out the ulcers of the well poisoning to the raw flesh' (Redlich, 1998).

That Hitler displayed 'suspiciousness and paranoid ideas' is beyond doubt. It is characteristic of all charismatic movements that as the group coalesces around its leader and celebrates its sense of being extraordinary, unparalleled and 'chosen', so it becomes increasingly hostile to all other groups. This is fuelled by a shared paranoia between the leader and the led. The actual nature of the paranoid belief system is usually revealed to the leader, and by him to his followers, with all the certainty of a delusional conviction: once formed it is unshakeable and all other beliefs centre round it. Hitler seems to have undergone a gradual 'mazeway resynthesis' which started during his pre-war period as a down-and-out in a flophouse in Vienna and reached its apogee in the autumn of 1919 when, revealing his vision to an audience of soldiers, he discovered that he could 'speak'.

For Hitler, with his obsessions about disease, germs and contamination, his conviction that the Jewish and Slavic peoples must be eliminated was represented as an act of public hygiene indispensable for the purification of the world in preparation for the millennial rule of the Master Race. Erik Erikson introduced the term *pseudospeciation* to describe the way in which one human group can identify and treat members of other groups as if they were lower forms of animal life and not human at all. It then becomes possible to exterminate them without feelings of guilt. Hitler commonly referred to the Jews as *Untermenschen* (subhumans). For him the Jew was the arch enemy, the Antichrist, and he prophesied an apocalyptic Armageddon in which the Jews would be destroyed, a prophecy which he all but fulfilled. Even at the end, when he knew the war was lost, Hitler expressed satisfaction that at least he had killed the Jews: 'we have lanced the Jewish abscess; and the world of the future will be eternally grateful to us' (*The Testament of Adolf Hitler: The Bormann Documents*).

As Anthony Storr (1996) pointed out, prophets, messiahs and gurus are both élitist and anti-democratic: they dominate their disciples, they don't make friends. This was abundantly so of Hitler, who, true to the DSM-IV criterion of schizotypal personality disorder, displayed a distinct 'lack of close friends or confidants'. According to his foreign minister, Ribbentrop, he did not want people to get close to him. As his architect, Albert Speer said: 'If Hitler had a friend, it would be me.' Hitler's relations with his general staff were always distant and wary – even more so after the plot of July 20th 1944. Towards the end of his life, Hitler said that he could rely only on Blondi (his dog) and Fraülein Braun (his mistress).

Finally, Hitler's 'social anxiety' depended for its relief on the adulation of the German people, and his 'paranoid fears' were never due to negative judgements of himself but to the unutterably evil projections which he put onto the Jews.

There can be little doubt, therefore, that Hitler fits the clinical profile of a schizotypal personality disorder, whatever additional traits he may have shown. Is there any evidence to suggest that he possessed a genetic predisposition to this disorder? Some evidence exists that he may. His paternal grandmother, Maria Schickelgruber, had a nephew called Joseph Veit, who had several children who were mentally ill. Two of his daughters suffered from mental retardation, another daughter died in a mental hospital, and a son committed suicide. In addition, Hitler's maternal aunt, who had a local reputation for being odd, ill-humoured and crazy, was diagnosed by the family physician as schizophrenic (Redlich, 1998). Hitler's preoccupation with questions of heredity, race and degeneration, would suggest that he was aware of having mental illness in his family and that this deeply worried him – as did the possibility that his paternal grandfather could have been a Jew, making himself a 'quarter Jew'. His involvement in the Nazi euthanasia programme to kill mentally retarded and schizophrenic patients as well as his genocide of the Jews could have been – at least in part – a symbolic effort to eliminate these traces of 'degeneration' from his own body as well as from the body politic of the Reich.

As is often the case with the relatives of schizophrenics, Hitler was a highly creative (as well as destructive) character. He had a life-long love of architecture and art and, even as the Russian troops closed in on his bunker in Berlin, he was still poring over the plans and models of the magnificent capital city he intended to build when the war was over. He viewed himself as an artist–politician, which fitted in with his charismatic style of leadership. But he was a creative artist who lacked talent, and this was his tragedy as well as Europe's. His rejection by the Vienna Academy of Fine Arts when he applied to become a student there in 1907 may have been one of the most fateful turning points of history: it helped to change him from a budding artist into a budding dictator.

Characteristic of borderline and schizotypal personalities is their capacity to put themselves in the liminal state (the threshold between conscious and unconscious processes). Hitler possessed this in full measure, especially when he addressed an audience, and it gave him his mesmeric power as an orator. Though he discovered this power while lecturing to troops just after the First World War, he recalled that his first intimation of its historic significance came to him as a young man after attending a performance of *Rienzi*, which recounts with Wagnerian majesty the tale of Cola di Rienzi, rebel and tribune of the people, who was alienated from his fellow men and destroyed by their failure to understand him. Hitler's sole boyhood friend, August Kubizek, was there on this occasion and described what happened when they strolled on the Freinberg above Linz after the performance. 'Words burst from him like a backed-up flood breaking through crumbling dams. In grandiose, compelling images, he sketched for me his future and that of his people.' When Kubizek met the Führer thirty years later in Bayreuth, Hitler remarked: 'It began at that hour' (Fest, 1983).

So it happened that, under Hitler's guidance, inspired as he was by the old Teutonic myths, the whole Nazi movement took on a pseudo-religious quality, with its rituals, parades and swastikas. Recognizing him as a Messiah, the German masses streamed to him, a contemporary account declares, 'as to a saviour'. Kurt Luedecke, who was to become one of Hitler's entourage, only to end up in Oranienburg concentration camp, described the spell Hitler cast on him, as an orator: 'Presently my critical faculty was swept away ... I do not know how to describe the emotions that swept over me as I heard this man ... the passion of his sincerity seemed to flow from him into me. I experienced an exaltation that could be likened only to religious conversion' (Fest, 1983).

As a party, the Nazis had not so much a coherent political programme as a set of prejudices rooted in Hitler's personal myth and his denial and projection of his own 'shadow' personality. A joke current in the 1930s referred to National Socialist ideology as 'the World as Will without Idea'! As with all charismatic leaders, the great puzzle is to explain the credulity and tremendous loyalty they inspire among their followers. Though Hitler's world view had its political roots in the perception he shared with the German people of the iniquities of the Treaty of Versailles, it was, in essence, no less crazy than that espoused by other schizotypal leaders. He openly endorsed

102

Hörbinger's 'world ice theory', which proposed a perpetual struggle throughout the universe between fire and ice, and his imagination was inflamed by visions of cosmic catastrophe: 'We may perish, perhaps', he said, 'but we shall take the world with us. Muspilli, universal conflagration.' He portrayed German nationalism as engaged in a life-and-death sub-Darwinian struggle against the forces of Darkness as represented by Bolshevism, the International Jewish Conspiracy, the spread of viruses and termites, and the spirochaetes of syphilis. It seems totally incredible that a highly educated nation could fight a world war on the basis of such a programme, causing the death of 55 million people and inflicting wounds on European civilization from which it has still not fully recovered.

Already in 1936, C.G. Jung, who has been unjustly accused of pro-Nazi and anti-Semitic sympathies (Stevens, 1994), foresaw this outcome. Teutonic mythology is unique in that its gods are overthrown by the powers of Darkness. The whole mythic drama ends in *Ragnorök* as Valhalla is consumed with flames, like the Third Reich in 1945: 'The impressive thing about the German phenomenon', wrote Jung (1936), 'is that one man, who is obviously "possessed", has infected a whole nation to such an extent that everything is set in motion and has started rolling on its course to perdition' (CW10, para. 388). There is no doubt that the Treaty of Versailles, the hyperinflation of the 1920s and the depression of the early 1930s, all contributed to Hitler's rise to power as the historians always tell us, but it is unlikely that his rise would have been as meteoric, or that his regime would have lasted as long as it did, had Hitler not possessed the terrible capacity to constellate the most awesome archetypes of the collective unconscious both in himself and in the people whose misfortune it was to follow him. The life of Adolf Hitler is a horrific example of the evil that can be inflicted on the world by one individual who combines a schizotypal ability to access the liminal state with a total abdication of all ethical responsibility for the enormous power placed at his disposal.

The alchemy of revolution

A nation is a society united in a delusion about its ancestry and
by a common hatred of its neighbours.   Dean Inge

By now the reader will be wholly familiar with the process of cult
creation. The prophet goes through his personal crisis (his creative
illness), experiences his mazeway resynthesis, and comes out of it
with what amounts to an intact delusional system. Lacking close
friends or critical mentors, he proceeds to elaborate his new belief
system in isolation. Unlike the ideas of artists, scientists or mathematicians, the ideas of prophets are not subject to the procedures of
'peer review', for this is the last thing that a prophet wants. What he
craves is not wise critics but a band of credulous disciples who will
hang on his lips and confirm that he is indeed the God-inspired
messenger he says he is, and wholeheartedly embrace his teaching.
As we have repeatedly observed, it is at times of crisis that people feel
in need of a guru; but it is all too easy to forget that the guru feels no
less in need of disciples. 'In studying gurus', wrote Anthony Storr
(1996), 'one constantly encounters the paradox that people who appear so supremely self-confident that they radiate charisma are those
who have a special need for disciples to reassure them.' The intensity
of the guru's conviction, so indispensable to his charisma, is often less
absolute than it appears, comments Storr, and his self-confidence
requires a constant transfusion of adulation and affirmation from his
followers, for 'it is difficult to sustain a belief in the authenticity of a
new revelation if no one else shares it.'

To accept the literal truth of the delusional system on which a new
cult is based requires willing collusion on the part of both sides – the
leader and the led. In the alchemy of cult formation, these are the
ingredients which are placed in the retort. How does the revolutionary reaction between them come about? What is the necessary
catalyst, or 'philosopher's stone'?

Many authorities have advanced sociological and psychodynamic
theories to account for the extraordinary ability of leaders to recruit
emotion from followers and channel it into feelings of loyalty for the
group and hostility for potential enemies; but these are partial
explanations which ultimately prove unsatisfactory because they fail

104

to recognize the existence of one crucial possibility: that, like other social primates, we are a leader-orientated species – we share a collective inclination to respect leaders and comply with their decisions. People will follow a leader and render him what services he may require provided only that they perceive his authority to be *legitimate*. In the majority of cases, this legitimacy is thought to have been conferred by the gods, as in the Divine Right of Kings.

To live co-operatively within a human group (Wenegrat's 'flexible mutuality'), and to gain admission to its social hierarchy, requires not only submission to the authority of its leader(s) but acceptance of its values, customs and beliefs. Generally, these beliefs are encoded in the religious doctrines and initiation rites prescribed by the community's gods, as articulated by charismatic 'hero–saviours' in the distant past. It is when the group and its accepted doctrines are under threat that the schizotypal leader arises to revolutionize the arbitrary belief system to which members of the community have been indoctrinated, so as to establish a new and no less arbitrary system of his own. It is a process as regular and predictable as a plant that propagates by sending out a runner bearing a replica of itself.

The archetypal stages of the process must be gone through, otherwise the inherent anticipations of the novices will not be met. Without the requisite miraculous conversion and mystical experiences, the voices and the visions, the road to charismatic leadership is blocked. Recital of these crucial events is necessary to create the legend on which the leader's charisma is based. Had Jesus not appeared to the Reverend Sun Myung Moon one Easter morning when he was 16 and informed him that he had been chosen to complete Christ's mission, there would have been no Unification Church (Barker, 1984; Galanter, 1979); and had Satya Sai Baba not been bitten by a scorpion at the age of 14 to induce the realization that he was the reincarnation of the legendary Indian saint, Sai Baba of Shirdi, his cult would never have come into existence. The splendour of the leader's association with divinity not only draws people to him, like bees to a pot of honey, but is rubbed off on his associates who experience powerful feelings of 'specialness' by virtue of being near him. The honey of charisma sticks to them and glues them to each other in the same way as Anton Mesmer conceived the transmission of 'animal magnetism' and Melanesian peoples ascribe to the adhesive properties of 'mana'.

However, acceptance of a group's ideology does not seem to be the primary requisite of membership. On the contrary, membership comes first and indoctrination follows later. As contemporary studies have established, cult recruitment is most successful when top priority is given to making the subject feel wanted and part of the group, rather than through the use of ideological persuasion. 'Potential recruits are invited to a dinner or social meeting at which they are fed and emotionally cobbled', reports Wenegrat (1989). 'Members go out of their way to make them feel special. They become the targets of "love-bombing" … Religious dogma is mentioned only after potential recruits are clearly attached to the group.' Then adopting the dogma merely becomes a process of accepting the opinion of one's friends. 'In terms of human mutualism, adopting the dogma is doing what comes naturally: accepting the consensual reality of what has become one's perceived social group … Observers are sometimes astonished by the things recruits will believe to maintain their newfound sense of belonging. The recruit's beliefs are sometimes likened to hypnotic or dissociative phenomena …' (Wenegrat, 1989). What potential members come to believe is decided through identification with the culture they find themselves in.

Being an evolutionary psychiatrist, and not a sociologist, Brant Wenegrat insists that the human predisposition to adopt the world view of one's in-group represents a process more fundamental than mere passive 'enculturation': it is an innate adaptation. As numerous studies have demonstrated, people actively want to conform to the views of those with whom they feel identified and bonded. When joining a new group, such as a political party, an army unit, a boarding school, a religious sect or a cult, people are willing to abandon previously held beliefs and embrace those of the group, even when they fly in the face of reason or contrary evidence.

Describing his experience of participating in the rituals of a cult he had infiltrated, William Shaw (1994) wrote: 'I realize I am acting out a fundamental, depressing lesson about how cults operate. Once the collective has been formed, no one dares break ranks and say, "Hold on. What we're doing is really stupid." Once you've started tearing up reality, and rebuilding it in a different shape, you don't want to step out of line or the whole precarious structure will crumble' (p. 38). Why should this be so? One possibility is that it's an adaptation which would have been particularly advantageous in small hunter–gatherer groups where a solid consensus of belief would reduce internal dissension and promote concerted action in the struggle to survive.

It is interesting that in English we have no noun for a person who is credulous, whereas we do for the sceptic. Could this reflect the English empirical temperament – the tradition of Locke and Hume? A 'credulist' is one who puts belief before the evidence of the senses, the sceptic puts evidence before belief. But, here again, we seem to have opposite poles of a continuum, for some people are evidently more credulous than others, but no one is so sceptical as to be incapable of believing anything. We, for example, are sceptical about the occurrence of alien abductions but credulous about the existence of Siberia, though neither of us has ever been there to see it with his own eyes. What one believes has much to do with the perceived authority of one's informant.

There is a very real sense in which we are all to a greater or lesser extent credulous because we possess, in all probability, an algorithm (an innate learning mechanism) for indoctrinability, which predisposes us to accept and endorse the consensual belief systems of the community in which we live. Social cohesion, defence and competitive efficiency depend on this willing acceptance of the consensus and the inclination to give credence to what we are told. Some similar kind of 'credulity' is apparent in all social animals for the same reasons. A bee colony would not survive very long if it were sceptical about the truth of the message conveyed by a successful forager with his orientation dance as to the whereabouts of new supplies of nectar. The survival of human communities depends on the readiness with which vital information can be passed from one generation to the next. Here the readiness to be indoctrinated is indispensable: the credulous child is a teachable child. As Dawkins (1995) has pointed out, belief in authority is a quicker and safer method of learning to survive in the world than having to learn everything afresh by trial and error.

Sociologists have long recognized the human propensity to co-operate with a social group larger than the family, but, here again, they

107

have lacked the phylogenetic understanding that affiliative behaviour and alliance formation, as well as in-group/out-group distinctions, are evolved adaptations whose selective advantage has rendered them characteristic of all human populations. In-group solidarity increases when the group finds itself ideologically or geographically isolated. In the ancestral environment, the ideological split would have been the necessary preliminary to the geographical split and the exodus to the 'promised land'. Should the group have been fortunate enough to find a vacant and isolated territory in which to establish itself, then its chances of survival and of creating a new settlement, with its own religion, mythology and language, would have been greatly enhanced. It is surely not without significance that many of the sects and cults that have thriven in the last 200 years are those which have embraced social isolation – the early Mormons, the Mennonites, the Amish, the Hutterites, the Shakers and many others, have survived and retained their identity through their insistence on maintaining their separate settlements.

Another factor supporting the solidarity of charismatic groups is the emphasis many of them place on communal living. This is as true of contemporary groups such as the Unification Church and the Hare Krishnas as it is of longer established communities such as the Hutterites and the Shakers, members of which tend to think of each other as belonging to the same 'family' (Foster, 1984).

The beliefs espoused by people once they have joined a cult often strike outsiders (who knew them before they joined) as so bizarre and incredible as to make them suspect that initiation into group membership must have involved the coercive procedures of 'thought reform' or 'brainwashing', like those employed by the Chinese during the Korean War to convert American POWs into communists. 'Brainwashing' was designed to break down the prisoner's sense of personal identity and cause regression to a childlike state of dependency in which he became susceptible to re-indoctrination at the hands of the Chinese 'parental' authority (Sargeant, 1957). There is little evidence, however, that contemporary cults indulge in such enforced 'reorganization of the mazeway' in new members.[2] On the contrary, as many studies have confirmed, the majority of recruits undergo what William James called 'conversion of self-surrender', having joined the cult voluntarily in the absence of any kind of coercion. It is also found that most of them just as voluntarily leave the cult, usually within about two years of joining. Increasingly, sociologists have come to see recruits less as the passive victims of unscrupulous cult leaders but rather as disaffected individuals seeking a creative transformation in their lives (Richardson, 1989). Indeed, the most striking examples of coercion have come not from studies of cults but from the behaviour of anti-cult activists who have forcibly abducted cult members at the request of their families so that they may be subjected to 'de-programming'.

However, the actual conversion is almost invariably experienced as something that happens beyond the subject's control. There is a sense of being thrown into the melting pot, a surrendering not only of one's old ego identity but of yielding to a transformative experience which takes over before one knows what has happened. A professional 'de-programmer' who infiltrated the 'Children of God' cult felt something of the kind happening to him: 'You can feel it coming on. You start to doubt yourself. You start to question everything you believe in. Then you find yourself saying and doing the same things they are. You feel like you're sinking in sand, drowning – sometimes you get dizzy' (Conway and Seigelman, 1978).

Clearly, people are drawn to cults because they provide something they cannot find in society outside. This is particularly true of young people passing through the college years, who provide the main target for cult recruiters. Traditional societies provided initiation rites to promote the transition from childhood in the context of the family to adulthood in the context of the group. Our society provides no such assistance, and it is in anticipation of finding emotional support and guidance during this period of transition that young people may join a cult. According to Saul V. Levine (1989), Professor of Psychiatry at the University of Toronto, who has been particularly interested in this age group, they generally become estranged from their parents during their period of maximum commitment to their cult. 'They feel especially sanctified and enhanced. Not only are their earlier feelings of alienation, demoralization and low self-esteem overcome, but they feel "wonderful" in all respects. They experience happiness, clarity of thought and high motivation. They feel healthier and want to share their sense of self improvement; they proselytize, they propound, they bore. Their bliss and happiness are,

109

however, not contagious. Their simplistic reasoning, their overriding commitment, their narrowed focus, their suspension of critical judgement – all these offend and concern us, but they are hallmarks of fundamental true believers of any ilk' (Levine, 1989).

The psychotherapeutic benefits of becoming involved in a new religion or cult have been summarized by Kilbourne (1989) and by Robbins and Anthony (1982). They list such factors as the termination of illicit drug use, renewed commitment to work, relief of neurotic distress, suicide prevention, decrease in feeling lonely and moral confusion, increased social compassion or social responsibility, self-actualization, decrease in psycho-somatic symptoms and a general sense of wellbeing. It appears that the extent of relief from distress is correlated with the intensity of the new religious affiliation. The probability is that many cults which receive little or no media attention perform some of these helpful functions for their members. It is the bad cults that exploit or destroy their followers that hit the headlines.

Psychoanalytic interpretations of the cult phenomenon have emphasized the importance of *transference* and *projection* in attaching followers to their leader. Just as patients will 'transfer' onto the person of the analyst feelings, hopes and expectations they have experienced in relation to important figures in the past (usually parental figures), so followers project similarly derived feelings, hopes and expectations onto the leader. Such transference may be accompanied by a 'regression' to earlier, more childish modes of dependency and a relative abandonment of independent, adult responsibility for organizing and running their lives.

In addition, the *superego* (an internalized moral authority, again usually based on the parents) may be projected onto the leader, with the result that his judgements are experienced as possessing a moral strength which must be obeyed with complete compliance. In addition to these Freudian insights, Jungians would add the archetypal components that may be activated in relation to an analyst or a charismatic leader – the Hero–Saviour, Father, Great Mother, the Healer/Shaman, as well as the Self (the term given by Jung to the entire archetypal endowment of the phylogenetic psyche, which, he argued, was collectively projected by people subscribing to a monotheistic religion onto the image of 'God').

110

The manner by which the leader's delusional system becomes adopted by his disciples has been compared to the phenomenon of *folie à deux*, whereby the delusions of a dominant psychotic person may be uncritically accepted by his or her subdominant but mentally healthy relative, friend or spouse. In the case of cult members, *folie à deux* would be more accurately described as *folie à plusieurs*. These psychodynamic formulations are all compatible with our hypothesis that the propensities to cult formation and group splitting are adaptive predispositions peculiar to the human species, acquired through natural selection.

The war of the generations

One generation passeth away, and another generation cometh.

Ecclesiastes, 1:2

One potential fault line along which all human communities can split is that which exists between younger and older generations, particularly with respect to the different ways in which they acquire the cultural traditions and physical resources of the group. Through evolution, culture has come to perform in human societies much the same function as instinct in mammalian societies, for culture is the means by which adaptive wisdom is passed from one generation to the next. Survival depends on how each generation relates to its cultural inheritance. While culture is a gift which each generation acquires, it cannot be taken for granted; it has to be *earned*. This is one reason why initiation rites have been of world-wide importance: they are enabling rituals through which the dying past is reincarnated in the living present.

In all human communities some sort of balance has to be achieved between the traditional forces of conservation and the progressive forces of change. Progress and survival demand that in the recurring conflict between the generations there should be no outright winner. A homeostatic balance must be maintained between the two opposing systems: the youthful revolutionaries and the elderly traditionalists. A complete break with tradition brought about by a walkover of the youthful progressives would imperil the competitive efficiency of society as would the triumph of conservative inflexibility through an implacable dictatorship of elders.

Freud considered that the older generation of males was wary of the rising generation because of the sexual threat that it posed; but this is only part of the story, and not the most significant part. Male adolescence is cued by a sudden dramatic increase in the amount of male hormone circulating in the blood: this fuels the sexual appetite, it is true, but it makes for much more aggressiveness as well. This is why young males challenge the status and authority of their elders and not merely their sexual prerogatives. More important still, they threaten the coherence of the group which cannot hope to survive in the struggle for existence if torn apart by inner strife between the generations. For this reason, all successful societies in the history of our species have had to find means of disciplining their young men and of channelling their energies into the service of society.

The dangerous moment comes at puberty, when intoxicated with a huge shot of testosterone, youths seek to shake off the constraints imposed by tradition and cast about for new ideals to pursue, new causes to embrace and new goals to be won. Konrad Lorenz (1970) has called this time 'the moult' (*die Mauser*). Declaring that 'it implies hazards quite as great as those threatening the newly moulted soft-shelled crab'! The pubertal moult is 'the open door through which new ideas gain entrance'. But these new ideas have to be compatible with the old and have to achieve balance with them: the arrogance of youth has to be countered by the wisdom of collective experience, as the young themselves come to appreciate when they get older.

However, the balances and counterbalances through which the conflicting perceptions of the generations are reconciled can break down at times of crisis, and the normal initiatory procedures on which social integration depends can fail. At such moments, the younger generation may seek to overthrow the hegemony of the elders by granting their allegiance to an alternative, God-given authority in the form of a charismatic leader. Should this leader prove powerful enough to displace the elders, as did Hitler in 1933, then the revolution succeeds and the 'young Turks' prevail. But should the elders prove immovable, then fissive pressures build up forcing the community to split. In either event, the archetypal con-figuration of charismatic leader empowering a charismatic group

112

would seem to provide both the necessary unit and the indispensable catalyst for cultural transformation to occur.

Of the two possibilities, the latter provides the more satisfactory solution, for it solves the resource problem of the parent group by promoting dispersal of its disaffected members. It is this function of group splitting and dispersal that the schizotypal personality is specifically adapted to perform.

6

Cult Politics

Power and Sex

Power is an aphrodisiac.   Henry Kissinger

The major problem confronting us is to explain how and why schizophrenia exists. How can the genetic predisposition to a 'low fertility' condition like schizophrenia remain so firmly established in the human gene pool that it is perpetually passed on from generation to generation throughout all the human populations that inhabit the globe? Many scholars have addressed this problem, and Crow (1995) has published a thorough and lucid review of the literature. Apart from general agreement about the teasing nature of the problem, there has emerged no consensus about its solution.

One answer is that the genes responsible, when present in not too heavy a loading, possess a selective advantage, in that they render people who carry them more creative and innovative. Provided these creative and innovative individuals were sufficiently fertile, their sexual activity would compensate for the low fertility of people who actually suffer from schizophrenia. This would then ensure the survival and transmission of schizotypal genes.

Could this be the genetic role for which nature has created the prophet? The idea that schizotypal personalities may possess the adaptive function of providing needy groups with charismatic prophets was first entertained by Erlenmeyer-Kimling and Paradowski in an article published in the *American Naturalist* in 1969. They rejected it, however, because they were under the impression that prophets have few children. They were wrong.

The prophet as stud

If a man believes he has been specially chosen by God, he is likely to conclude that he is entitled to special privileges.

Anthony Storr

Though some cult leaders advocate celibacy among their followers, few of them apply this injunction to themselves. Most of them behave like Jim Jones, David Koresh, Charles Manson, Georgei Ivanovitch Gurdjieff and David Berg: they exercise *droit de seigneur* over their community, siring numerous offspring in the process. David Brandt Berg (1919-94), founder of the Children of God, is a prime example. Subjected to a strict, sexually repressive upbringing by fundamentalist evangelical parents, he gives the classic schizoid or schizotypal history, describing himself, in capitals, as 'A VERY LONESOME LITTLE BOY'. He says, 'I had hardly any friends ... I was frail, shy and very reticent, a veritable bookworm and recluse who preferred to retreat to the world of study of other times and other places rather than participate in the foolishness and horrors of the hard, cruel world around me.'

He spent the first half of his life touring the United States with his parents as an itinerant preacher and did not experience his divine revelation until after the death of his domineering mother, when he was 49. Up to that point he had preached the conventional morality of a fundamentalist Christian. Then, one night, he reports that 'THE SPIRIT OF GOD ROSE UP WITHIN ME' and forced him to make a 'PUBLIC DECLARATION OF WAR ON THE RELIGIOUS SYSTEM'.

This transformation occurred in California in 1968 at the height of the 'sexual liberation movement'. It struck an immediate chord among the hippy 'beat' generation, and thousands flocked to him to become 'Children of God'. Steven A. Kent (1994) of the University of Alberta, whose *Lustful Prophet* is a psychohistory of Berg and his movement, declares: 'With the death of his mother, Berg's sexual guilt died as well, just in the very period that his own ministry was growing. For the rest of his life he engaged in a wide range of sexual activities with little if any apparent shame.' Making full use of his 'unique position of authority over thousands of people ... he un-

116

leashed his now guilt-less passions, and sanctified his deviance through scriptural interpretation and claims of divine revelation.' He employed religious sanctions to justify incestuous relations with his daughters and granddaughters, to justify his abandonment of his wife for a much younger woman, and to justify wildly promiscuous relations with his female disciples. As Kent records, 'he granted himself access to all COG women, and effectively destroyed monogamous marriages among his followers.'

Though remaining with his second partner, Maria, he established a personal harem, through which he rotated new women. He even took a teenage girl, called Rachel, as an additional wife, although he had overseen her marriage to a young man two years earlier. Such behaviour seems to have proved acceptable to most members of the cult. Any woman who experienced reluctance to accede to Berg's demands nevertheless felt compelled to do so through a powerful combination of peer pressure and the threat of religious censure. 'We have a sexy God', he preached, 'and a sexy religion and very sexy leader. If you don't like sex, you better get out while you can.'

Having successfully eroded the strength of marriage bonds between COG couples, Berg extended his control over his disciples' sexuality by commanding them to recruit new converts to Jesus through 'sexual love'. This form of sacred prostitution he called 'flirty fishing' to be performed by his personally ordained 'hookers for Jesus'. As Kent demonstrates, Berg was able to depend on the loyalty of his followers because of his success in using religious justifications to legitimate his rampant sexuality and 'liberated' beliefs. 'Berg established a social system in which followers equated resistance to him with hostility to God, which meant that members controlled one another with the same fierce consciences that they used to regulate themselves. Although hundreds (if not thousands) of people have left COG over the years, many of the apostates had difficult times doing so, partly because they felt they would be ungodly by their disloyalty.'

Similar techniques are available to all charismatic leaders, and it is not surprising that few can resist making full use of them. Jesus Christ seems to have been a shining exception in this regard, and Christian saints tended to follow his example, thus giving some scholars the false impression that holy men are people of low fertility. Virtually all cults come to assume a fixed social structure which is hierarchical and pyramidal, with the leader indisputably placed at the summit, his position rendered unassailable by divine sanction. Each cult is a small theocracy ruled by the prophet through an inner circle of trusted 'elders', 'lieutenants', or eldest sons and daughters, who are the enforcers of the cult's rules and the protectors of its doctrinal purity, however bizarre or immoral it might appear to outsiders. The leader may display great spontaneity, flexibility and imagination in coming up with his extraordinary notions and with religious justifications for his outrageous sexual behaviour, but, as Saul Levine (1989) has observed, 'Those on the rung below are the epitome of true believers – unwavering, inflexible, even intolerant.' Even in sexually exploiting their disciples, with full backing from the 'lieutenants', charismatic leaders prove strangely unpredictable. The Polynesian prophet, Yali, was so beset by willing followers, that he charged them five shillings a time for his sexual favours. Yet he was eventually imprisoned for rape. Bhagwan Shree Rajneesh, notorious for his collection of 93 Rolls Royces, taught his followers that sex is the path to enlightenment, and boasted that he himself had enjoyed intercourse with more women than any man in history. The fact that he suffered from premature ejaculation need not have diminished his reproductive success. However, he maintained that there were too many children being born into the world and encouraged female disciples to be sterilized and males to be vasectomized. As many as 200 complied, some bitterly regretting having done so, but many more may have been made pregnant by him. True to the antinomian spirit of gurus, Rajneesh's insistence on sexual freedom was the very opposite of traditional Hindu teaching, and it caused widespread offence.

Both Jim Jones and David Koresh were equally rapacious sexually and considered themselves divinely authorized to have sex with anyone they wished, using sex to dominate their followers rather than expressing erotic love. At Ranch Apocalypse, Koresh forbade married couples to have sexual relations, insisting that only he was permitted that privilege. Accordingly, he physically segregated partners, the men having their sleeping quarters on one floor of the building, the women on another. He taught that God had commanded him to take 140 wives and that it was a crucial part of his mission to fill the world with righteous children. It has been estimated that 17 of the 22 children who perished in the fire of April 1993 had been fathered by him. Anthony Storr suggests that it is possible that Koresh sacrificed the children of cult members because he was not their father. As several of his ex-followers testified, he taught that ritual sacrifice of children might be required by God. If this appalling possibility in fact occurred, it would go even further towards ensuring the propagation of his own genes at the expense of his male disciples.

The Maori, Rua, whom we met in Chapter 1, lived in a monogamous society, yet he had no less than twelve wives and a large number of children. His wives described the ecstatic experience of having intercourse with him as like being impregnated by the Holy Ghost (Webster, 1980).

Examples could be multiplied to illustrate the truth that, in contrast to the opinion of Erlenmayer-Kimling and Paradowski, charismatic prophets are notoriously, and one might almost say heroically, promiscuous. In those cults that endure, the leader's numerous offspring come to form an aristocracy which is responsible for perpetuating his divine memory, sustaining his ethos for the group and for passing on his schizotypal genes.

In using their power and status to acquire large numbers of sexual partners, charismatic leaders are doing no more than most men would in their position. Evolutionary psychology has moved a long way towards establishing the different sets of conscious assumptions and unconscious motives with which males and females approach one another as sexual partners.

The ease with which males can get their genes into the next generation is apparent from the simple fact that men produce infinitely more sperms than women do ova. In the course of her reproductive lifetime, a woman will produce little more than 400 eggs, while a man produces between 100 million and 200 million individual sperms, each containing a unique combination of his genes, every time he ejaculates. It follows that each man could, given the opportunity, inseminate and fertilize large numbers of women, and this disparity is reflected in the psychology of the two sexes. George Williams (1966) was the first to draw attention to the unequal sacrifices that males and females have to make in order to achieve reproductive success. For males, the necessary sacrifice is virtually zero in terms of energy and resource expenditure: their essential role

119

ends with copulation. For females, on the other hand, copulation is only the beginning. The relative cost to the mother in time, effort, calories, energy and pain, is so much greater than to the father that it confirms one's impression that nature can have no sense of justice at all. Yet the father's genes benefit equally with those of the mother. It is in the female's genetic interest, therefore, to assume the burdens of reproduction only when the social and economic circumstances are propitious and when she has taken great care to select the fittest available male.

The relative promiscuity of the male makes opportune sex far more appealing to him than it does to the female, with her need for masculine commitment; and anthropology has established that polygyny seems to be the natural state for humanity in the sense that men, given the chance of taking more than one wife, are strongly inclined to do so. Of the 1,154 societies for which anthropologists have data, no less than 980 of them (and that includes practically all known hunter–gatherer societies) have allowed a man to have two or more wives.

These differences are further underlined when communities of homosexual males are compared with communities of lesbians, for, in such communities, men and women are free to express their sexual proclivities without having to take into account the demands, wishes or needs of the opposite sex. It is found that male homosexuals are sexually more active than lesbians and, before the AIDS epidemic, they were much more promiscuous. In 1981, Bell *et al.* estimated that 25 per cent of male homosexuals had sex with more than a thousand partners. Lesbians, on the other hand, show no greater tendency to promiscuity than heterosexual women, their mean number of partners being only three in the course of their lifetime (Loney, 1974). While some homosexual males seek and find a lasting sexual bond with one partner, they are an exception. Close and lasting relationships are much commoner among lesbians. These findings are completely in accordance with the differential sexual strategies for heterosexual males and females as described by behavioural ecologists.

That heterosexual men generally do not have as many partners as their homosexual counterparts is because society – and more particularly women – will not allow them to get away with it. The leader of a cult, however, operates under few such inhibitions. Surrounded by devoted female disciples, in a community in which the rules are entirely of his making, he is in a position to indulge his sexual wishes wherever his fancy may take him.

As David Buss (1994) has pointed out, females normally select a long-term sexual strategy, preferring marriage and fidelity to a partner who they believe will provide for and protect them and their children. In exceptional circumstance, however, a woman will adopt a short-term sexual strategy, involving what is known, rather inelegantly, as 'extra-pair copulation', so as to take advantage of an opportunity to be fertilized by a man who is judged to possess more promising genes than her husband. Like the pop star or TV 'celebrity', the charismatic prophet is able to beguile his female devotees into adopting this short-term strategy. Just as a 'groupie' will yield herself to her pop-idol without any thought of obtaining vows of marriage from him, so the disciple will obey the summons to the prophet's bed in unconscious anticipation of impregnation by high-quality genes rather than vows of long-term support.

Similarly, a prospective wife may have to choose between becoming the only wife of an ordinary man or joining the harem of an exceptional one. If the prospective husband is important enough, she may be pulled across the 'polygamy threshold' and so abandon any aspiration she may have had for marital exclusiveness. Just as charismatic prophets are good at inducing some women to adopt the short-term strategy of occasional, opportunistic sex, so they appear accomplished in the art of lifting potential marriage partners over the 'polygamy threshold'.

One important question remains to be answered. Our theory may account for male proneness to schizophrenia, but how are we to account for the enormous populations of female schizophrenics who exist throughout the world? Schizophrenia is no respecter of gender. There are just as many schizophrenic women as men, though in women the age of onset is a few years later. This would suggest that both sexes are equally endowed with the capacity for mazeway resynthesis. But if so, why are the great majority of cult leaders men? Is schizophrenia the price that women have to pay so that male schizotypal prophets can split groups, collect harems, and sexually exploit their followers? Is the schizotypal propensity adaptive only in men? And if so, why has its manifestation not declined in females in the course of evolution in the same way as the prominence of breasts and nipples has declined in males?

For a trait to become less salient in one sex rather than the other requires a huge stretch of evolutionary time. The capacity for maze-way resynthesis, and its communication to followers, is dependent upon the evolution of language and consequently cannot be more than 5 million years old. This is not long enough for its expression to have become limited to one sex only, for deselecting a trait which is disadvantageous is an extremely slow process. Despite the number of deaths occurring in every generation as a result of burst appendixes, for example, the appendix is still present in us all, even though it conveys no advantage that we are aware of. Could the schizotypal propensity in women be similar? It is not possible at this juncture to say. But we know that schizotypal prophets attract schizotypal followers (Peters *et al.*, 1999).[1] The chances are, therefore, that many of a prophet's sexual partners will be schizotypal. This can only enhance the transmission of schizotypal genes to the next generation for both sexes. In those relatively rare instances where women become cult leaders, their fertility may be increased, but not nearly to the same extent as in their male counterparts. Their progeny will, however, be granted high status and thus stand a greater likelihood of reproductive success.

The main answer to the problem of female schizophrenia probably lies in the different strategies and biosocial goals of males and females. Whereas males are orientated to the political issues of group leadership and group allegiances, females are primarily committed to the personal issues of marriage, childbirth and child-rearing. With the exception of our own society during the last twenty years, this distinction is apparent across all cultures and is the result of both innate imperatives and social influences. Not surprisingly, it affects the kind of delusions characteristically experienced by men and women in ways we have described in Chapter 4. Men tend to become possessed by the Hero–Saviour archetype with its built-in propensity to recruit and lead followers, while women become identified with the Great Mother archetype with its inclination to protect, nurture and give succour. The public orientation of the male would thus account for the preponderance of male prophets and the relative scarcity of female ones.

Considerable though the female contribution may be, the greater reproductive success of male prophets ensures the continuance of schizotypal genes in the human gene pool and may well compensate for the poor reproductive success of those carriers of both sexes who are unfortunate enough to develop schizophrenia. The necessary mathematics to verify this could conceivably be worked out. The data would prove extremely difficult to collect, but this should not put off anyone determined enough to undertake the task.

A question of heredity

The web of our life is a mingled yarn, good and ill together.
William Shakespeare, *All's Well That Ends Well*,
Act 4, scene 1

The question is, what form does the inheritance take? Is it monogenic (caused by a single gene), polygenic (caused by the cumulative effect of several genes) or heterogeneous (caused by a number of genes which express themselves in different aspects of the disorder)? Despite all the research devoted to these questions, we still do not know the answer. One theory that has received favourable attention is that of Gottesman and Shields (1982), who proposed a model which they described with the term 'multifactorial-polygenic-threshold'. It holds that the genes responsible for the predisposition to schizophrenia are widely dispersed, in varying degrees, throughout the general population. In order to develop clinical schizophrenia, an individual has to cross a threshold, beyond which the genetic predisposition becomes manifest. The critical point at which the threshold is fixed is determined by the genetic loading that an individual carries, combined with his or her accumulated life experience. This model deservedly commands respect, for it has been applied successfully to physical diseases, such as diabetes mellitus.

Just as diabetes mellitus is the price paid by some people today for an adaptive mechanism which enabled our ancestors to survive in food-scarce environments in the past, so schizophrenia may well be the exorbitant price that some of us pay for humanity's possession of a valuable adaptive asset, such as forming a tightly knit group of migrants under the leadership of a schizotypal and highly sexed guru. In a sense, schizotypal genes could be like the genes responsible for sickle-cell anaemia, which enhances the well-being of carriers by protecting them from malaria while impairing the health of those with greater genetic loading by afflicting them with anaemia. Parallels are to be drawn from other psychiatric disorders where adaptive traits inherited by all human beings – for example, anxiety, phobias, depression, jealousy, excitement – may become maladaptive in certain individuals.

If, then, the predisposition that may result in schizophrenia is inherited in graded form, it could account for the kinds of personality organization which lie on the continuum between normality and psychosis – the schizoid, schizotypal and paranoid personality types. In prophets, as in both schizotypal and schizophrenic people, similar perceptual aberrations occur as we have shown, together with highly eccentric patterns of thinking, speech and belief, the same self-referential sensitivity to outer events, and a heightened awareness of unusual ideas and images emanating from their minds. We would suggest that the biological advantages of these bizarre traits became apparent in the ancestral environment when groups split and their outcasts wandered off into the wilderness, a schizotypal guru striding purposefully at their head.

7

Schizotypal Dispersal
and Genocide

> When thou comest nigh unto a city to fight against it, then
> proclaim peace unto it ... And if it will make no peace with thee,
> but will make war against thee, then thou shalt besiege it: And
> when the Lord thy God hath delivered it into thine hands, thou
> shalt smite every male thereof with the edge of the sword: But
> the women, and the little ones, and the cattle, and all that is in
> the city, even all the spoil thereof, shalt thou take unto thyself:
> and thou shalt eat the spoil of thine enemies, which the Lord
> thy God hath given thee. Thus shalt thou do unto all the cities
> which are very far off from thee, which are not of the cities of
> these nations.   *Deuteronomy*, 20:10-15

It is now nearly a century since William Graham Sumner of Yale
University introduced his distinction between the 'in-group' and the
'out-group' into sociology. That this theoretical contribution has survived, while those of many other sociologists have perished, is an
index of its phylogenetic provenance: it describes a basic feature of
the social programme for our species.

Sumner's distinction was itself a sociological elaboration of the
view promulgated by the nineteenth-century philosopher, Herbert
Spencer, that human beings adopt two essentially different modes of
social functioning – the 'mode of amity' (which typifies conduct with
familiars) and the 'mode of enmity' (characterizing conduct with
strangers). The operation of these two modes is not only apparent in
our behaviour but in our language. The Latin word *hostis*, for example, from which we derive *hostility*, originally meant *stranger*. This
etymology reflects the ever present possibility that a stranger will be
unconsciously classified by us as a potential enemy. In Brazil a tribe

called the Mundrucus make a distinction between themselves (whom they call 'people') and the rest of the world's population (whom they call *pariwat*). *Pariwat* rank as game; they are spoken of exactly in the same way as huntable animals. A similar distinction is made by all human societies between killing a member of one's own group – 'murder' (which is universally regarded as bad) and killing a member of an out-group in warfare (which is regarded as heroic). In other words, the Biblical Commandment 'Thou shalt not kill' in fact means 'Thou shalt not kill *Israelites*' (the in-group). The 'philistines', the 'uncircumcised' (the *pariwat* or out-group) are fair game.

Though Spencer and Sumner contributed greatly to our understanding of such distinctions, they failed to recognize their biological roots. It was not until 1965 that this deficiency was rectified at a meeting of the Royal Society in London, when it was addressed by Erik Erikson: 'I took it to be my task,' recalled Erikson, 'as one of the few representatives of developmental psychology in a hall filled with natural scientists, to note that mankind from the very beginning has appeared on the world scene split into tribes and nations, castes and classes, religions and ideologies, each of which acts as if it were a separate species created or planned at the beginning of time by supernatural will. Thus each claims not only a more or less firm sense of distinct identity but even a kind of historical immortality. Some of these pseudospecies, indeed, have mythologized for themselves a place and a moment in the very center of the universe, where and when an especially provident deity caused it to be created superior to, or at least unique among, all others' (Erikson, 1984).

Our human ability to adapt to the conditions prevailing in widely different environments has enabled us, as a result of group splitting and aggressive conflicts with our neighbours, to spread out all over the globe. When travel and communication were very difficult, as in the environment in which we evolved, pseudospeciation rapidly developed. People who migrated and settled in different geographical locations – separated from other groups by natural boundaries, such as oceans, mountains, rivers and lakes – developed different cultures, different languages, different religions, different loyalties, and made basic distinctions between themselves and all other peoples who walked the earth. Schizotypal leaders would, we believe, have been implicated in shaping the essential characteristics of these distinc-

126

tions. For a number of the schizotypal characteristics we have been discussing in earlier chapters, especially in their *strong* or 'positive' form as manifested in an acute schizophrenic episode, lend themselves to leadership of a migrating group seeking to establish a new settlement and a new cultural identity – for example, the cognitive dissonance, the preoccupation with religious themes, belief in the occult, the disordered language and use of neologisms from which new dialects and linguistic patterns could emerge, the startling mood changes, as well as the delusions and hallucinations which typify the condition.

Let us take each of these in turn:

(1) *Cognitive dissonance*:[1] Since the beliefs propounded by the prophet are often incompatible with reality, there must be some means of reconciling followers to these discrepancies when they occur – as, for example, when the prophet makes a prophecy that fails to come true. For many years, Jehovah's Witnesses have periodically proclaimed the date of Armageddon, only to have to revise it when the day arrived and passed with no sign of the predicted catastrophe. Since the sect has become institutionalized and lost some of its original charismatic fervour, it has reached the same sensible compromise as that adopted by other Christian churches and sects, issuing a bland assertion that Armageddon will happen 'at some time in the future.' But the charismatic leader of a newly formed group would have to deal effectively with his followers' 'apocalyptic disappointment', or risk the fragmentation of the group. This is where the cognitive dissonance of schizotypy could prove indispensable, for it not only permits the prophet to ignore the embarrassment of his failure but also to demonstrate to his flock that his faith is in no way affected by it. Hence the very striking finding of Festinger (Festinger *et al.*, 1964) who, having infiltrated a millennial cult, discovered that the non-occurrence of the leader's prediction of the world's end actually intensified the loyalty of his group. It was Hitler's 'cognitive dissonance' that enabled him to go on talking of victory as the Russian troops approached the suburbs of Berlin in 1945, and to move about on his war map divisions that had long ceased to exist. Without this fatal schizotypal characteristic, the Second World War may have ended somewhat earlier.

(2) *Religious preoccupations*: The belief systems, moral values and

ruling ideology of the great majority of human communities have been rooted in their religion. The religious tenets to which a group subscribes, and which differentiate it from all other groups, are held to have been 'revealed' to the founding father by the gods at the beginning of time. Such revelations commonly come in the form of visions, dreams and supernatural voices. The probability is that those responsible for receiving such divine messages were well endowed with schizotypal genes. Revelations of this kind would have sustained the migrating group on its perilous quest for the promised land and have been indispensable to the preservation of its ideology once established there. Messiahs appeared in Islam at the time when the faithful embarked on the conquest of the known world in the seventh century AD. The history of Islam demonstrates the power of religion as a great unifying (pro-'us') and dividing (against 'them') force. 'Before Mohammed, Southern Arabian peoples lived in a sort of political-cultural chaos. Families waged blood feuds. Robbers and warlords plundered towns and caravans. Jews, Christians and Mazdaists killed each other in wars and persecutions. There was little or no sense of wider social cohesion. Mohammed's vision united Southern Arabians and gave them a sense of fellowship they had never before experienced. Within several centuries, this previously despised racial and cultural group had mastered much of the civilized world' (Wenegrat, 1989).

(3) *Disordered language*: Language is both a uniter and a divider, in that it is fundamental to in-group/out-group distinctions. All geographically separated populations develop their own language on the basis of the 'language acquisition device' and 'deep structures' implicit in the human brain (Chomsky, 1965; Pinker, 1994). Even within the same nation, or tribal affiliation, dialects develop which strengthen in-group loyalty and out-group discrimination. Class distinctions, age group differences, cultural affiliations (e.g. punks, drug addicts, bikers, football supporters), professional identities (doctors, lawyers, soldiers, oil rig operatives) are all served by the use of special accents, terminologies, slang, acronyms, and tones of voice. As Aldous Huxley once observed, language is more effective at separating people than in keeping them together. 'The Americans and the English have everything in common,' said Oscar Wilde, 'except, of course, the language.'

128

7. Schizotypal Dispersal and Genocide

The link between population dispersal and linguistic diversity, leading to differences between human groups making it impossible for them to collaborate with one another, is precisely described in the eleventh chapter of *Genesis*, in the story of Babel. Originally, we are told, humanity consisted of one family speaking a common tongue. But men got above themselves and decided to build a city and a tower that would reach up to the heavens. Yahweh interpreted this as a threat, and said to the Celestial Council: 'Let us go down, and there confound their language, that they may not understand one another's speech. So the Lord scattered them abroad from thence upon the face of all the earth: and they left off to build the city. Therefore is the name of it called Babel; because the Lord did there confound the language of all the earth: and from thence did the Lord scatter them abroad on the face of all the earth' (*Genesis*, 11:7-9).

The speed with which a new group begins to assert its identity through the invention of new linguistic forms can be very rapid, and this probably played a significant role in group splitting, especially if it took place along generational lines. The schizotypal penchant for the production of idiosyncratic language, speech patterns and neologisms would have promoted this. The charismatic leader's verbal mannerisms would be adopted by the subgroup and this would further vitiate relations with the old, parent group, thus facilitating the split. Geographical isolation from other groups would naturally facilitate the process of linguistic innovation.

Examples of Hitler's neologisms have already been given Saul Levine (1989) has provided other examples originating from different contemporary cults. In the Divine Light Mission *satsang* meant spiritual discourse and *darsheen* meant seeing the Master, Maharaj Ji; while in the Church of God 'litnessing' meant witnessing and a 'systemite' was an evil, devil-influenced person. Such usages, commented Levine, provide a source of pride in being privy to special meanings, and they give members a sense of being part of a privileged, unique group of people.

Another form of linguistic innovation, encouraged by some schizotypal leaders, is 'speaking in tongues' in fulfilment of the *Acts of the Apostles*: 'And they were all filled with the Holy Ghost, and began to speak with other tongues, as the Spirit gave them utterance.' William Shaw (1994) describes a meeting of the Jesus Army cult in London: 'I have never heard anyone speaking in tongues before: eyes closed, brows knitted, the Irishman next to me starts to talk in a long, low unstoppable alien babble. Others in the room are speaking in strange, unrecognizable never-before uttered languages too. It is the language of God.' At another meeting: 'between songs, Big Tom, standing next to me, speaks in tongues: "Masur a basur. Aramash-te, armamar, karama, lash-ante ..." the words that emerge from these devoted mouths are all vaguely similar; mock middle-Eastern, full of rolling consonants and wide vowels' (pp. 146-52).

Leo, charismatic leader of The Eminent Theatre Journey Centre in London used language that struck Shaw as not only original but 'oddly pretty'. For example he gave his books and lectures such titles as 'The Opal Inbreath', 'Gemrod Call-Over', 'Cobwebs and Tears', 'The Amethyst Sigh'. 'Gatherings of followers, called by Leo, are also given wonderful mystical-sounding names: The Random Emin Keep, The Blue Emerald Classroom, The Quiet Gathering.' Shaw comments that 'when followers talk, it's as if they are talking in the mythical tongue of a race of futuristic hobbits. Newcomers only understand a fraction; they can end up with the distinct impression that those who have been in the Emin for years are visitors from a rare secret world' (p. 43).

(4) *Mood changes*: The mercurial mood changes typical of borderline personalities and often found in schizotypal people contribute to their 'uncanny' charismatic appeal to their followers. When depressed, the prophet sits brooding on the iniquities of his enemies, biding his time. When elated, the spirit enters into him, he proclaims his message, recruits supporters, and finds the necessary energy to lead them out of 'bondage' into the Promised Land. This pattern was apparent, as we have seen, in Mother Earth and Sabbatai Sevi. It was also evident in a number of other charismatic leaders, such as L. Ron Hubbard, the founder of Scientology, Joseph Smith, founder of the Mormons, and Bhagwan Shree Rajneesh.

(5) *Delusions and hallucinations*: Since group solidarity is maintained by a communality of belief, it is clear that a new group, if it is to split off, must create a new consensus which is at odds with the old. It is here that the schizotypal leader, with his genius for delusional and hallucinatory originality, becomes indispensable. Once his delusional belief system has been established in his mind with all the

force of a divine revelation, the unshakeable, absolute conviction with which it is held, gives the prophet a charismatic intransigence which is deeply attractive to people in crisis, who feel disaffected, bitter, and uncertain about what to think or what to do. We are all to some extent both sceptical and credulous, and whether we embrace or dismiss a new idea depends very much on our state of mind when we encounter it. People who join cults usually do so when they have become alienated from their friends and families and have fallen into a state of pessimism and despair. The bizarre belief system of a new cult holds out to them the promise of salvation and, if they can make the necessary cognitive leap, then they experience an ecstatic transcendence to their previously miserable existence. They have found the light and the way. Hence Marc Galanter's (1989) finding that the more bizarre the belief system, the more cohesive the group, and the more elevated the mood of its members. It was probably ever thus. And it squares with the anthropological finding that the belief system to which every human population subscribes appears arbitrary and irrational to outsiders. It is this that differentiates it from all other groups.

The hostility of other social groups to the emergence of a new religious movement is a universal phenomenon. Indeed, Johnson (1963) has suggested that religous groups can be categorized according to the degree of hostility they display towards the surrounding milieu. Such hostility is enhanced by the perception that the members of a new religious movement must be mentally disturbed. All societies define the boundaries within which people are perceived as being mentally ill: *'The greater the social distance between persons, the greater will be the tendency to perceive unfamiliar beliefs and behaviours as abnormal and even pathologic'* (Horowitz, 1982). Quoting this observation, Pattison and Ness (1989) comment, 'Regardless of individual attributes, members of an entire class or group are likely to be labelled as "mentally ill" if the social distance is great.' They go on: 'Factors producing social distance include geographical distance, ethnic difference, social class distinctions and cultural differences.'

Erik Erikson saw the establishment and development of a new culture as being broadly analogous to the biological processes which result in the evolution of new and different species of animals and plants. New species, once they have evolved, become established in their ecological niche and remain remarkably stable. The emergence of yet newer species out of this ancestral stock occurs when small populations become isolated and begin to diverge in a manner peculiar to themselves and to their environmental circumstances.[2] A new species can be said to have come into existence when it has achieved 'reproductive isolation' – i.e. it can no longer interbreed with the ancestral stock.

The creation of a new species is thus irreversible. This has never happened with human beings. Although pseudospeciation may create *cultural* barriers to breeding between the people and the pseudospeciated 'subhumans', both groups nevertheless biologically remain members of the same species and are able to interbreed should the cultural barrier be sufficiently eroded to permit it. Genetics has established that the genotypical differences between the widely dispersed human groups in the world are trivial, relating to such relatively unimportant matters as skin colour and whether hair is crinkly or straight.

There is, therefore, no *biological* basis for pseudospeciation in the sense that there *are* no different human species. However, there is a biological basis for our propensity to pseudospeciate; it is the propensity we share with all mammals to distinguish 'us' from 'them'. It is this propensity that incites us to xenophobia, racialism, militant nationalism and to war. It would have us conceive ourselves as 'chosen people' possessing a monopoly of goodness and decency and being the unique recipients of divine gifts of immortality and central position in the universe, while, at the same time, it encourages us to see the out-group as subhuman adversaries with virtually limitless capacities for treachery, hostility and evil.[3] In this manner, out-groups make ideal repositories into which the in-group can project its collective *shadow* (i.e. the sum total of all those qualities and values which the in-group ethos holds in disrepute).[4]

Herbert Spencer's two modes – amity and enmity – were evidently selected because they promoted survival through successful competition for the finite resources available. Our species has seldom met with ease and plenty in the course of its evolution, and human populations share with other animal species the tendency to increase more rapidly than the supplies on which they depend. If we have always banded into groups it is because the struggle for existence left us little alternative. Together we could achieve far more than individuals striving on their own, however great their strength and determination to survive; and it is only in groups that our biosocial needs can be satisfied. In groups we have struggled to scrape a living from tight-fisted Nature, and in groups we have competed with all other groups which were not in alliance with our own and, as often as not, with those that were. Usually, when rival groups came into contact a conflict of interests arose; and when it was settled by force, men called it war.

Such behaviour is very ancient indeed. Evidence for the existence of anatomically modern humans – *Homo sapiens* – in Africa is apparent for the last 140,000 years. They spread to other parts of the world over the next 60,000-80,000 years.[5] During this period, their behaviour seems to have remained unchanged and not to have differed in any very significant way from that of contemporary archaic populations, such as the Neanderthals. 'Indeed', writes Robert Foley (1996) of the Cambridge Department of Biological Anthropology, '*it is the high potential for dispersal itself*, rather than any specific behaviour, that seems to characterize modern humans' (italics added). Foley maintains that they lived in moderately large communities with coalitions of males linked by kinship and with unrelated females attached to specific males. 'Assuming conditions of net local population growth, two significant characteristics would arise from this ancestral social organization. The first is that with male kin-bonding groups, communities would be at least partially closed to each other and hostile, resulting in some form of territorial or agonistic behaviour between communities. A consequence of this would be that overall group or community size would be an advantage, particularly in terms of numbers of males within a coalition. The competitive advantages that would arise from this would, however, also lead to both social and ecological pressures. As group size goes up, competition for both resources and reproduction would increase. This would lead to the second of the two ancestral tendencies occurring – demographic fission of communities. Primate social groups tend to split into two when they reach group sizes that are greater than can be socially or ecologically maintained. Fission of groups would in turn be a factor promoting geographical dispersal and leading to the

133

colonization of new regions and localities, whether or not they might already be occupied by hominids.'

In the past 50,000 years there have been over thirty major recognizable migrations of human beings, such as the movement of Mongolian peoples from China through North America and into South America (Cavalli-Sforza and Cavalli-Sforza, 1995). Unfortunately, it is not possible to be sure whether these migrations were made by intact populations or whether they occurred as a result of sub-groups splitting off for ideological or other reasons from parent groups that had settled along the route. In the light of Foley's deductions, however, the latter possibility seems likely, and the long, slow trek south would have been as conflict-ridden and blood-soaked as migrations in other parts of the world.

Understandably enough, a direct relationship exists between out-group hostility and in-group co-operation. The more intensely the enemy is loathed and feared, the greater the loyalty and cohesion within the group. As a result, one would predict that groups should tend to split only in times of peace, or when inner dissensions became so extreme as to cause polarity and drive opposing factions apart. This prediction is supported by the inverse relationship so frequently observed as existing between conflicts within groups ('civil wars') and conflicts with out-groups ('international wars') in both primitive and civilized circumstances.[6]

In Paleolithic times, group splitting and intergroup aggression not only spread human populations over the planet, it probably served to keep them in balance with one another and with the resources available to them (Vayda, 1968). Wars would have tended to occur when neighbouring populations became too large for the territories sustaining them. To nourish a group of 50 people by hunting and gathering, a large range was required. Tribal boundaries were invariably well defined and any trespass would have resulted in resistance and, if it persisted, war. In Australia and Tasmania the commonest cause of war between Aborigines was killing game on the lands of another tribe. This was also true of the Maoris in New Zealand and the Ainu of Japan. Similar economic forces were at work among those who ceased hunting and became herders of cattle. In southeast Africa wars over waterholes and grazing grounds were virtually incessant and resulted in heavy loss of life. Writing in the 1920s, Davie observed, 'Groups come directly into conflict in carrying on their struggle for existence; they fight over hunting and grazing grounds, for food, for watering places, for plunder.' The effect of such wars was to reduce the size of the populations involved through death in battle and, in cases of decisive or repeated victory, to drive vanquished populations out of their territories which could then be used to support the victors. This primitive form of 'ethnic cleansing' must often have been tantamount to genocide, and wars of this kind have been recorded in many parts of the world, but especially in New Guinea (Bureau, 1959; Vayda, 1968).

Andrew Vayda (1968) suggested a theory which accommodated the facts of primitive warfare very convincingly. He proposed the following sequence:

(1) A reduced per capita food supply, associated with increasing competition within the group for fewer resources, generates intense domestic frustration and other in-group tensions.

(2) When these tensions reach a certain level, the group may split, or alternatively seek release in warfare with an enemy group.

(3) A result of the warfare is reduction of the pressure of people upon the land, either because of heavy battle mortality or because of the victorious group taking over the territory of its defeated and dispersed enemy.

(4) The reduced pressure on the land brings improvement in the per capita food supply and reduction in competition for resources within the group. As a consequence, domestic frustrations and other in-group tensions are brought within tolerable limits, and the group does not split.

Vayda believed these variables all operate in a self-regulating (homeostatic) manner – 'according to this hypothesis (or set of hypotheses),' he wrote, 'psychological, demographic, and economic variables are all being regulated, with the regulation of one variable being dependent upon the regulation of another'.

Vayda's hypothesis has the advantage of squaring with the historical and paleo-anthropological evidence which indicates that war and peace are, and always have been, essentially *cyclic* phenomena, and he provided a biological insight into why this should be so. That a self-regulating (homeostatic) principle should be involved in so characteristic a human activity is also in accordance with our knowledge of how different systems maintain operative equilibrium in our brains, throughout our bodies and on our planet.

Leadership, secular and religious

Render therefore unto Caesar the things which are Caesar's; and unto God the things that are God's.   *Matthew*, 22:21

Study of populations indulging in warfare, whether civil or international, reveals the vital role played by two different kinds of leader, the politician and the prophet. Max Weber took this distinction a step further, detecting three types of charismatic leader: the 'exemplary' prophet, the 'ethical' prophet and the politician. We will accept Weber's categories and add our own gloss to them:

(1) The 'exemplary' prophet is the shaman or charismatic leader who experiences a mazeway resynthesis through which he comes to identify with the gods, and promotes heteropistic splitting of the group.

(2) The 'ethical' prophet is the 'messiah', who does not deify himself but becomes God's messenger in order to provide 'revitalization' of the group.

(3) The 'politician' is the political or military leader responsible for organizing the group and mobilizing its resources for the purpose of defence or aggression.[7]

So far we have confined our examination to the first two kinds of leader, both of whom are responsible for the spiritual and ideological underpinnings of the group; the politico-military leader has been of primary interest to historians. He tends to be more concerned with practical secular matters, with dominance striving, and exercising social assertiveness than his schizotypal counterpart. His function is to ensure group cohesion, take strategic decisions and maintain discipline.

Whereas the prophet seeks power through ideology, the politician seeks it through force. Human warfare has been described by many as the 'last resort' of individuals and groups in the struggle for power. All are fought for the benefits that power brings – material resources, access to sexual partners, feelings of group solidarity and superiority, escape from fears of being subjected by the enemy, the imposition of one's own ideology, and so on. As the great German authority on war,

136

von Clausewitz, put it: '[War is] an act of force to compel our enemy to do our will' (Clausewitz, 1976).

From the purely biological standpoint, one of the most important consequences of warlike assertiveness is that it promotes differential reproduction – that is, the fittest, more aggressive, more dominant males have the pick of the most desirable females and thus sire the next generation. So doing, they pass on genes which are selectively advantageous for the continued survival of the population. This is the basis of the mythic union of Ares with Aphrodite.

The schizotypal prophet is not noted, however, for the size of his muscles or competence in the arts of warfare. To get his genes into the next generation he has to cultivate more introverted gifts of persuasion. The prophet is needed to reorganize the mazeway of the group and point it in the direction of the promised land; the warrior–politician is needed to ensure that it gets there – and stays there once it has arrived. Consequently, the prophet–messiah has to attach himself symbiotically to the politician–general. Their bond is indispensable to group identity and survival. Sometimes both roles coincide in the same leader, as they did in Adolf Hitler. Circumstances may turn the prophet into a general, especially when paranoia gets the better of him, as in the case of Jim Jones, David Koresh, or Shoko Asahara. In the ancestral environment a migrating population was under constant threat from the populations through whose territory it was marching. It had to be vigilant and prepared to beat off attacks. Having reached what it believed to be the promised land it had to be prepared to fight, expel or annihilate those who might already be in possession. If not himself expert in the martial arts, the prophet needed men close to him who were. To survive and become established in the promised land the new community had to be ready to hold onto and defend it. If charisma is to be institutionalized it has to assume a military dimension.

Group splitting and dispersal are high-risk activities, only embarked upon in dire circumstances. To stand any chance of success the departing group needs *conviction* as well as determination. Having undergone his personal mazeway resynthesis, the prophet's conviction is unshakeable. This gives him his charisma and his power. His followers stick to him and are convinced by him because their situation is desperate: they *need* to believe he is right in everything he says. Once embarked, their credulity becomes their most priceless – indeed their only – possession.

As was emphasized in Chapter 2, schizoid, paranoid and schizotypal personality disorders as well as schizophrenia are all *spacing* disorders. That is the adaptive function underlying all of them – to disperse human populations round the full range of their potential habitat. In Chapter 4 we argued that the schizotypal prophet played an important role in group splitting, but group splitting serves merely as a preliminary to dispersal. It is in convincing his group that it must move off to exploit a new ecological niche that the schizotypal leader realizes his ultimate biological objective. That, in evolutionary terms, is what he is for.

In the monotheistic tradition of the Middle East, there are two outstanding examples of 'ethical' prophets who combined the roles of Messiah and politician: these are Abraham and Moses. In the biblical record, Abraham, father of the three great monotheistic religions, Judaism, Christianity, and Islam, is the original prototype of the prophet who receives the divine call. Yahweh tells him to leave his native land and people in Ur of the Chaldees in Mesopotamia and to lead them in a migration to Canaan, between Syria and Egypt: 'Get thee out of thy country, and from thy kindred, and from thy father's house, unto a land that I will shew thee: And I will make of thee a great nation ... And I will bless them that bless thee, and curse them that curseth thee: and in thee shall all families of the earth be blessed' (*Genesis*, 12:1-3).

Of the split which must have occurred in the natal group on Abraham's departure from Ur, the Bible tells us nothing. But we do hear of a later split which occurs in the migrating group when it has taken up a temporary abode on land to the south of Beth-el. The division occurs between Abraham and his brother, Lot, and it occurs for the usual reason: 'the land was not able to bear them, that they might dwell together' (*Genesis*, 13:6).

Having arrived in Canaan, Abraham receives Yahweh's assurance that the land will be his and his descendants' in perpetuity: 'For all the land which thou seest, to thee will I give it, and to thy seed for ever. And I will make thy seed as the dust of the earth: so that if a man can number the dust of the earth, then shall thy seed also be numbered' (ibid., 12:15-16).

138

The story of Moses presents some interesting variations on our theme. To start with, the group of people that he leads is not split so much as oppressed and longing to be freed from thraldom to their Egyptian masters. But more interesting still, Moses is, unlike all our other examples, a *reluctant* prophet: when he receives the divine call, he begs to be excused!

The call comes from the midst of a burning bush, which is unconsumed by the fire: Moses hears Yahweh's voice calling him: 'Moses, Moses … Draw not nigh hither: put off the shoes from off thy feet, for the place whereon thou standest is holy ground.' God tells Moses that he has come to deliver the Hebrews from their captivity, 'and to bring them up out of that land unto a good land and a large, unto a land flowing with milk and honey: unto the place of the Canaanites …' Moses is to be instrumental in their delivery: 'I will send thee unto Pharaoh', says God, 'that thou mayest bring forth my people the children of Israel out of Egypt.' But instead of exaltation at being chosen for this sacred mission, Moses is appalled by the responsibility. He actually has the audacity to argue with God: 'Who am I, that should go unto Pharaoh and that I should bring forth the children of Israel out of Egypt?' he asks. 'They will not believe me, nor harken to my voice: for they will say, the Lord hath not appeared unto thee.' But God is adamant and will brook no refusal. Moses tries one last desperate plea: 'I am slow of speech', he says, 'and of a slow tongue.' At this, God gets angry with him and tells him that if he cannot speak persuasively then his golden-tongued brother, Aaron, will speak for him, but he must nevertheless go to Pharaoh (*Exodus*, 3:8-11; 4:1; 10). Moses evidently has no alternative, and does as he is bid.

Having led his people out of Egypt, Moses brings them to mount Sinai, 'the mountain of God', where Yahweh had appeared to him in the burning bush. There, Yahweh again manifests himself, this time in the kratophany of a great storm: 'And all the people saw the thunderings, and the lightnings, and the noise of the trumpet, and the mountain smoking: and when the people saw it, they removed and stood afar off … and Moses drew near unto the thick darkness where God was' (*Exodus*, 20:18; 21). There a covenant is made: in return for Yahweh's special love and protection, the Hebrews will pledge their obedience to his will, and will worship no other gods but him. So that their society may be stable and just, Yahweh insists that

139

they must obey his Commandments: they must respect each other and avoid murder, theft, adultery, lying and covetousness, because such conduct leads to chaos and breakdown of the community. Moses relays all this to the people, but they give him a hard time, for they are stubborn and rebellious. Moses has to intercede for them with Yahweh, and he sets up judges and courts to regulate the civic affairs of the community.

Already married to Miriam, Moses takes a Cushite woman as a second wife, and leads his people northwards across Transjordan, heading for Canaan, the Promised Land. He requests permission to pass through the states of Edom and Moab, which are vassals of the Midianites, but his request is not granted. Accordingly, he circles to the east of them to conquer Sihon, King of the Amorites, and Og, King of Bashan. But this evokes the hostility of the Moabites and their Midianite overlords, and Moses embarks on a successful holy war against them, shortly before his death. Thus Moses performs a number of roles: a divinely inspired prophet, mediator of the Covenant, founder of the community, legislator, politician, general. The historical accounts revere him as the greatest of the Old Testament prophets and one of the great personalities of all time. 'And there arose not a prophet since in Israel like unto Moses, whom the Lord knew face to face' (*Deuteronomy*, 34:10). Yet he could not avoid leading his people into a destructive war and to genocide: it was his role, and Yahweh demanded it.

On those occasions when human populations split, and one portion moves away, leaving the other portion behind, they display behaviour similar to that observed by behavioural ecologists in other social species. These researchers make a distinction between two types of phenotype: a *maintenance* phenotype, which is optimally adapted to the existing habitat, and a *dispersal* phenotype, which performs the same function as the schizotypal leader. In schizophrenic patients we can discern a similar propensity influencing individuals to leave the natal group (in which they have been born, brought up, and indoctrinated) and to disperse into uncharted social, psychological or geographical terrain. Both attractive and repulsive forces promote this propensity. On the one hand, the patient is drawn to the new domain and goes there under the influence of some inflated messianic delusion; on the other hand, the patient is driven from the natal area

140

by paranoid delusions of persecution, often accompanied by hostile voices. Fortunate schizophrenics may attract a following of disciples to take care of the practical aspects of life, much in the manner of psychiatric nurses; or they may remain in the natal group, inhabiting the curious inner world of the shaman, mystic or holy eccentric. In less fortunate cases the process goes awry and they end up not in a promised land but in community care.

Both maintenance and dispersal phenotypes are apparent in some species of birds, such as the robin. After the autumn battle for territory, a successful territory-holder stays put; but robins that do not win territories migrate. Perhaps the swallow in Oscar Wilde's story of *The Happy Prince* did not really stay to look after the prince. Maybe he stayed because he was a genetic stayer and the myth of caring for the prince was merely a rationalization to justify his bizarre conduct! Most of us are probably genetic stayers, until adverse circumstances force us to move. Then we need the guidance of a genetic migrator, and we wait around anxiously for a schizotypal leader to oblige.

Many human communities have a traditional migration myth which schizotypal personalities can adapt to their own purposes – examples are the Aryan myth of *Lebensraum* in the East, the English myth of 'empire building' and colonization justified as a 'civilizing mission', the American myth of the ever-extending frontier ('Go West, young man!'), and the pre-colonial South American myth of 'the Land without Evil'. Every so often prophets have arisen to personify the myth and carry their followers a stage further along the route to population dispersal. In the case of successful migrations, a form of religious and cultural colonization often occurred: charismatic leaders not only indoctrinated their followers but also had a profound impact on those people who were unfortunate enough to be residing in the promised land when he and his followers arrived there. For the residents, conversion to the prophet's way of seeing things becomes an absolute condition of survival. To resist conversion is to invite persecution, ejection or death, as the Incas discovered when the Spaniards arrived in the sixteenth century. Those who convert are then integrated, albeit at a lowly level, within the social hierarchy of the occupying power. This certainly happened again and again after the discovery of agriculture 10,000 years ago, and the likelihood is

141

that something similar occurred on a much smaller scale in the ancestral environment. The consequence was that the charismatic prophet's leadership, his belief system and his genes contributed to the survival not only of his own group but of those residents who were spared by his invading forces. One of the many appalling characteristics of human warfare, whether practised at the most primitive or the most sophisticated level, is the annihilation of enemy males and the rape, enslavement or acquisition of enemy females. Since the schizotypal leader could enjoy first choice of the spoils, this would inevitably lead to yet further distribution of his genes.

For those leaders, who during the last two millennia have drawn their inspiration from the Holy Bible, there is ample justification for such behaviour and it comes directly from the voice of God: 'And the Lord spake unto Moses, saying, Avenge the children of Israel of the Midianites ... And Moses spake unto the people saying, Arm some of yourselves unto the war, and let them go against the Midianites, and avenge the Lord ... And they warred against the Midianites, as the Lord commanded Moses; and they slew all the males ... And the children of Israel took all the women of Midian captives, and their little ones, and took the spoil of all their cattle, and all their flocks, and all their goods. And they burnt all their cities wherein they dwelt, and all their goodly castles, with fire ... And Moses said unto them Have ye saved all the women alive? ... Now therefore kill every male among the little ones, and kill every woman that hath known man by lying with him. But all the women children that have not known a man by lying with him, keep alive for yourselves' (*Numbers*, 31:1-18).

Again: 'When thou goest forth to war against thine enemies, and the Lord thy God hath delivered them into thine hands, and thou hast taken them captive, And seest among the captives a beautiful woman, and hast a desire unto her, that thou wouldest have her to thy wife; Then thou shalt bring her home to thine house; and she shall shave her head, and pare her nails; And she shall put the raiment of her captivity from off her, and shall remain in thine house, and bewail her father and her mother a full month: and after that thou shalt go in unto her and be her husband, and she shall be thy wife' (*Deuteronomy*, 21:10-13).

That present-day cult leaders can shift with apparent ease from an emphasis on love, personal growth and salvation to armed preparation for war is evident in the case of Jim Jones, David Koresh, Shoko Asahara and Bhagwan Shree Rajneesh. Bainbridge (1978) has told the story of an English architect who defected from Scientology to found his own psychotherapeutic cult, composed mainly of other architects. Initially strongly affiliative (though also rigidly hierarchical) its contacts with outsiders was conciliatory and largely limited to the distribution of literature and the solicitation of funds. But within a few years, the previously peace-loving leader was advocating mayhem on an apocalyptic scale. As he declared to his followers:

> The final march of doom has begun. The earth is prepared for the ultimate devastation. The mighty engines of WAR are all aligned and brought together for the End ... Release the Fiend that lies dormant within you, for he is strong and ruthless and his power is far beyond the bounds of human frailty ...
>
> Rape with the crushing force of your virility; kill with the devastating precision of your sword arm; maim with ruthless ingenuity of your pitiless cruelty; destroy with the overpowering fury of your bestial strength; lay waste with the all-encompassing majesty of your power ...

With the leader-imposed ideology and fierce loyalties engendered within a charismatic group, the advocacy and the actual accomplishment of genocide is always a terrible possibility.

8

Apocalypse and Armageddon

Our minds are designed to generate behaviour that would have
been adaptive, on average, in our ancestral environment ...
Behaviour itself did not evolve; what evolved was the mind.

Stephen Pinker

Whether or not Stephen Pinker's view is correct, it is true to say that
evolutionary psychology has confined its attention to the *behavioural*
manifestations of the 'modules' (innate psychological propensities)
with which, it proposes, the human mind is equipped. These modules
have been put in place by natural selection operating over aeons of
time. Charles Darwin would have welcomed this proposal. 'Psychology will be based on a new foundation', he predicted in the final pages
of *The Origin of Species* (1859). 'Light will be thrown on the origin of
man and his history.' That it has taken psychology nearly a century
and a half to begin fulfilling Darwin's prediction is due to the powerful resistance put up throughout the twentieth century by those
wedded to the 'Standard Social Science Model' (SSSM), which insisted that evolutionary biology had little or nothing to contribute to
the study of human behaviour.

One of the few disciplines to buck the baleful influence of the
SSSM was Jungian psychology, which inevitably paid the price of
such defiance by being relegated to a position of scientific obscurity.
However, being something of a schizotypal guru himself, who had
experienced a mazeway resynthesis after his break with Freud, Jung
remained unshakeably convinced that human psychology proceeded
on the basis of innate propensities, which he termed 'archetypes'.

A profoundly introverted man, Jung was less interested in the
behavioural manifestations of archetypal structures than in their
influence on *mental* processes, as manifested in dreams, visions,
hallucinations and free use of the imagination, as well as in such

cultural[1] products as myths, folk tales and religions. He devoted his life to comparing and contrasting data derived from such personal and cultural manifestations in an effort to discern the archetypal patterns underlying them (Jung, 1959, 1960; Stevens, 1995, 1998, 1999). The eternally recurring themes of childhood and youth, love and sex, hunting and warfare, sickness and healing, death and rebirth, fertility and sacrifice – everything that constitutes a core experience of life – has been put into symbols and tales which, for all their manifold variety, often share striking resemblances to one another, wherever on this planet they have been brought into being.[2]

Mythological and religious themes are, as the evolutionary biologists now say, 'environmentally stable'. While Jung acknowledged that similarities could be brought about by the combined operation of migration, tradition and trade, he nevertheless argued that some form of transmission through heredity must also occur since he was able to discover instances where such motifs arose spontaneously, without any previous encounter with them on the part of the subject. Jung, therefore, concluded that these motifs[3] must correspond to 'typical dispositions', 'dominants' or 'nodal points' within the structure of the psyche itself. All cultures, it seems, display a large number of traits which are in themselves diagnostic of a specifically human culture. These have been independently catalogued by the anthropologists George P. Murdock (1945) and Robin Fox (1975).[4]

More recently, Walter Burkert (1996) has emphasized the world-wide similarities in religious phenomena: 'they include formalized ritual behaviour appropriate for veneration: the practice of offerings, sacrifices, vows and prayers with reference to superior beings; and songs, tales, teachings and explanations about these things and the worship they demand'. A religion, Burkert argues, is a system of symbols incorporating ideas and beliefs which are emphatically accepted as true even though they cannot be verified empirically. They are confirmed, however, through meditation, trance and ecstatic experiences which purport to establish a direct encounter with supernatural forces.

These universal and prehistoric phenomena cannot be explained or derived from any single cultural system, maintains Burkert: 'The search for the source of religion calls for a more general perspective, beyond individual civilizations, which must take account of the vast process of human evolution in the more general evolutionary process of life ... Cultural studies must merge with general anthropology, which is ultimately integrated into biology.'

A leading authority on the religious symbolism of different cultures who consistently adopted a similar position to Jung's was Mircea Eliade. Eliade maintained that a symbol or motif does not depend for its existence on being understood, known or even recognized, since it preserves its inherent structure long after it has been forgotten. Thus, myths and rituals involving immersion in water (baptism), purification (lustration), the deluge (the flood), the submersion of lost continents (Atlantis), the dissolution of the old order and the precipitation of the new (the stories of Noah and of Deucalion, or of Armageddon and the Apocalypse), all fit together so as to 'make up a *symbolic system which in a sense pre-existed them all*' (Eliade, 1958; italics added).[5]

A question of great psychological interest is how the personal symbols of dreams and the collective symbols of myths, religions and folk tales are related to one another. The general consensus is that the relationship is very close. As Otto Rank (1961) put it, 'The myth is the collective dream of the people.' If people everywhere tend to dream of similar themes and produce common symbols, then cultural traditions help shape these symbols and give them their particular ethnic quality; and the innate propensity to produce symbols of this generic type will go on as long as human beings survive, whatever their cultural circumstances. Joseph Campbell (1990) summed up this line of thought in his aphorism: 'A myth is a public dream, a dream is a private myth.' All symbols are the product of interaction between innate propensities and personal experiences. For this reason, collective symbols transcend geography and history, while personal symbols relate to the here and now. It would be wholly artificial, however, to attempt a clear distinction between the two forms, since all symbols are the product of both collective and personal influences. What may be said with some degree of certainty is that some symbols are more personally inflected than others: the more archaic the symbol, the more collective or universal it will be; the more differentiated the symbol, the more coloured it is by the personal peculiarities of the individual producing it.

It is our contention that in the actual process of myth creation, the schizotypal leader, with his ready access to normally unconscious symbolic activities, would play a highly significant role. For it will be *his* private myths that, through the cultural impact of his charismatic personality, will be transformed into the public dreams and, ultimately, the religious beliefs and practices of his people.

The archetypal symbolism of the Apocalypse and the Promised Land

I wonder if we are not moving to some final cataclysm. I expect a catastrophe, I know not what, in which we shall all be swallowed up ... I really believe in the end of everything.

Emile Zola in a letter to a friend in 1899

To what extent, then, can we understand the symbolisms of the Apocalypse, Armageddon and the Promised Land to be collective rather than personal? Could we be justified in suggesting that charismatic prophets are not merely recycling, in idiosyncratic form, the traditional symbols of their culture, but are in fact articulating symbolic propensities inherent in the evolved psyche of the species?

To attempt to answer this fascinating question we must examine the content, the provenance and the distribution of the symbols involved, and relate them to the facts of group splitting, prophetic utterance, and population dispersal to a new and more desirable location.

Every prophet exploits the potential fault lines in the fabric of the natal group, in the sense that his message is both positive and negative, both attractive and repulsive; and the prophet presents these dual oppositions as being the direct consequence of a divine revelation. The negative revelation depicts all that is rotten in the present state of the natal group; the positive revelation describes the path to salvation, the immense attractions of his new teaching, and the Promised Land that awaits all 'born-again' true believers. The prophet then proceeds to widen the developing chasm between opposing factions by identifying his own group (the in-group – 'us') with the positive and attractive forces of 'Good' (under the protection of God or the gods and goddesses) and stigmatizing the parent group, or any

148

other potentially hostile group (the out-group – 'them') with the negative and repulsive forces of 'Evil' (in league with the Devil or with evil spirits).

The necessary preliminaries for splitting the natal group, and for the departure of the daughter group, are now complete, and the trek to the Promised Land begins. Since the chances of reaching their objective without a struggle are slight, the prophet has to prepare his followers for the likelihood of a life-or-death struggle which will ultimately decide the fate of their mission and the fulfilment or frustration of their quest.

These events have occurred again and again throughout the history of our species, and it is these that are symbolized in the apocalyptic fantasy of Armageddon, the ultimate struggle between the forces of Good and Evil, the rediscovery of Paradise Lost, and the establishment of the Millennium. It is interesting how often arrival at the Promised Land is represented as a home-coming – a reacquisition of what was formerly ours 'by right'. In the Judeo-Christian tradition it is commonly equated with the Garden of Eden, the archetypal womb from which we have been excluded and to which, by God's will, we are now restored. It is interesting that members of an established cult experience it as 'home' and other members as 'kin' – 'family'. Hugh Milne, Rajneesh's bodyguard, described his reaction to meeting Rajneesh and joining his ashram: 'I had an overwhelming feeling of coming home. He was my spiritual father, a man who understood everything, someone who would be able to convey sense and meaning into my life' (Milne, 1987, p. 13). The followers of Baba, an American guru who established his ashram round a bench on the edge of Central Park in mid-Manhattan in 1972, referred to themselves as 'family', and embraced new members with the greeting, 'welcome home!' (Deutsch, 1975).

Throughout the history of Christendom the most salient apocalyptic fantasy has been that of St John the Divine, received by him on the Greek island of Patmos and famously recorded in the Book of Revelation. St John's vision of Armageddon, followed by the Second Coming of Christ, was in many ways a reworking of the much earlier Prophetical Books of the Jews dating from over 2,000 years ago which foretold how, out of an immense cosmic catastrophe, there would arise a Palestine which would be nothing less than a new Eden,

Paradise regained. The positive and negative aspects of these prophecies is at once apparent. The negative message concerned the plight in which the Chosen People found themselves. It was due to their neglect of Yahweh. For this they would be punished by famine and pestilence, war and captivity, and subjected to a judgement of such severity that it would cancel out their guilty past. There would come a Day of Wrath, when sun and moon and stars would be darkened, when the heavens would be rolled up, and the earth shaken to its foundations. This would not be the end, however. A 'saving remnant' of Israel would survive these terrible chastisements and Yahweh would dwell among them as ruler and judge. Then, we are told, 'freed from disease and sorrow of every kind, doing no more iniquity but living according to the law of Yahweh now written in their hearts, the Chosen People will live in joy and gladness' (Cohn, 1970).

As we would expect, each of these apocalyptic visions occurred to prophets at times of crisis, oppression or persecution. St John's revelation occurred at a time of Roman persecution of the Jews under Domitian, while the Book of Daniel, the first Jewish apocalyptic text, was composed about 165 BC at the time of the Maccabean revolt against the Jewish oppression of Antiochus Epiphanes. The Apocalypse of Ezra, which belongs to the first century AD, followed the destruction of the Temple in Jerusalem, while earlier prophets, like Amos and Isaiah, spoke out at times of upheaval in the eighth century BC.

These apocalyptic visions tend to follow the same structural pattern: revelation → judgement → struggle between Good and Evil → destruction or punishment → renewal:

(1) *Revelation*: Apocalypse comes from the Greek *apo* = away, from or off, and *kalyptein* = to cover or to hide. *Apokalypsis* therefore means to uncover what was hidden. In other words, it reveals the true nature of the problem – just as Hamlet's vision of his father's ghost reveals what is rotten in the state of Denmark. With the passage of time, the word 'apocalypse' has come to mean more than 'the uncovering of things hidden' and to encompass the notion of a 'huge final catastrophe' from which only an élite few survive.

(2) *Judgement*: When God passes judgement on evil-doers who have broken the Law, He publicly confirms the truths He has privately

revealed to His prophet. In Israel this conformed to a well-established tradition, for times of affliction were construed as acts of God, which only God Himself could undo. Yahweh was a tyrannical God who demanded subservience as the price for His protection. Only through total submission and obedience could you hope to have Him on your side. The moment you displeased Him you were in dire trouble. By a circular logic it followed that if you were in trouble then it must be because you had displeased Him. To get back into favour you must suffer His punishment. Then, when you had suffered enough, He would send you a messiah to lift you out of your predicament.

(3) *Struggle between the forces of Good and Evil*: This can be symbolized in many forms, ranging from the conflict between light and darkness to the deadly tournament between a hero–saviour and a monster. This symbolism is very ancient indeed and displays the primordial human tendency to categorize phenomena in antithetical pairs, which may well owe its origins to the natural opposition between day and night. Light and darkness are, after all, fundamental data of existence on this planet. They must have been among the first phenomena of which consciousness became aware. So it's not surprising that light should have become a universal symbol of both consciousness and divinity, and that darkness – the time when, in the ancestral environment, we were most vulnerable to natural predators and attacks from our fellow humans – should be symbolically equated with unconsciousness, fearful mystery and evil. Accordingly, light and darkness symbolism has shaped the mythologies, cosmologies and religions of peoples of all parts of the earth, darkness being equated with an original chaos, light with the bringing of order, as in the first chapter of Genesis. The dawning light of a new day is a primordial symbol of psychological awareness, spiritual transformation, new life and inspiration; the failing light of dusk, on the other hand, symbolizes contracting awareness, spiritual decline, death and despair. In numerous cultures, art, mythology, narrative poetry and theology make use of this symbolism. This complementary yet antithetical dynamic is at the heart of all phenomena as represented in the *T'ai Chi*, the binary symbol of Yin and Yang.

In dreams, myths and fairy tales, moral issues are commonly represented by the symbolism of light and darkness and, as we saw in the teaching of Mother Earth of Trinidad, by the symbolism of right and left. Of undoubted significance for the traumatic effects of group splitting, the archetypal battle between Good and Evil is also represented by pairs of warring siblings, such as the Gemini, the twins Osiris and Set, and Romulus and Remus, or the brothers Cain and Abel, and Jacob and Esau. Frequently, warring twins are represented as being one light and one dark, further emphasizing their links with day and night, good and evil. The struggle in ancient times between Apollo and Python is also linked to this symbolism, as is the battle between the eagle and the snake. The Christian splitting of the godhead into All-Good Almighty God and All-Evil Satan, Prince of Darkness, is but a further example of this fissive polarity.

The progress of separation and opposition from the intra-familial to the inter-tribal is summed up by a Bedouin proverb:

> I against my brother
> I and my brother against our cousin
> I, my brother and our cousin against our neighbours
> All of us against the foreigner.

The painful though necessary implications of group splitting are commonly addressed by the founders of new cults. Jesus was no exception: 'Think not that I am come to send peace on earth: I come not to send peace, but a sword. For I am come to set a man at variance against his father, and the daughter against her mother, and the daughter in law against her mother in law. And a man's foes shall be they of his own household. He that loveth father or mother more than me is not worthy of me: and he that loveth son or daughter more than me is not worthy of me' (*Matthew*, 10:32-7). When followers abandoned their children to enter Rajneesh's ashram, he told them they had done the right thing. 'The greatest relationship is between a Master and a disciple', he said; beside that all other relationships pale into insignificance. To develop the fortitude to split from the group and move off, devotion to the Master was probably indispensable. It had to usurp the place given to old loyalties previously felt for members of the natal group, who stayed behind.

At the basis of human imagery of evil lies the archetype of the predator, the quintessence of malevolent hostility – the huge-jawed, slavering, heavily clawed dragon–serpent, capable of seeking us out wherever we hide. His natural adversary (and our welcome ally) is the hero–saviour. In apocalyptic visions, the symbol of ultimate evil, the Antichrist, is the Beast. Often he appears in two forms as in the biblical monsters Leviathan and Behemoth. Leviathan is the sea monster and Behemoth the land monster. They may be understood as representing the primeval potential still actively present in the reptilian and old mammalian parts of the human brain (MacLean, 1985; Stevens, 1998). It is these neuropsychic centres which are activated when human communities become engaged in a life-or-death struggle for indispensable resources, culminating in pseudospeciation and genocide. Here is St John's description:

> And I stood upon the sand of the sea, and saw a beast rise up out of the sea, having seven heads and ten horns, and upon his horns ten crowns, and upon his heads the name of blasphemy. And the beast which I saw was like unto a leopard, and his feet were as the feet of a bear, and his mouth as the mouth of a lion: and the dragon gave him his power, and his seat and great authority ... And I beheld another beast coming up out of the earth; and he had two horns like a lamb, and he spake as a dragon. And he exerciseth all the power of the first beast before him ... (*Revelation*, 13:1-2; 11-12).

The story of a predatory dragon–serpent and its heroic destruction occurs in so many mythic traditions that it must have been one of the earliest dramas to excite the human imagination. Humbaba, the Babylonian monster, is slain by Gilgamesh and Enkidu; the Minotaur, who required a regular diet of seven youths and seven maidens, is destroyed by Theseus with the aid of Ariadne in the Labyrinth at Knossos; the great Python is overwhelmed by Apollo at Delphi; the Medusa with her macabre coiffure of writhing serpents is killed by Perseus through divine assistance; while Cerberus, the guardian of Hades, a three-headed dog with snakes down his back, is indestructible and may only be placated with barley-mead cakes, yet Herakles manages to drag him away from the gates of Hell.

How are we to understand these loathsome products of the human mind, and how do they relate to the apocalyptic saga of the prophet and his people approaching their Promised Land?

We can conceive monsters as the result of evolutionary, neurological and psychological constructs. From the evolutionary standpoint, the struggle between the hero and the monster represents the actual struggle which occurred within the immensity of biological time between our ancestors and the dangerous predatory beasts with whom they were forced to compete for survival (Sagan, 1977). The evolution of intelligence and speech, together with our capacity to make and use weapons, provided us with the necessary 'magic powers' of the hero for our species to prevail.

From the *neurological* standpoint, one might dare to suggest (though it is pure speculation) that monsters could represent a synthetic amalgam of the reptilian and paleo-mammalian components of the brain. Could it be that monstrous images are created through a collusion between these ancient cerebral components and the powers of imaginative invention at work below the threshold of consciousness?

At the *psychological* level of analysis, the monster is the 'monster within' – the greedy, self-serving, destructive predator and rampant violator of innocents at the core of the shadow complex in Everyman. The Minotaur is the beast lurking in the labyrinth of men's minds, the symbolic precursor of the Freudian Id which emerges in dreams: 'Then the Wild Beast in us', wrote Plato in the *Republic*, 'full-fed with meat and drink, becomes rampant and shakes off sleep to go in quest of what will gratify its own instincts'. The monster may also be understood as a demonic personification of the terrible, destructive aspect of the Great Mother archetype, who devours her children and crunches up their bones rather than grant them freedom and independence. The hero's victory over the monster has to be accomplished anew in every generation, for this victory alone can guarantee the survival of civilization and, in the ancestral environment, the survival of the group in the Promised Land.

The etymological derivation of the word monster is from the Latin *monstrum*, meaning a divine portent or warning, and *mostro*, to show, *monstrator*, a teacher, and *demonstrator*, one who points things out. The monster thus shows us our own destructive power and warns us how capable we are, given the opportunity, of devouring the

154

finer aspects of human nature. It is a ghastly image of the vicious, unredeemed and, perhaps unredeemable, part of the unconscious psyche.

Each culture and every generation breeds its own monsters and its own heroes to defeat them. In our culture it has been Christ's struggle with the Devil and his animal forms and familiars. Within this cultural context other monsters have emerged: Shakespeare's Caliban, the Marquis de Sade's debauchees in *The One Hundred and Twenty Days of Sodom*, Mary Shelley's monstrous creation in *Frankenstein*, Bram Stoker's *Dracula*, Hannibal Lecter in Thomas Harris's *The Silence of the Lambs* and *Hannibal*, all play on the archetypal keys of predation, fear and heroic struggle, which are still as responsive in us as they were in our ancestors. Films like *Jurassic Park* and *Jaws* likewise play games with the monster-predator and his destruction.

It must not be forgotten, however, that there are positive fabulous beings as well as monsters – for example, Pegasus, the Griffin and the Phoenix. These may be understood as representing unlived, unconscious potential which can be highly creative for both the individual and the group. Christianity, with its insistence on the importance of love, obedience and the avoidance of sin, represented an attempt on the part of Western civilization to keep human atavistic destructiveness under control. Now that the church has lost its moral authority, the danger becomes more acute that the monster in us may gain the upper hand and, with his post-nuclear apocalyptic powers, drive us to mutual genocide and extinction. To recognize and deal with the monsters in our minds could be the critical issue for the survival of our species now and far into the future – always provided, of course, that the monster allows the future to occur (Cawson, 1995). (4) *Destruction or punishment as the consequence of the judgement*: At this stage God's wrath becomes manifest and 'justice' is meted out in cataclysmic devastation. In the Book of Revelation it is portrayed by the destruction of the city of Babylon, and St John gives a devastating description of how easily may be cast away the things we value and most strive for. Like the conflagration of Hiroshima, it all happens in an hour:

Alas, alas that great city Babylon, that mighty city! For in one hour is thy judgement come. And the merchants of the earth shall weep and mourn over her; for no man buyeth their merchandise anymore ... Alas, alas that great city, that was clothed in fine linen, and purple and scarlet, and decked with gold, and precious stones, and pearls! For in one hour so great riches is come to nought (*Revelation*, 18:10-17).

To those of us who lived through the decades of nuclear confrontation in the cold war, the idea of global destruction is familiar, but it has a much older pedigree – the biblical story of Noah's flood, the inundation of Deucalion and Pyrrha, and other Middle Eastern tales of flood disaster. Halley's idea that a great comet had crashed into Russia and created the Caspian Sea was the precursor of the contemporary theory that cataclysmic discontinuities in the fossil record – the sudden disappearance of dinosaurs, for example – were due to the impact of giant meteorites plummeting into the oceans and causing massive tidal waves which inundated the land. Similar tales of deluge were being told by Australian aborigines long before the European settlers arrived there. The prospect of a huge meteorite crashing into the earth or of a supervolcano erupting within the next fifty years is a subject which has been seized on gleefully by tabloid newspapers. But in all the myths of world destruction, the cataclysm is inflicted by the gods as a punishment for man's transgressions. Then, after the great catastrophe, a new beginning follows.

(5) *Renewal in a New World*: 'And I saw a new heaven and new earth: for the first heaven and the first earth were passed away; and there was no more sea. And I John saw the holy city, new Jerusalem, coming down from God out of heaven, prepared as a bride adorned for her husband. And I heard a great voice out of heaven saying, Behold, the tabernacle of God is with men, and he will dwell with them, and they shall be his people, and God himself shall be with them, and be their God. And God shall wipe away all tears from their eyes; and there shall be no more death, neither sorrow, nor crying, neither shall there be any more pain: for the former things are passed away' (*Revelation*, 21:1-4). However, this state of bliss is only for the Godly, the chosen few: the rest are to be slain, cast into hell or sold into slavery. Soon after Christianity became the state religion of Rome, and Christ's Second Coming was still expected, Lactantius, tutor to the son of the Emperor Constantine, described the sorry fate

of the ungodly in what sounds uncomfortably like a prediction of Hitler's Third Reich: 'That multitude of the godless shall be annihilated, and torrents of blood shall flow, [and Christ] will hand over all heathen peoples to servitude under the righteous ... and his kingdom of the righteous shall last for a thousand years' (Weber, 1999). The consequences of the 'us' and 'them' dichotomy prevail even in paradise.

*

Taken together, these elements form part components of what we might loosely call the 'archetype of the apocalypse' (Edinger, 1999), a mosaic of interrelated ideas and images making up a complex symbolic system with a rich dynamic of its own. The archetype is constellated at times of collective crisis and articulated by charismatic leaders who manage to tap its energy to galvanize their group into collective action. If it is indeed an archetype, we must ask to what extent apocalyptic symbolism is phylogenetically determined?

The term *phylogenetic psyche* (Jung's 'collective unconscious', of which 'archetypes' are dynamic component structures) is best reserved to describe the psychological potential of humanity which is encoded in the brain. The *personal psyche* refers to what the individual makes of the phylogenetic psyche in the course of growing to maturity. Intermediate between these is what Joseph Henderson (1991) has usefully termed the *cultural psyche*, which incorporates the shared unconscious assumptions of every family, neighbourhood and nation. Clearly, the cultural psyche is not genetically transmitted in the manner of the collective psyche: it is the product of traditional influences over the actualization of archetypal imperatives arising from the phylogenetic psyche through the development of generations of individuals living out their lives in a given geographical location.

When, therefore, Edinger refers to the apocalypse as 'an archetype of the collective unconscious' he is, to our mind, guilty of misrepresentation. The apocalyptic myth is evidently a product of the cultural psyche, the result of historical Judeo-Christian influences on the actualization of the archetypes of in-group loyalty and out-group hostility, the archetypal categories of 'friend' and 'foe', the 'familiar'

157

and the 'strange'. It is these categories which are incorporated in the theological language of 'Good' and 'Evil', and the archetypal symbolism of 'light' and 'dark'.

Many popular forms of science fiction are dominated by the bloody tumult of interplanetary conflict, interstellar wars, revolutions against galactic tyrants and struggles to the death between the forces of Good and Evil. Such films, videos and books illustrate the powerful influence exerted on our imagination by the archetypal imperatives leading to group conflict and to war, and almost inevitably, it seems, they make dramatic use of apocalyptic imagery.

However, stories of hero–saviours, their slaying of the monster and the consequent salvation of their people, are by no means confined to Jewish or Christian populations: they have arisen at different times all over the world. Every culture has its great heroes from the past, many of whom assume legendary stature. That a messiah should be recognized and acclaimed presupposes both a collective demand for salvation and an established set of ideas as to how the demand should be met. As a result, different messianic traditions have arisen in different parts of the world, their forms being influenced to a certain extent through the diffusion of messianic concepts from one culture to another. But they all broadly conform to the same archetypal pattern, of the divinely empowered hero who comes at a time of collective disaster to save his people and to guide them to some Utopia where they will live in peace and security for evermore. An almost universal corollary to the history of the successful messiah is the idea that he will return at some time in the future to fulfil those prophecies which were left unfulfilled at the time of his death.[6]

Among numerous preliterate peoples anthropology has recorded the existence of beliefs that conform to this pattern and which *preceded* the arrival of Christian missionaries among them. Indeed, the arrival of Europeans in their lands was often explained in terms of these indigenous beliefs. For example, according to Fijian myth, two grandnephews of Ndgengei will return to usher in the millennium. When the first Europeans arrived at Fiji, it was generally believed that these were the descendants that the myth foretold. As happened in many other parts of the world, Christian teaching was then assimilated into the native mythology, as in the *tuka* cult, founded by the Fijian prophet, Ndungumoi, which combined elements of the Ndgengei cult with Christianity, and developed rituals which were a mixture of Fijian war dances and European military drill. Ndungumoi predicted that on a certain day many generations of dead Fijians would arise against the Europeans, drive them out and restore all tribal lands to the faithful. Similar movements arose among the Maori of New Zealand in the form of the Hau-Hau (Babbage, 1937) and the cult established by Rua, and among the Indian tribes of North America in the form of the 'Ghost Dance' movement and the 'Old Way of Handsome Lake'.

Although Judeo-Christian versions of the archetypal motifs of the Apocalypse and the Promised Land have proved widely influential in shaping the particular visions, hallucinations and delusory beliefs of charismatics since the European expansion of the sixteenth century, they are by no means *prototypical*. The Tupi-Guarani, an indigenous people originating in the basin of the São Francisco in the interior of Brazil, had already settled along the Atlantic coast before the Europeans arrived. In the course of the centuries *before* the sixteenth century they had migrated in great waves towards the coast. These mass displacements were inspired by native messianic movements centred on charismatic prophets who predicted their eventual arrival at what they called the 'Land without Evil' (the homeland to which, according to their myths, the Divine Hero retires after creating the world). The paradise they dreamed of was of their own mythic making and owed nothing to Judeo-Christian teaching. The Land Without Evil was, however, similar in many ways to the earthly paradise promised by Christian and Muslim prophets. The harvest would be produced without human toil, there would be great abundance for all, the old would become young, all enemies would be defeated, and youth and happiness would last for ever. Thus does the archetypal pattern assert itself in similar lineaments among peoples geographically separated by 25,000 years of time.

When Jesuit missionaries eventually arrived in South America, they observed and recorded this migratory messianic activity. One of the most recent of these had started in 1539. Thousands of Tupinambas (of the same stock as the Tupi-Guarani), fearing the death and destruction of the end of the world forecast by their shamans, abandoned their settlements on the Brazilian coast and set off, impelled by a messianic urge, to find the 'Land of Immortality and Perpetual

Rest'. After nine years they had traversed the South American continent at its widest point and had arrived at Chachapoyas in Peru. (Here they recounted their experiences; and their fantasies evidently meshed with those of the Spanish, for they told of rich lands and fabulous cities of unheard-of wealth and majesty. As a result, the Spanish set off in the counter-direction, under Pedro de Ursua, in quest of El Dorado). Oral tradition still relates the ordeals, perils, hardships and famine the Tupinamba suffered on their great trek. However, when they reached the Pacific coast and found there was no Land of Immortality, they, like countless other charismatic groups afflicted with 'apocalyptic disappointment', gave up, and many of them resumed the long journey back to the East (Lanternari, 1963). A few, however, remained and are still to be found in villages on the Peruvian coast.

Many other such native migrations were recorded. Almost without exception they were inspired by fears of the end of the world and the hope of finding refuge in an earthly paradise. As late as 1921, Nimuendajú discovered that the lives of the Tupi-Guarani were still dominated by the same fears and hopes. Those whom he found on the Brazilian coast had not given up the prospect of crossing the Atlantic to find the wondrous place their ancestors had been unable to see. He also found people from other tribes who were still trying to reach the Land without Evil, hoping to avoid the end of the world foretold by their shamans many generations earlier.

The contemporary scientific notion that universes come and go, and possess a life cycle of their own, has long been current among the Tupi-Guarani, who believe that a world preceding the present one was destroyed by a cosmic cataclysm and that the same terrifying event will occur again in the near future. While in some instances this idea was influenced by the preaching of Jesuit missionaries, Vittorio Lanternari (1963) was quite certain that, among the Mbua of Paraguay, the fear had no connection with Christianity and was a direct survival from ancient native tradition.

Arrival at the Promised Land

And Moses went up from the plains of Moab unto the mountain of Nebo, to the top of Pisgah, that is over against Jericho. And the Lord shewed him all the land of Gilead ... and all the land of Judah, unto the utmost sea. And the south, and the plain of the valley of Jericho, the city of palm trees, unto Zoar. And the Lord said unto him, 'This is the land which I sware unto Abraham, unto Isaac, and unto Jacob, saying, I will give it unto thy seed: I have caused thee to see it with thine eyes, but thou shalt not go over thither.'   *Deuteronomy*, 34:1-4

How would a migrating group recognize the Promised Land when it got there? The schizotypal leader's fantasies may have given some idea what to expect, but the probability is that both his and his followers' anticipations would be strongly coloured by what Gordon Orians and Judith Heerwagen (1992) call 'evolved responses to land-scapes.' They propose that our aesthetic responses to landscape have been derived, at least in part, from evolved propensities that function to help hunter–gatherers make crucial decisions as when to give up one location and move onto another, where to settle and what kind of places to avoid.

Studies of picture preferences among people from widely differing backgrounds have confirmed not only that natural as opposed to man-made environments are consistently preferred (Kaplan, 1992) but also that savannah-like landscapes are liked better than all others, particularly by young children (Balling and Falk, 1982). On the whole, people prefer environments that have large trees, semi-open spaces, hills and valleys, streams, rivers, lakes and estuaries, and a distant view of the horizon. They also like there to be an element of ambiguity or mystery which invites further exploration – for example, roads or paths that lead out of sight round hills, or the representation of partially blocked views which hint at interesting but hidden possibilities. All such research findings indicate that parallels exist between what people prefer and the environmental circumstances in which humans evolved and flourished.

Environmental adaptation depends on the perception of natural cues, the recognition of their significance and the capacity to react appropriately when their significance has been recognized. This is as true of humans as of any other animal. We assess things in terms of their significance for us and the behavioural opportunities they provide according to the motivational or psychological state we happen to be in at the time.

Clearly, habitat selection is crucial for the survival and reproductive success of every organism and, in our own case, our perceptual, cognitive, emotional and behavioural responses to environmental cues have been under powerful selection pressure for hundreds of thousands of years. While the survival requirements of contemporary human beings differ in many ways from our ancestors, the story has not changed all that dramatically. We still have to orientate ourselves to the physical environment, obey inner imperatives to explore our surroundings and construct inner cognitive maps; we have to assess lurking threats and dangers as well as locate promising resources. Indeed, many of the phobias from which our contemporaries suffer (agoraphobia, arachnophobia, acrophobia, claustrophobia, etc.) are exaggerated responses to environmental cues that signalled actual danger in the surroundings in which we evolved (Stevens and Price, 2000). Biological sources of danger include potentially hostile strangers, spiders, snakes, predatory animals, heights, confined spaces from which there is no escape, parasites, poisonous foods, and so on. It is surely significant that the kind of Promised Land described by prophets is free of all such dangers.

Orians and Heerwagen suggest that, when on the move, our hunter–gatherer ancestors selected suitable habitats in three stages:

Stage 1: A new and unfamiliar landscape is rapidly assessed: individual responses to the landscape are strongly emotional, based as they are on innate propensities as well as previous experience.

Stage 2: If the response to Stage 1 is positive, then the environment is explored to assess its resource potential. Here again, evolved responses guide investigation and focus attention on those aspects of the habitat which are relevant to survival and reproductive success.

Stage 3: The decision is taken whether to settle in the environment or to move on.

There are good biological reasons why behavioural response patterns should have evolved to guide these decisions. As Orians and Heerwagen point out, time is important, and automatic responses leave the brain free to focus on those aspects of behaviour that urgently require attention. Thus, an open environment, devoid of protective cover, is perceived as undesirable, as is a dense forest within which movement and visual surveillance are difficult. Humans can, of course, inhabit such environments, but more extensive experience and learning is required for inhabitants to survive in them.

It seems likely, therefore, that the kind of environment that migrating populations would perceive as corresponding to their profoundest anticipations of the promised land would be the primordial landscape of our kind – the African savannah. Biomass and the availability of meat are much higher in savannahs than, for example, in forests and, as a result, they provide an attractive environment for large terrestrial, omnivorous primates like ourselves. Savannahs provide distant views, grassy ground cover favourable to nomadic life, trees which offer protection from the sun and a refuge from predators, and plentiful sources of food. One resource that is relatively scarce in this environment, however, is water, and this could explain the great sensitivity of people worldwide to water symbolism (Orians and Heerwagen, 1992).

One fascinating experimental finding is that participants in studies of landscape preferences were usually unable to explain or justify the choices that they made; yet they made them readily and with conviction, providing results which were regular, repeatable and predictable. 'When questioning participants about the bases of their preferences,' reports Kaplan (1992), 'we have found that they are usually quite unaware of the variables that proved so effective in predicting what they would prefer ... Perhaps there is an evolved bias in humans favouring preferences for certain kinds of environments, just as there is an evolved bias favouring reproductive activities. In the case of sexual behaviour we do not expect people to explain their inclinations on adaptive grounds, although such inclinations must ultimately derive from an adaptive basis.'

When human populations have found and taken up residence in such a highly preferred landscape, which seems to embody all that makes life worth living, it is not surprising that they should experience a joyous sense of 'homecoming' and be willing to defend it to the death.

The Noah complex

Just as the disappearance of the moon is never final because a new moon inevitably follows, so the disappearance of man is

never final either, for after flood or whatever a new humanity is
born.   Mircea Eliade

In myths of world destruction, the cataclysm is commonly inflicted
by the gods as a punishment for man's transgressions. Then, after the
great deluge or terrible fire, a new beginning follows. A small group
of 'chosen people' survives to establish a new order, infinitely better
than the old, and purified of its sin, error, and hopelessness. Noah's
flood eventually subsides and the world is repopulated by a God-fear-
ing elect. Deucalion, the son of Prometheus, and his wife Pyrrha,
survive the deluge visited upon the earth by Zeus in his wrath, and
reconstruct the human race. Monsters slay the Nordic gods at Rag-
narok and the world is destroyed by fire and flood, but the world tree
Yggdrasil survives and bears a new man, Lif, and a new woman,
Lifthrasir, to regenerate the human race.

In the Teutonic 'twilight of the gods', the destruction of Valhalla is
not the end. Baldur is reborn and creates a new world. In the Hopi
myth of four great empires, each one of them begins and ends with a
cataclysm. Every time a few people survive to build a new world.
In the third century BC, the Babylonian priest, Berosus, endorsed
the Chaldean doctrine of the Great Year, according to which the
universe is periodically destroyed and reconstructed every
Great Year, consisting of two millennia. In the alchemical work
to create *Adam secundus*, the purpose of the 'opus' is to reconcile
the intolerable oppositions of human life by bringing about the
total destruction of the old incomplete man so as to create the
new whole man.

Recent advances in genetics give some indication of the biological
reality of the 'Noah phenomenon' – namely, that on one or more
occasions the human race has almost suffered extinction and has
only survived through the reproductive success of a tiny handful of
people, who, if not 'chosen', at least were fortunate enough to be in
the right place at the right time. Through the study of mitochondrial
DNA, researchers have identified 'genetic bottlenecks' in the distant
past, when the total population of Homo sapiens was reduced to a
small number of progenitors. It is thought that one such bottleneck
occurred between 100,000 and 200,000 years ago in one of the radia-
tions of Homo out of Africa.

8. Apocalypse and Armageddon

For the last half of the twentieth century, myths of world destruction, together with the eschatological expectations of the early Christians, were unconsciously activated in association with the idea of nuclear holocaust. The German analyst, Hans Dieckmann has detected in us what he calls the *Noah complex* – the desire to wipe everything out and start afresh. Our instinct for self-preservation permits us to enjoy these apocalyptic fantasies because it tells us that *we* should be the ones to survive. We identify with Noah, Deucalion and Baldur. As Dieckmann (1986) put it: 'The horror evoked by images of the end of the world frighten us even as they fascinate, and they grip us perhaps precisely because, with the "end", the Christian hope of redemption and the glorification of the triumphant Christ unconsciously makes itself felt. This may be why in our soul the fear evoked by the horrors of this end of the world cannot really take effect and influence us to work for its preservation. An unconscious fascination pushes us to realize the end of the world.'

When we think like this, we are subject to the same archetypal imperatives as our migrating ancestors, as they flung themselves in sheer desperation into the final apocalyptic struggle for the Promised Land. Should our Noah identification rise into consciousness, we rationalize it: we think to ourselves that there are too many people, anyway, and that they are using up the world's resources and polluting the environment at an exponential rate. In a hundred years or so the planet will be uninhabitable because our shortsightedness will neither let us take the necessary steps to reduce the population nor return to simple methods of agriculture and production. Therefore, it is better to wipe out 95 per cent of the world's population and let the enlightened ones – 'us' – start again with a new order that will not make the same terrible mistakes. This apocalyptic fantasy of the new beginning has found expression in the 'post-nuclear holocaust' novels and films which have achieved enormous popularity in recent decades.

It is as if we have reached the stage, in this global village of ours, at which foraging communities would split. Unfortunately, there is nowhere left for our disaffected members to go. The Promised Land is shut.

9

Love, Rank and Religion

Man is by his constitution a religious animal. Edmund Burke

There is a growing body of opinion that religious behaviour is 'prepared for' by the genetic structure of our species. According to this
view, religions are biological phenomena which enhance the welfare
of those who have them.[1] As a social animal, our personal survival
depends on being accepted as a member of a successful, well-organ-
ized and reasonably co-operative human group. It is to guarantee the
long-term cohesion of such groups that initiation rituals evolved.
Religion sanctions all such rituals and grants the tribal elders their
spiritual authority and political power. Biologically, this is the most
crucial function of religion. Not only does it ensure group cohesion but
it induces individual members of the group to sacrifice their narrow
self-interests to the wider interests of the community as a whole.[2]

In this respect, religion acts as a social reinforcer of more basic
genetic propensities. In the neo-Darwinian view, our genes make use
of us in order to satisfy their own selfish ends – namely, to get into
the next generation. If this is so, how can selfish genes produce
unselfish people? The answer is, say the neo-Darwinists, that our
genes see to it that we behave altruistically because it is to their
advantage that we should do so. Our co-operativeness is driven by
genetic self-interest. The grocer sells vegetables to make a living, not
to help us. We buy his vegetables to live, not to help him. But the
result is that both sides benefit from the exchange. Accordingly, it is
of advantage to our genes – and to ourselves – that we should live in
a society with a structure and a moral code sanctioned by religion.[3]

The very universality of religious phenomena, combined with the
unquestioning way in which the great majority of people have traditionally retained the beliefs of the culture into which they were born,
suggests the existence of an innate imperative to learn a whole

167

complex of religious, mythological, political, ethical and social rules. Together these rules constitute the 'mazeway'.

This innately determined 'rule-learning device' functions as an 'open programme' much like Chomsky's language acquisition device:[4] it is a neurologically based complex primed to accept the religious and moral 'vocabulary' of the culture. Children are born with the built-in assumption that their community will possess not only a language, which they will quickly pick up, but also an interrelated system of beliefs and values which they must acquire and conform to. The survival and reproductive value of such a rule-learning device is evident. All societies codify themselves, and their successful continuity depends on the readiness of new members to learn the code. The alternative is social anarchy, and a collective incapacity for competition or defence. If societies fail to codify themselves efficiently, therefore, or lose faith in their doctrines, they are gravely at risk. It is at such moments that schizotypal traits reveal their adaptive significance.

Attachment and rank

Although we are co-operative creatures, we are also fundamentally competitive: we compete with one another for love, resources and social rank. The dramas generated by this rivalry are the very essence of human social life, and it seems that they are derived from two fundamental biosocial complexes:

(1) one concerned with attachment, affiliation, care-giving, care-receiving and altruism, and
(2) one concerned with rank, status, discipline, law and order, territory and possessions.

These two fundamental systems – and the contrasting forms of social organization they give rise to – find numerous parallels in the history of ideas. One example is Empedocles' distinction between love and strife, from which Freud derived his Eros and Thanatos instincts; other examples are Aristotle's distinction between the hedonic and political life, and Tonnies' classical sociological distinction between *Gemeinschaft* and *Gesellschaft*.

The natural history of competitiveness began over 300 million years ago, when our ancestors competed for resources (food, territory and mates) on an individual basis, as many vertebrates continue to do to this day. Then, as group living became established and territory began to be shared, individuals ceased competing directly for territory and instead started to compete for rank. Once acquired, high rank brought with it access to the resources that were desired.

Sometime in the last ten million years, a new form of social competition has evolved: instead of threatening or trying to intimidate rivals in order to dominate them, the competitor seeks to attract them. This form of competition is apparent, for example, among chimpanzees, and its significance was first recognized by Michael Chance (Chance, 1988; Chance and Jolly, 1970). In addition to threat displays, male chimpanzees indulge in a form of display that is not threatening at all, and does not demand the submission of a subordinate. Rather it is a form of social solicitation, which, Chance noted, results in affiliative behaviour.

From extensive observations of social primates, Chance recognized that they had two quite distinct modes of functioning, which he termed 'agonic', and 'hedonic'. The *agonic mode* is characteristic of hierarchically organized groups where individuals are concerned with warding off threats to their status and inhibiting overt expressions of aggressive conflict; while the *hedonic mode* is associated with affiliative behaviour in more egalitarian social organizations, where agonic tensions are absent. These two modes are as apparent in human social groupings as they are in those of chimpanzees. In the hedonic mode, the competitor seeks to disarm potential rivals and attract potential mates as well as achieving status in the eyes of other members of the group.

Whereas in the agonic mode, high rank is the reward of the more aggressive, assertive, dominant type of individual, in the hedonic mode, it is attractive people who are granted prestige.

These distinctions are of interest for our discussion of charismatic leaders, for, as our examination of them demonstrates, they seek both to attract and dominate their followers – in that order; and the cults they form tend to function in the hedonic mode initially but, as they come into conflict with other groups, their organization tends to become hierarchical and agonic. In either mode, the reproductive fitness of the leader is increased, for he can assert *droit de seigneur* both through attraction and dominance.

Unfortunately, the phylogenetically ancient form of agonistic competition has not been eradicated from human nature. It has, after all, been present and evolving on this planet for 300 million years, and it is deeply embedded in the human genome; whereas hedonic competition has been in existence only about one-thirtieth of that time. As a result, human social behaviour is still heavily influenced by both modes of competition.

Essentially, the two possible outcomes of competition through intimidation (the agonic mode) are dominance or submission; and the two possible outcomes of competition through attraction (the hedonic mode) are affiliation (social co-operation, love and integration) or detachment (withdrawal and social isolation).

These can be represented orthogonally: (1) physical competition for dominance on the vertical axis, and (2) competition by attraction for approval and social integration on the horizontal axis.

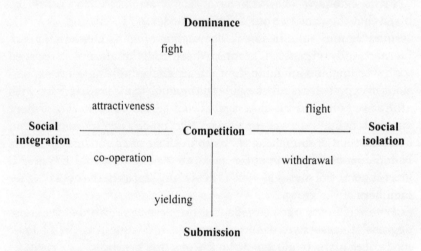

Figure 1. A schema for possible outcomes of competition through dominance and attraction

The horizontal dimension may also be labelled closeness – distance, approach – withdrawal, in-group – out-group orientation, extraversion – introversion, and so on. In other words, the horizontal dimension is concerned with attachment, the vertical dimension with power. This schema carries significance for our understanding of

170

charismatic leaders and their groups as well as providing a theoretical basis for the classification of psychiatric disorders.

In our book *Evolutionary Psychiatry: A New Beginning* (2000), we propose links between the basic dimensions of love and power and the disorders encountered in psychiatric practice. These may be summarized as follows:

(1) Successful affiliation tends to be associated with social adjustment and mental health.
(2) Dominance tends to be associated with high self-esteem and hypomania.
(3) Submission tends to be associated with low self-esteeem, feelings of shame and humiliation, dependent or anxious personality disorders, and depression.
(4) Failure in affiliation tends to be associated with a *spacing disorder*, namely schizoid, paranoid and schizotypal personality disorders as well as schizophrenia.

As suggested in Chapter 3, a crucial factor is whether or not a vulnerable individual continues to feel himself or herself to be an 'insider' (a member of the in-group, whether loved or unloved, of high status or low), or an 'outsider' (not a member of the in-group, not involved in attachment relationships or status conflicts). If an insider develops a psychiatric disorder, it will tend to be a *disorder of attachment and rank* (neurotic or manic-depressive disorder), whereas an outsider will tend to develop a *spacing disorder*. Vulnerable people who are uncertain as to their allegiance and who hover uneasily on the cusp between 'insider' and 'outsider' status will, if they develop a psychiatric disorder, tend to present with a borderline personality disorder. This means of reclassifying the major psychiatric disorders is summarized in Figure 2.

The significance of these two fundamental biosocial complexes subserving affiliation and rank is as great for the study of symbolism as it is for the diagnosis and treatment of psychiatric disorders (Stevens, 1998). The symbolisms of tragedy, loss, demotion and despair, like the psychiatry of bereavement and depression, are expressions of natural and universal experiences which human beings share with other mammalian species. They are manifestations of adaptive mechanisms that, in the ancestral environment in which we evolved, contributed to survival. Thus, depression (and all the

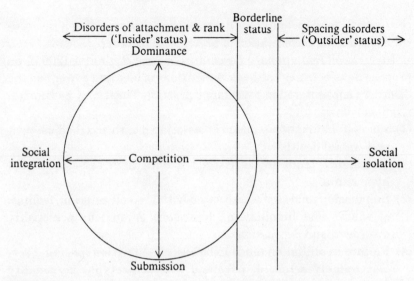

Figure 2. A schema for the classification of the major disorders

symbolism it gives rise to) is an adaptive reaction to loss or deprivation. The loss in question may be loss of a loved-one (the affiliative
biosocial complex) or loss of status (the rank biosocial complex) or
both. The adaptive function of the depressive reaction is to enable
individuals so afflicted to adjust to their loss. By becoming depressed
and displaying behaviour which symbolizes defeat, the demoted
individual is forced to adapt passively to his or her lower status and,
at the same time, to avoid provoking further attack or hostility from
a more powerful individual who has displaced him or her. Depression
(and its symbolism of descent, oppression and loss) is thus linked to
the ubiquitous mammalian tactic of submission; while its opposite,
mania (and its symbolism of ascent, triumph and gain) is linked with
the tactic of dominance. We may conclude, therefore, that manic-depression, and its non-pathological manifestations in elation and
despair, as well as all the symbolism that these states give rise to, are
inextricably linked to our evolved propensities to seek affiliation and
rank within the context of a stable human group.

These manifestations are relevant to our understanding of charismatic prophets. Throughout this book we have argued that the
majority of such figures have schizotypal personalities. However, it
must be acknowledged that many seem to have episodes of elevated

172

mood, and some have been diagnosed as manic-depressive – for example, Mother Earth,[5] Sabbatai Sevi[6] and L. Ron Hubbard.[7] How are we to explain this? Are prophets, nearly all of whom exhibit 'borderline' characteristics, potentially manic-depressive or potentially schizophrenic? Or is it possible that they are both? And if they are both, where does this leave our hypothesis that the high fertility of prophets accounts for the continued existence of low fertility schizophrenics in the population at large.

The major 'functional' psychoses (manic-depression and schizophrenia) are biologically implicated in three phases of the natural history of groups: (1) group cohesion, (2) group splitting, and (3) competition with other, potentially hostile groups. Mood disorders (mania and depression) evolved to serve phase (1); while spacing disorders evolved to serve phases (2) and (3).

Mood disorders serve to maintain group cohesion by sustaining the social hierarchy and facilitating the allocation of leadership and follower roles within the hedonic group. In contemporary social situations, the issue of dominance does not immediately arise, for all encounters are normally conducted in the hedonic mode. Should people be called upon to work together or live in close proximity to one another, as they would in ancestral groups, this agreeable state of affairs may continue indefinitely, provided they are well-adjusted individuals and do not have to make too many controversial decisions. If conflicts should arise between them, as in ancestral groups outstripping their resources, then the hedonic mode may switch into the agonic mode, and conflicts for status may well ensue. Success in a status conflict results in feelings of elation, while failure results in demotion and feelings of despair. If they persist, feelings of despair may develop into the dejected state we recognize as 'depression'. The adaptive function of the depression is to facilitate losing and to promote accommodation to the fact that one has lost. In other words, the depressive state evolved to promote the acceptance of a subordinate role and the loss of resources which can only be secured by holding higher rank in the dominance hierarchy. The function of this depressive adaptation is to prevent the loser in a status conflict from suffering further injury and to preserve the stability and competitive efficiency of the group by maintaining social homeostasis.

The selective advantage of an evolved capacity for the recognition

173

and acceptance of rank difference in social groups is that it reduces aggressiveness and establishes precedents in granting rights of access to indispensable resources such as territory, food and potential mates. It naturally follows, therefore, that gaining rank is associated with elevated mood and losing rank with depressed mood. These adaptive patterns of response, which evolved over 300 million years ago in reptiles, are still with us, encoded in the reptilian portions of our own brains (Maclean, 1985). They provide the *templates* for the manic or depressive reactions in human beings. But whereas our reptilian ancestors won or lost the fight for territory, social animals like ourselves win or lose in the competition for status and for love.

What light does this throw on the psychology of charismatic leaders and their groups? Being at the top of the social hierarchy, leaders commonly feel loved and respected, and their spirits are high, if not frankly hypomanic. Followers closely identified with the leader may well share his high mood; but, if they resent the leader, their spirits tend to be lower, which effectively inhibits their capacity to rebel. So it is that, with confident, energetic leaders, and with any subversive elements too depressed to act, a group's cohesiveness is maintained and it is able to compete with other groups in the struggle for existence. However, when group tensions develop, and social organization shifts from the hedonic to the agonic mode, then the depressed subversives become ready meat for a charismatic prophet with a message of salvation. Group dynamics now move from phase (1) through phases (2) and (3); and the schizotypal phenotype, rather than its manic-depressive equivalent, displays its adaptive function.

The adaptive function of the schizotypal phenotype is, as we have seen, to promote group splitting and population dispersal. This it achieves by producing (a) a mazeway resynthesis which creates a new belief system incompatible with that of the parent group, (b) paranoid delusions which drive the daughter group away, and (c) fantasies of a promised land which draws the daughter group to a new habitat.

Thus the manic leader, being adapted to phase (1), tends to stay with the parent group and, if he revitalizes its mazeway, the subsequent shift in the belief system tends to be homopistic; while the schizotypal leader, being adapted to phases (2) and (3), revitalizes the mazeway so as to create a belief system which is essentially heteropistic.

What then about schizotypal personalities who experience elevation or depression of their mood, are they not manic-depressive? The answer is no, because their mood is secondary to the success or failure of their (schizotypal) mission. The schizotype gets high mood from the adulation of his followers, and, presumably, in anticipation of acquiring followers, so that he has the energy and confidence to preach his message. It is only if his message is repeatedly rejected, and thus invalidated, that he becomes depressed. But this particular form of schizotypal dejection resembles less the clinical picture of a depressive illness than the 'negative' symptoms of schizophrenia – inertia, lack of drive and willpower, complete withdrawal into the self.

Unlike the manic-depressive, the schizotype undergoes a mazeway resynthesis which leads him into a different world, with the result that he becomes alienated from his previous world. In the absence of followers to share and support him in this new world, there is little to prevent him from sliding into a schizophrenic psychosis. Alienation is the hallmark of schizophrenia, and that is why psychiatrists were called 'alienists'. What protects the prophet from schizophrenic alienation is the loving reverence of his followers, and this he retains by representing himself to them as God's representative on earth.

Just as the two major biosocial systems of affiliation and rank rule the relations between the prophet and his flock, so, in monotheistic religions, they have ruled relations between God and the faithful. God is always in the supremely dominant position: we are enjoined by the scriptures to love, fear and obey Him. 'The fear of God is the beginning of knowledge' (*Proverbs*, 1:7). Subordination is the *sine qua non* of religious life: 'Fear God, and keep his commandments, for this is the whole duty of man' (*Ecclesiastes*, 12:13). The alternative to such subordination to the Almighty is banishment: excommunication, expulsion from the Garden of Eden and the Fall from Grace.

The essential difference between the messiah and the charismatic prophet is that the messiah advocates renewed submission to the Almighty whereas the charismatic advocates heresy. Consequently, they find themselves on opposite sides when the community splits. The messiah continues to subordinate himself to God, preaches a

175

homopistic message to his people and anathematizes the charismatic for his heresy; for his part, the charismatic refuses to submit, preaches heteropistically and becomes the embodiment of God for his people as they grow as alienated from the parent group's orthodoxy as he is himself.

Sometimes the messiah and the charismatic prophet coincide in the same man, but then, as the group dynamics constellated round him change, he is forced to adopt one role or the other. This was true of Jesus Christ. The Jews, having suffered defeat and occupation at the hands of the Romans, hoped for the restoration of the Royal House of David under the rule of a great King, the Messiah (*Christos* in Greek). The messiah would be a warrior hero, who would bring together the dispersed tribes of Israel, and, after 70 AD, would rebuild the temple of Jerusalem.

When Jesus proclaimed himself to be the Messiah, the majority of Jews were incredulous because he did not fulfil the anticipated pattern. He was not a warrior prepared to fight military battles, or a politician prepared to enforce Yahweh's rule of law, but a prophet who warned people that the end was at hand, and preached a heteropistic message as to what they must do to survive it. What mattered was not military victory, political power or righteous behaviour, but the religious spirit in which life was to be lived.

What was both subversive and revolutionary about Jesus was his teaching that God demanded not obedience but *love*. Jesus sought to transform the agonic world of the Old Testament into the hedonic community of the New – to replace fear with love, dread with hope, and punishment with forgiveness. The archetype of the patriarchal father was to be transmogrified through the power of Love. When the Kingdom of God failed to materialize in the absence of Christ's Second Coming, the Apostles dealt with their 'apocalyptic disappointment', as have thousands of followers of other cults before and since, by reinterpreting the prophet's message into another form – in this instance, a form which has persisted up to the present time. The Kingdom of God is not to be conceived, they said, as something that will arrive from outside. On the contrary, it has already arrived. It is here inside you *now*. 'Now is the accepted time', declared St Paul. 'Behold, now is the day of salvation.' Thus is the Promised Land redefined: it becomes *inner space* to be experienced *symbolically*.

176

There is a diastole and systole in the affairs of groups, particularly religious groups. Christianity began as a small cult centred on a charismatic prophet, and became institutionalized as a world religion, with a bureaucracy centred on the Holy City of Rome, only to split into Eastern (Orthodox) and Western (Catholic) halves. Then a further split occurred in the Great Schism between the Avignon and Roman Papacy, followed by the great fragmentation of the Reformation. Although a large fraction of the world's population is still nominally Christian, the proportion of communicants, who actually participate in the ancient ritual of 'eating the god' in memory of Christ, has been diminishing rapidly throughout the past century. Nevertheless, the cult started by Jesus of Nazareth has survived in all its multitudinous forms, for two thousand years.

In their study of religious movements, Pattison and Ness (1989) distinguish between *church*, *denomination*, *sect* and *cult*. The history of modern religious groups shows how they may grow to assume any of these forms, according to their size and social context. The Church of Jesus Christ of Latter-Day Saints (the Mormons) provides a good example of how a cult is founded, leads to population dispersal and the propagation of its charismatic leader's genes, eventually to become institutionalized as a sect, denomination or church.

According to Mormon history, Joseph Smith, an uneducated 14-year-old farmhand, went into the woods near his home in Palmyra, New York State, one spring morning in 1820, to pray. There he had a vision in which both God and Jesus Christ appeared, telling him that further revelations would be granted him. He had to wait three years. Then, during the night of September 21st 1823, he had a second vision in which an angel appeared, called 'Moroni'. Moroni identified himself as the last of the Old Testament prophets, who had sailed from Israel to found the ancient civilizations of Central America. The history of this migration, so Moroni said, was inscribed in a language called 'Reformed Egyptian' on gold plates buried in the hillside near Joseph's home. Joseph claimed that, with divine help, he was able to find them, dig them up and translate them into English. This translation was dutifully written down by Joseph's friend, Oliver Coudery, and printed in 1830 as *The Book of Mormon: Another Testament of Jesus Christ*.

The original gold plates then mysteriously disappeared. However, eight of Joseph's followers were prepared to testify that they had actually seen them, and their testimonials are printed at the front of every copy of The Book. Its publication brought a flood of converts, and by 1839 the movement had grown so large that Joseph Smith led his followers in a migration to the banks of the Mississippi, where they built a town called Nauvoo (from the Hebrew meaning 'beautiful city').

One of the most significant of Joseph Smith's divinely inspired pronouncements occurred on July 12th 1843, when he decreed that full restoration of the Gospel demanded introduction of the practice of polygamy. Smith is said to have acquired 84 wives. This outraged puritanical opinion throughout America, with the result that Joseph and his brother Hyram were arrested. Such was the bitter hostility they evoked that a mob broke into their jail and murdered them on June 27th 1844.

Persecution of the Mormons persisted after Jospeh's death, with the result that his charismatic successor, Brigham Young, led an exodus of 20,000 faithful from Nauvoo along the terrible Oregon trail. After much hardship, a small pioneer group trekked through Nebraska and Wyoming to the Salt Lake in Mexican territory which is now Utah. Mormon teaching attracted immigrants from all over Europe, particularly from Britain, and many Mormon townships were given such names as Leeds, Chester and Wales. Eventually, over 350 townships were settled, including the first English-speaking communities in Colorado, Idaho, Nevada and San Francisco. It is probably true to say that most of the inter-mountain States were colonized by the Mormons. Instead of practising genocide, they adopted a policy of peaceful reconciliation with the native Indians, believing that the Indians were descendants of the original settlers from Israel, who had, according to Moroni's gold plates, begun to arrive in America over 4,000 years previously. Many Indians were baptized into the Mormon church.

The story of Joseph Smith and his cult is thus a persuasive example of how a charismatic leader can inspire mass migration and settlement in a Promised Land, while at the same time ensuring that copies of his genes are replicated in large numbers. Mormons still exist in many parts of the world, but whether they are regarded as a church or a sect depends, as Pattison and Ness point out, on where

178

they happen to be and in what force: 'Mormonism assumes the form of the universal church cosmology in Utah, but functions as a denomination in the democratic pluralism of California. In the Midwest, Mormons exist in tension with other competing Christian sects, while in the South the Mormons are viewed as a dissident cult.'

Pattison and Ness also demonstrate how groups may undergo transformation with time: 'The tragic Jonestown saga illustrates the process whereby a typical Baptist denominational group retreated into an independent sectarian stance, and ultimately to a dissident revolutionary cult.' The same can be said of David Koresh's Branch Davidians.

Access to the sacred

> When a great storm lashes the lake into fury, God is walking on the face of the waters; when the roar of the waterfall is louder than usual, it is the voice of God. The earthquake is caused by his mighty footstep, and the lightning is ... God coming down in anger.   Sir James Frazer, *The Worship of Nature*

We have examined a number of reasons why people may join cults, but so far we have not discussed what is, perhaps, the most important of all – the powerful, overwhelmingly powerful, sense a prophet can give to his followers of being in touch with the *sacred*, the *numinous*, what Rudolph Otto called the *mysterium tremendum et fascinans*. This can be, for those who have had it, a profoundly exciting, literally hair-raising experience, for it induces a psychophysical state of immense biological antiquity – one that biologists call 'arousal'.

Arousal is remarkably similar in a number of emotional conditions: sexual desire, anger, fear and numinous excitement are all associated with increased heart rate, raised blood pressure, increased muscular tension, characteristic changes in the brain waves as recorded by the EEG, diminished electrical resistance of the skin, piloerection (the hair stands on end), dilatation of the pupil of the eye, respiratory changes and so on. These changes typify arousal. And they give rise to a challenging question: if the physical signs of anger, fear, sexual desire and numinous experience are all broadly similar, what distinguishes one from the other? The answer can only lie in the

179

psychological perception of what is being experienced, and this is determined by the actual circumstances that are being responded to. It is the charismatic prophet's special gift that he can not only access this state in himself, but successfully induce it in others.

The charismatic guru who has contributed most to our psychological understanding of numinous experience, and who was himself susceptible to it, was C.G. Jung. He explained it in terms of the psychodynamics of what he called the Self – the nucleus at the core of the personality which incorporates the entire archetypal potential of the phylogenetic psyche. The central importance of the Self, its powerful autonomy in sustaining and co-ordinating our psychic existence, would explain, Jung maintained, the ease with which we humans have ubiquitously identified it with (or projected it onto) a Supreme Being, or God, conceived as a transpersonal entity outside ourselves and responsible for everything that happens to us. Jung saw all religions, all churches, all theologies as a metaphysical consequence of this projection of the Self and its enormous psychological potential. To enter the realm of the sacred is to mobilize the powerful energy of the Self and to put one's ego at its mercy. As a result, the sacred is something that human beings have always approached in fear and trembling, surrounding it with taboos and prohibitions, and elaborate systems of belief and ritual. But what appears sacred to a member of one culture appears profane to a member of another. For this reason, there is no such thing as a false religion: all religions are true for those who believe in them. And, in the Jungian view, the Self is the living embodiment in each and every one of us of the numinous power that has always and everywhere been attributed to 'the gods'.

To approach the sacred and have a numinous experience is to glimpse what is felt to be of 'ultimate importance', and it inevitably demands some kind of religious belief. Whether or not the belief is 'true' is completely irrelevant. All that matters is that one has it. To us, belief in Zeus, Osiris or Ahura Mazda may seem to have been delusory, but the experience induced by such belief was not. The goose pimples, the sense of awe in the presence of the *mysterium tremendum*, experienced by believers entering a precinct sacred to one of these deities were *real*. An idea, an object, a symbol, or a place is experienced as numinous if it refers to something tremendous and

180

is perceived as sacred in the sense that it relates to something infinitely greater than oneself.

Anthony Wallace has calculated that since our species began to behave in this way, we have created somewhere in the region of 100,000 different religions; while Mircea Eliade (1958) has said we cannot be sure that there is anything that has not at some time in human history been somewhere transformed into a holy object imbued with sacred power: 'Anything that man has ever handled, felt, come into contact with or loved *can* become a hierophany' (from the Greek *hieros* = sacred and *phanein* = to reveal; a hierophany is thus a sacred revelation). How can this happen? How is the common made special? How does the sacred symbol or belief come into being? If you put these questions to people belonging to different cultures from all over the world, they will tell you that their holy symbols are sacred because 'the gods' made them so. Somehow, the gods manage to convey their intention that the object, ritual or belief system selected by them must become things of collective veneration. How is the message conveyed? Through the visions and auditory hallucinations of a charismatic prophet.

It is all a matter of selection and choice. Coming from the other side of the thin partition, the great artist can perform a role similar to the prophet, in drawing collective attention to the Truly Important, the Ultimately Real. Painting and music were initially sacred in the sense that they were created as religious acts. Indeed, for many of us, art galleries and concert halls have replaced churches as the buildings we enter in search of the divine or sacred – of what strikes us as beautiful and eternally valid on the transpersonal plane. The unfailing characteristic of great art is to reveal what is eternal in the transitory, and universal in the particular. Whenever art achieves this it keys us into the *phrike* which the Greeks recognized as the hair-raising shudder, the sacred spine-tingling shiver of awe and dread that is the quintessence of numinous excitement. It arises from the unconscious dynamics of the Self; it is not something that we can induce through conscious exercise of the will.

In addition to inspired charismatic teaching and great works of art, anthropology reveals a further factor capable of generating awareness of the sacred: anything powerful, monstrous, extraordinary or startling – what Eliade called a *kratophany* (from the Greek

181

kratos, meaning power, and *phanein*, a revelation – a revelation through power). Anything that is unaccustomed or extraordinary possesses the capacity to arrest our attention, inspire awe and fascination, or provoke fear and withdrawal – not only in ourselves but in all mammals to a greater or lesser extent. Anything exceptional can inspire this response: enormous size, great strength, loud noise, bright light, extreme beauty or great ugliness. Shamans, sorcerers, holy madmen and inspired prophets, can be hideous and frightening: their gross eccentricity and behaviour are the stigmata that mark them out as being special and chosen. Ritual confirmation of the role of the shaman or prophet is merely a collective affirmation of a sacred choice that has apparently been made by a suprapersonal power. Such individuals are frighteningly charismatic. They are sacred.

But, kratophanies are not in themselves sufficient reliably to invoke the numinous experience. A crucial additive is needed: story, narrative, myth. As Eliade (1958) has abundantly demonstrated, something is dependably imbued with sacred numinosity if it has been hallowed by a tribal hero–saviour whose activities in the remote past are celebrated in a myth. His activities mark the beginning of time – *in illo tempore* to use Eliade's phrase, in that time when the world began – what Australian Aborigines call the Dreaming Time. Typically, the place and time at which sacred events are believed to have occurred are the centre of the cosmos at the moment of the Creation.

For Christians as well as Jews, Palestine has, more than anywhere else in the world, carried the image of the Promised Land. To Christians the centre of the world was Golgotha. Golgotha means literally 'the place of the skull'. This may have been because the hill on which the Crucifixion occurred was shaped like a skull, but legend insisted that it was also the place where Adam was created and where his skull was buried. It was the centre of the world where the two most important religious events occurred: Adam's fall and the Saviour's redemption of his sin. By being crucified on Golgotha, Christ redeemed Adam directly with his blood, and this holy site has been imbued with sacred numinosity ever since.

For preliterate peoples, the place of crucial religious significance was the totem centre of their homeland. It was the ultimate sacred spot designated by Hero–Saviours who had lived at the beginning of time. The original place of creation, it was the cradle of the ancestors, the centre of the earth; and the rites performed there in the name of the early heroes and the gods, guaranteed the sacred power of the place. This was the lasting achievement of the saviour–prophet: to designate the *heart* of the promised land and to endow it, in perpetuity, with holiness.

A religious outlook

Among all my patients in the second half of life – that is to say over thirty-five – there has not been one whose problem in the last resort was not that of finding a religious outlook on life.

C.G. Jung

Jung did not regard this as a problem confined to his patients: it was, in his view, the collective problem of a culture no longer capable of meeting the religious needs of its members. 'About a third of my cases', he wrote, 'are not suffering from any clearly definable neurosis, but from the senselessness and aimlessness of their lives. I should not object if this were called the general neurosis of our age' (CW16, para. 83). It is people suffering from 'the senselessness and aimlessness of their lives' who are particularly liable to join cults.

We are a meaning-making animal. And that is why we create religions and sciences. We create sciences so as to discover how things work and how they came into being; we create religions to make sense of their meaning and purpose, and to fathom why the vast cosmic experiment was started off in the first place. Only religion attempts to address the *meaning* of existence, an issue on which science remains speechless. That is why a religious approach to reality will continue to be needed, despite the advances of science and technology, and why charismatic gurus will continue to attract people questing for a religious meaning for their lives. 'Religion consists in believing that everything that happens is extraordinarily important' wrote Cesare Pavese. 'It can never disappear from the world for that reason.'

Where scientific and religious modes of enquiry overlap is in the actual experience of meaningful discovery – what Albert Einstein called 'the most beautiful emotion' which arises when one contemplates what lies beyond our immediate sensory perceptions and one achieves a genuine scientific insight, or intense religious experience, when 'the truth' is perceived. At such moments one steps outside Plato's cave of shadows and encounters the phenomenon of transcendence, *satori* (enlightenment). When such experience is successfully communicated to others, it may become a scientific hypothesis or the nucleus of a new religious belief; and so great is the value attributed to such insights that those who are gifted at attaining them will always be venerated – as scholars, Nobel Laureates, shamans, saints, messiahs, gurus and prophets. They are the seers who seem to perceive more than is vouchsafed to the rest of humanity and are consequently credited with a higher level of being. They are 'mana personalities', endowed with special powers.

That neurobiological structures have evolved to mediate the experience of the *numinosum* is because numinous experience is adaptive: it has promoted the survival and reproductive success of our ancestors in the ecological context on which human survival depends. But while neuroscience can give us 'explanations' of how the numinous experience occurs, it can never deputize for the experience itself. Our religious intuitions have always led us to assert that we – humankind – alone among all the animals of creation, speak with authority on account of our special relationship with the gods. We are their privileged servants here on earth, and all that we do is in their name. Primitive religions, in their various ways, portray human beings as the messengers between heaven and earth. More advanced religions express the same idea. To the Muslims, humanity is the viceroy placed by God over creation; to the Hindu, the human spirit is one with the eternal and infinite Brahman; to the Christian, humanity is made in the image of God.

To the humanist, we have made God in the image of humanity; and this means that we must ourselves assume full responsibility for the welfare of our planet. But this, in itself, demands a religious rather than a scientific attitude. The religious archetype informs us that we are here to serve God *hermeneutically* – that we are the means of communication between our portion of the cosmos and all that lies beyond it. This is our sacred mission and, inasmuch as we truly understand and perform it, we experience the *numinosum*. Anything less debases the meaning and impoverishes the experience of life. The worship of profane idols – social justice, sexual equality – is simply not enough, for if we abrogate all that is sacred and render the world profane, we make possible its wholesale profanation. We lose our capacity to experience the *numinosum*, we lose our ability to feel awe and respect for creation, which we then treat as a thing alien, exploitable and devoid of all rights. And we degrade ourselves to the level of parasites too stupid to recognize that we are destroying the host off which we live.

Viewed in this perspective it is possible to sympathize with those thousands of contemporary prophets who voice their millenarian forebodings of apocalyptic catastrophe, for never before in the history of our species have we been in a position, through our own selfish wickedness, to destroy everything that lives on our planet. But we are now. And, with our numbed religious sensibilities, we could well do so. 'Where there is no vision', says the Book of Proverbs, 'the people perish' (*Proverbs*, 29:18). For our planet has become a nuclear arsenal as well as a global village, and biological weapons of mass destruction are relatively easy to manufacture and deploy, yet we continue to be moved by the archaic imperatives to split, disperse and pseudospeciate. Rationally we can agree with Bhagwan Shree Rajneesh that what we need at this moment in our history is a 'religionless religiousness' – a religious attitude which lacks commitment to any particular creed or god, but which asserts a renewed form of Christian love and Buddhist all-compassion on a transpersonal, transnational and transideological plane. For our survival will depend on a mazeway resynthesis on a global scale, generating a massive shift in human consciousness if we are to contain our genocidal propensities.

To us, the destruction of our planet and our species would be the ultimate disaster. But to the cosmos, it would be an event of little significance. There are, in our expanding universe, another eleven billion galaxies, each containing eleven billion stars and planets. This great cosmic experiment will continue, unmoved by our minute apocalypse.

Only to human consciousness does the prospect of a universe without human beings matter. And only human consciousness can prevent the universe from learning to do without us. This new century could decide our fate. Will some schizotypal genius arise with the necessary vision and charisma to transform our eco-system into a Promised Land? Perhaps it is our only hope.

10

Personal Afterword

Summary and Conclusions

> To be accepted as a paradigm, a theory must be better than its competitors, but it need not, and in fact never does, explain all the facts with which it can be confronted.　　　Thomas Kuhn

The authors of this book met for the first time in the summer of 1992 as members of a study group which had grown up round the intellectually generous and saintly figure of Michael Chance, the primatologist who discovered the hedonic and agonic modes. We soon found that we had one formative experience in common: in addition to training in medicine and psychiatry, we had, while still medical students at Oxford in the 1950s, read 'PPP' (Philosophy, Psychology and Physiology) – though not in the same year. In John Price's time, PPP had been located in a disused preparatory school in the Banbury Road, where the Professor of Psychology's study consisted of the boys' former latrines. When Anthony Stevens arrived on the scene two years later, it had moved to somewhat more salubrious quarters in South Parks Road, but it remained small (limited to about twelve undergraduates) and was looked on as a rather esoteric course of study, although one obtained a BA (Hons) to add to one's medical degree at the end of it. Probably because of PPP's maverick status, *esprit de corps* was high, and lectures, seminars and tutorials tended to be nothing if not controversial. The climate of opinion was trenchantly critical of theoretical formulations in psychology, especially those emanating from the various schools of psychoanalysis. This did not, as it happens, deter Anthony Stevens from finding an ecological niche in Jungian psychology, though it made him aware of a need to set Jung's archetypal hypothesis in the context of evolutionary biology.

187

Largely, we suspect, because of Niko Tinbergen's presence in the Department of Zoology, Oxford was to the forefront in seeking to build a bridge between psychology and ethology (the study of the behaviour of animals living in their natural habitats), and this gave both of us a theoretical orientation which has influenced our thinking ever since. We were both attracted by ethological descriptions of animals living in the wild (rather than the performance of endless experiments on rats running in mazes, which provided the primary focus of study in psychology departments at that time) and by the brilliant demonstration by Konrad Lorenz that behaviour could be studied *comparatively* – in precisely the same way as anatomy. This crucial insight – that all species have behavioural characteristics which are as distinctive and as classifiable as their physical attributes – created an extraordinary situation: it made it possible to trace the evolutionary history of basic patterns of behaviour from reptiles through mammals and primates to ourselves. We both felt that this must have a profound impact on all branches of the human sciences, not least psychiatry, where it might permit a definition of the basic adaptations with which all human beings are equipped and an understanding of how their malfunction could result in mental disorder.

Our careers had diverged long before we met. We had both qualified and worked as psychiatrists, but then in 1970 Anthony Stevens gave up his job as a Senior Registrar at a large mental hospital just outside Epsom to develop a private practice in analytical psychology in London and the West of England, and went on to write books which explored the implications of evolutionary theory and Jungian theory for the practice of psychotherapy. For his part, John Price went into genetics research, became a consultant psychiatrist working in the NHS, and pursued his interest in the evolutionary history of mental disorders, especially mood disorders, about which he published pioneering work in the 1960s (Price, 1967, 1969). Our eventual meeting was a heady experience for us both. Despite our different career trajectories, we found that over a range of psychiatric issues our ideas had been running on parallel lines. We shared a similar disappointment in the slow progress psychiatry had made in our lifetime and attributed this to the same causes, namely, its uncritical embrace of the medical and standard social science models, and its failure to adopt a Darwinian view of the adaptive function of psychiatric symptoms.

By embracing the medical model, psychiatrists had been seeking to emulate the clinical precision of their medical and surgical colleagues: they examined their patients, diagnosed their illness and prescribed drugs for its treatment, persuading themselves that they were dealing with clinical entities, which, like thyrotoxicosis, diabetes or piles, possessed a known origin, a definable course and a definite cure. We knew this to be largely an illusion. For although psychiatrists continued to define, classify and treat 'illnesses' like schizophrenia, depression and obsessive compulsive disorder, they had little idea what these conditions could be or why human beings should suffer from them. Kraepelin's descriptive classification of mental illnesses towards the end of the nineteenth century had certainly brought order into a previously chaotic back ward of medical practice, but it offered no definite indications as to the cause or treatment of the 'illnesses' it defined. Since then research had made some progress towards establishing a genetic and neurophysiological basis for the major psychoses, and powerful psychoactive drugs had been developed which went some way to remove symptoms and relieve suffering. But, as a branch of medicine, psychiatry had failed to achieve the scientific status confidently predicted for it by such pioneers as Kraepelin, Bleuler and Maudsley at the beginning of the twentieth century. We agreed that the main reason for this failure had been the persistent reluctance of psychologists and psychiatrists to come to terms with the scientific revolution wrought in biology by Charles Darwin. Their formulations were still tinged with special creationism, their findings lacked the unifying cohesion of a conceptual framework linking the basic features of human life with the natural history of our own and other animal species. There were powerful religious and political reasons why this had been so in the past, but it seemed to us that these had lost their salience, and that developments in behavioural ecology and evolutionary psychology had made it possible to bring psychiatry within the ambit of a new and rapidly evolving science of humanity.

In adopting this point of view, we were in a tiny but robust minority. By the early 1990s, a small number of us had begun to think of ourselves as evolutionary psychiatrists and psychologists – Paul

Gilbert and John Archer in Great Britain, Russell Gardner, Brant Wenegrat, David Buss, Randolph Nesse and Michael McGuire in the United States, and Alfonso Troisi in Italy, each of whom had detected and announced the presence of neuropsychic propensities in human beings which were virtually indistinguishable from Jung's archetypes. These 'evolved psychological mechanisms', 'master programmes' or 'propensity states' were held responsible for crucial patterns of behaviour that evolved because they maximized the fitness of the organism to survive, and for its genes to survive, in the environment in which they evolved. All agreed that these strategies are inherently shared by all members of the human species, whether they be healthy or ill, and that psychopathology occurs when these strategies malfunction as a result of environmental insults or deficiencies at critical stages of development.

Though we were few in number and were disappointed by the lack of interest shown in our ideas by the majority of our hard-working colleagues in the profession, we were convinced that a paradigm shift was under way, and that the Darwinian evolutionary model was destined to replace the old SSSM. In our isolation, we took comfort from that great authority on paradigm shifts, Thomas Kuhn. 'Any new interpretation of nature', he wrote (1968), 'whether a discovery or a theory, emerges first in the mind of one or two individuals. It is they who first learn to see science and the world differently ...' (p. 143). Part of the excitement of our contacts with one another derived from our sense that we were in the vanguard of a new way of seeing things. For Anthony Stevens the main interest of this work was the opportunity it afforded to extend archetypal theory to psychiatric aetiology and therapeutics. It represented the first systematic attempt to put psychopathology on a sound evolutionary basis.

It was against this background, and with these thoughts in mind, that we eventually decided to embark on the ambitious – and some would say presumptuous – project of writing a textbook of 'Evolutionary Psychiatry', applying evolutionary thinking to a whole range of psychiatric disorders. Our collaboration on this book, the first edition of which was published by Routledge in 1996, was a source of enjoyment and stimulus to us both. But, as we anticipated, its publication was not greeted with universal acclaim by our colleagues. Though some were generous in their praise ('one of the most fruitful developments in psychiatry in recent years', wrote Anthony Storr in the *Financial Times*[1]) and declared that we had made a substantial contribution to a deeper understanding of such disorders as manic-depression, anxiety, phobic states, sadomasochism, bulimia and anorexia nervosa, others castigated us for indulging in speculative thinking in the absence of hard empirical data and, as one reviewer put it, 'seeking the glory of the winning tape without running the race'![2] The proposal that drew most flack from our critics was our group-splitting hypothesis of schizophrenia, for which, they insisted, we had produced very little evidence to support or refute. To attempt to meet this criticism we began collecting the material on which the second edition of *Evolutionary Psychiatry*, and much of the present book, is based.

The group-splitting hypothesis was the brainchild of John Price, and it had a long period of gestation in his mind. Its original conception occurred when he was working at the Psychiatric Genetics Unit of the Medical Research Council in the 1960s with Eliot Slater, James Shields and Leonard Heston, who were interested, among other things, in a possible adaptive function of schizophrenia. They were impressed by the finding that there was a high incidence of schizophrenia in a northern Swedish island and by the suggestion put forward by the Swedish psychiatrist Dr Essen-Moller, that schizotypy helped people to tolerate life in Lapland, where it was necessary to endure long periods of relative isolation during the winter. Sitting for hours over a hole in the ice waiting for a fish or a seal to appear, auditory hallucinations would provide companionship and a modicum of entertainment, rather like a personal Walkman! It was about this time that Price read Erlenmayer-Kimling and Paradowski's (1969) paper proposing (and rejecting) the hypothesis that the adaptive function of schizotypy could be the production of prophets. Despite their rejection of the idea, Price remained interested in the incidence of religious delusions among schizophrenic patients, and, together with a colleague, Jim Birley, drafted a paper comparing the prevalence of religious beliefs in first-degree relatives of schizophrenics with relatives of controls. They found no difference. But since the data were derived from case summaries, they felt that their paper was not good enough to merit publication. Price then switched his attention to the adaptive function of depression, and thinks he must have written off the schizophrenia problem as insoluble – until, that is, we were presented with the challenge of writing a chapter on the disorder for *Evolutionary Psychiatry*.

John Price had first become interested in cults as a result of being asked to write an anonymous leader on the subject for *The Lancet*,[3] and we both read and discussed *Cults and New Religious Movements* (1989) which Marc Galanter had edited for the American Psychiatric Association. Charles Lindholm's *Charisma* (1990) and Anthony Storr's *Feet of Clay* (1996) also had a powerful impact on our thinking. A crucial breakthrough occurred during one of our brainstorming sessions on Dartmoor, where it was our practice to walk every afternoon when working together on the book. With mounting excitement, we entertained the idea that the adaptive function of cult formation under the influence of delusions of charismatic leaders could be to promote the break-up of ancestral communities when they had grown too big for their resources. Our consideration of mood disorders had brought home to us the powerful pressures to conformity needed to sustain group cohesion. If these pressures were to be reversed so as to compel the group to split, a profound reorganization of group dynamics would be required to disrupt the cohesive pattern of conformity. The notion of cyclic periods of growth and peaceful coexistence alternating with periods of internal disruption, splitting and fighting with neighbouring groups was analogous to the cycles of war and peace undergone by neighbouring tribes and states which Stevens had described in *The Roots of War* (1989). We began to see that human investment is, and always has been, more devoted to group goals than behavioural scientists had recognized. When not actively engaged in pursuing such goals, it is as if people feel themselves to be 'asleep' – as Gurdjieff (1950) and other gurus have described the 'unawakened' state of people who have not had the good fortune to become their disciples! It is when involved in politics and warfare (splitting and fighting), or in crusading for a cause, that they 'wake up' and feel truly alive (the feeling that people commonly report on joining a cult and embracing its ideology).

The more we thought about it, the more things seemed to fit into place. For example, we could explain the difference between mood disorders ('linking disorders') and schizophrenia (a 'spacing disorder'). Mood disorders were by-products of the need for group cohesion, serving to sustain the group hierarchy, if necessary, at the expense of individual suffering. The schizophrenic predisposition, on the other hand, was involved in group splitting, providing a vector responsible for pushing cult members away from the parent group and drawing them onwards to a 'promised land'. The complex occurrence of both linking and spacing disorders in the same individual could be due to the fact that, when splitting is sufficiently advanced, two groups emerge, each of which has to become cohesive. Cohesiveness within the new group is associated with elevated mood among its members as well as in the charismatic leader, who commonly becomes grandiose in manner as he asserts his dominance over the group.

From the moment we began planning *Evolutionary Psychiatry* we recognized that schizophrenia presented us with the greatest challenge. Not only was no adaptive advantage apparent for those afflicted with the disorder, but a growing body of evidence indicated that schizophrenia was associated with abnormal changes in the brain. Among other things, these included enlargement of the cerebral ventricles, decrease in size of the temporal lobes, and abnormal blood flow and glucose metabolism in the prefrontal cortex. Yet, if schizophrenia should indeed turn out to be an organic disease (like Alzheimer's or Huntington's Chorea), how was it possible that an illness which induced low fertility in its sufferers continued to manifest itself in every human population, generation after generation? Mutation could be ruled out because the gene frequency required would be too high to be maintained by what we know of the normal mutation rate. So we, like other psychiatrists before us, inclined to the view that, although schizophrenia is not itself adaptive, the genetic *tendency* to the disorder could be.

As long ago as 1962, Paul Meehl (1962; 1992) had introduced the term 'schizotaxia' to denote this genetic tendency; and suggested that a large dose of schizotaxia could result in schizophrenia, while a smaller dose could result in a schizotypal personality. If it could be established that schizotypy carried some genetic advantage then it was possible that it could compensate for the genetic disadvantage of schizophrenia itself. Since environmental factors played a role in determining whether or not susceptible individuals became schizophrenic, it was also possible that some degree of phenotypic plasticity

193

was involved, so that the same amount of schizotaxia caused schizophrenia in some people and schizotypy in others.

It was in considering these possibilities that we became increasingly attracted by the idea that the adaptive advantage of schizotaxia could be its manifestation in the charismatic and sexually charged role of the cult leader. We extended our reading list so as to familiarize ourselves with the lives of prophets and gurus other than those described by Lindholm and by Storr. The more we read the more our conviction grew: a very large number of them were schizotypal personalities.

We found added support for our idea when we turned to the writings of that rare breed, the psychiatric anthropologists. There are three of them with whose work we became acquainted: Anthony Wallace,[4] an anthropologist attached to a psychiatric unit in Philadelphia, Edward Foulks,[5] now a Professor of Psychiatry in New Orleans and Roland Littlewood[6] of University College, London. The work of these three researchers provides a shining example of the highly significant insights that can grow out of the cross-fertilization of anthropology and psychiatry. All three drew attention to the fact that beneficial cultural change sometimes emanates from the apparently psychotic experience of a single individual.

From our point of view, the most important contribution came from Wallace's concept of 'mazeway resynthesis', on which we have drawn extensively in the present volume. Wallace's description of the radical reorientation of the mazeway occurring at a time of crisis in a charismatic leader (such as the Seneca Indian, Handsome Lake) immediately resonated with our clinical experience of working with schizophrenic patients in the acute stage of their psychosis. Any psychiatrist could have reached the same conclusion. Here, for example, is a description of the typical schizophrenic episode published by Sir Martin Roth (1996), a recent President of the Royal College of Psychiatrists:

> the patient may have already begun to see the outside world as transfigured by elements of threat, mystery, danger and unreality, the 'delusional atmosphere' common in this disorder. It is at this stage that an overwhelming idea of wide-ranging significance often erupts out of a clear sky in the minds of

194

schizophrenic patients and leaves an indelible impression. It arrives direct and unmediated by any relevant or under- standable antecedent even of experience. Such a 'primary' delusion instils in the patient the total conviction that he is the new Messiah or the reincarnation of St John the Baptist or Mohammed or a delusion of similar character. The fear-laden perplexity and confusion of the patient abates for a period. The world is once again perceived as whole and authentic. The delusion explains it all. This symptom marks perhaps the most clear break in the continuity of psychic life of the schizophrenic patient.

For their part, both Foulks and Littlewood provided data which supported the contention that identical mental experiences could lead either to schizophrenia or to the role of prophet, the actual outcome being decided by the individual's psychological resources as well as the social situation in which he found himself.

What fascinated Anthony Stevens in this material was the light it cast on the *liminal* state and on its therapeutic implications.[7] In his analytic practice he had found that much creative mileage could be obtained from enabling non-psychotic patients to enter that border- line where conscious and unconscious processes meet. The patients in whom the most profound personal transformations occurred in the course of treatment were those who had a rich dream life which they experienced as being full of affect and meaning. This was in line with Jung's view that dreams contribute to the well-being of the whole psychic economy by performing an essentially *compensatory* func- tion, the purpose of which is to balance one-sided or unduly constricted conscious attitudes. This compensatory view of dreams, which finds echoes in recent biological theories of REM (rapid eye movement) sleep (Stevens, 1995), is consistent with Jung's concept of psychic homeostasis. Jung viewed the psyche as a self-regulating system which strives perpetually to maintain a balance between opposing propensities, while, at the same time, seeking its own growth and development. Schizotypal personalities are highly gifted at accessing the liminal state and it is this ability that enables them to have such a profound impact on their culture. Just as their dreams may in time become the myths of their people, so the sudden eruption

195

into their conscious minds of a new belief system can result in a fundamental reorientation of the mazeway in their followers. It is as if a mazeway resynthesis in a charismatic guru can perform the same compensatory role for a moribund culture as can a dream for an unhappy or maladjusted patient. The unconscious mind has access, it seems, to revolutionary insights which some individuals – particularly those with schizotypal personalities – can mobilize and channel into the minds of people susceptible to their charismatic influence. It is possible that all important cultural movements are generated in this way.

It occurred to us that a belief system is like a flag. Every group has one, and it forms an indispensable component of the group's core identity. The really interesting point about this is that irrational beliefs make more effective 'flags' than rational ones. A cult wedded to a bizarre set of beliefs successfully marks itself off from groups with different beliefs, an observation that Bigelow stressed in his book *Dawn Warriors* (1969): 'Each group requires something intimate, unique to itself, around which its members can cohere', he wrote. 'Irrational beliefs serve this purpose far better than rational ones: they are not only easier to produce, but also less likely to be confused with enemy beliefs. Irrational fantasies produce a continuous supply of "group uniforms", promoting and maintaining internal cohesion within each group, and segregation between groups.'

When group splitting occurs, as in the early stages of cult formation, a highly significant change ensues with the rejection of the old flag and the unfurling of the new. Not only is the mazeway resynthesized but new customs and new modes of behaviour are adopted. These changes may have highly adaptive consequences, as when Handsome Lake induced his fellow tribesmen to build houses and till fields; or they may be entirely arbitrary, as when Mother Earth instructed her followers to go naked into Port of Spain. Such arbitrary aberrations are not futile, however: they are yet another form of flag-waving, enhancing separate group identity, and forcing different groups apart in the interests of population dispersal. The great diversity of customs between groups permits a variety of different social strategies to be tested on a trial-and-error basis, thus promoting more rapid cultural evolution than would occur with homopistic group splitting. It seems likely that the high degree of cultural flexibility attendant upon heteropistic splitting would have been adaptively valuable during the rapid climatic changes of the last 600,000 years. Indeed, the possibility should not be ruled out that, during this late period in human evolutionary history, selection for cultural flexibility has taken precedence over selection for individual patterns of behaviour. When humans disperse, they must disperse as a group or not at all Potts (1998). In the ancestral environment, a lone human being was a dead human being. The capacity of our ancestors to survive lay in their use of intelligence within a collective context. It follows, therefore, that human dispersal must have involved group splitting.

This does not mean, however, that group splitting invariably requires the development of a cult round a charismatic prophet. There are, of course, other ways in which groups can divide. In Chapter 4 we examined the homopistic fissioning apparent among the Yanomamo, 'the fierce people' of the Amazon basin, where village communities split as a result of violent quarrels between men over sexual access to women. The Yanomamo are in a sense fortunate because they are surrounded (or were until recently) by 'empty bush' into which disaffected groups can disperse. Most other societies have been surrounded by more populous regions and, for those who departed, splitting often necessitated a long and potentially hazardous journey. Colonization is a case in point: Greeks and Romans dispatched colonists throughout the ancient world, while in recent centuries Europeans, especially Anglo-Saxons, colonized huge areas of the globe. Other examples are afforded by successful raiding parties, like the Vikings, who, having found plunder elsewhere, failed to return to base. 'When the missionaries arrived the Africans had the land and the missionaries had the Bible', declared the Kenyan leader, Jomo Kenyatta. 'They taught us to pray with our eyes closed; when we opened them, we had the Bible and they had the land!'

What is striking about such examples is the fact that the split-off colonists continued to share the same mazeway with the parent group they had left behind. It was this realization that caused John Price to make a distinction between homopistic and heteropistic splitting. Heteropistic splitting demands a prophet. The cohesive parent group cannot tolerate heresy: the subgroup is driven away not by quarrels about women but by a schism over theology. In these circumstances paranoia flourishes. Pursued by real or delusory fears of persecution, and drawn on by apocalyptic visions of a promised land, the migration proceeds – a pattern repeated from prehistory right up to the times of Jim Jones, David Koresh and the Bhagwan Shree Rajneesh.

When considering how the sexual athleticism of schizotypal prophets might compensate genetically for the low fertility of schizophrenic people, it is evident that those groups which dispersed successfully would have enjoyed an enormous genetic advantage. We have seen this in the (largely homopistic) colonization of America, Australia and South Africa, where even deleterious genes (such as those responsible for acute intermittent porphyria) have spread widely throughout the habitat. In those cases of colonial radiation which involved heteropistic splitting (as in the case of the Mormons, for example) schizotypal genes would doubtless have taken advantage of the rich opportunities for dissemination. Against this advantage must be set the very high risks that attend the dispersal phenotype. Not only may the migrating charismatic group be eliminated, but the schizotypal leader may become overtly schizophrenic, he may lead his people into an unfavourable habitat, or hand them a pathogenic mazeway resulting in sterility (as in the case of St Ignatius Loyola with the Jesuits) or mass suicide (Jim Jones and Marshall Herff Applewhite).

It would be absurd to minimize the difficulties involved in calculating the balance of risks and advantages of the dispersal phenotype in quantitative terms. One can do no more than draw attention to the possibility that the reproductive success of cult leaders could be sufficient to compensate for the reduced fertility of schizophrenic patients and to sustain schizotaxic genes within the human gene pool. The disruptive upheaval involved in group splitting and migration is so enormous, and the potential benefits so great, that it could well require the evolution of an extreme psychological and behavioural condition like that which we encounter in its most dramatic and disturbing form in people with schizophrenia.

10. Personal Afterword

Criticisms, research and the future

Madness in great ones must not unwatched go.
William Shakespeare, Claudius in *Hamlet*

As we talked over our ideas, we tried to anticipate the sort of criticisms that would be made of our position. How, for example, could we account for the negative symptoms of schizophrenia – the apathy, loss of motivation and the withdrawal – which, to say the least, are not particularly apparent in cult leaders? Our answer was that the existence of cult followers acts as a preventive which serves to inhibit the development of negative symptomatology in the leader, should he teeter over the brink into a psychosis. Reflecting on the history of the many schizophrenics we had treated, we could point to the deep sense of invalidation a patient suffers with the onset of the psychosis. His behaviour inspires fear and hostility in others, his statements evoke perplexity and even ridicule, and his beliefs are not shared by a single human being. His psychological isolation is total. As a result, he becomes confused, demoralized and depressed. Incapable of coping with even the simple necessities of life, he just gives up. Would not this go some way towards accounting for the negative features of the condition?

In a variety of psychiatric disorders, the support of just one other person can make the difference between sustained morale and complete psychological collapse, as, for example, George Brown was able to demonstrate in the case of women suffering from depression (Brown and Harris, 1978). The same factor was noticed among Western military prisoners subjected to communist brainwashing during the Korean War. In schizophrenia, there are many recorded instances of the sustaining support another person can provide in cases of *folie à deux* in which a dominant individual indoctrinates a subordinate friend or relative with his delusional system – a cult in embryo, one might say: in such cases, the severity of negative symptomatology appears to be much reduced.

During one of our discussions, the image developed in Price's mind of a semicircle of disciples, sitting with patient expectancy before their guru, anticipating the *darshan* which will grant them their share of numinous experience. Like a parent bird presented with the

199

gaping red mouths of a nest full of hungry chicks, the prophet regurgitates his message, creating for himself and his followers a shared mazeway of new thoughts and new terminologies. As he gratifies their spiritual hunger, he visibly swells with self-validation and renewed self-esteem, finding rich nourishment in their love and rapt attention, putting himself as he does so beyond the reach of the alienation and despair that is the lot of a schizophrenic patient.

The most obvious criticism that these ideas have so far attracted is the one that is directed against all evolutionary arguments in psychology – namely, that they are inherently untestable. To suggest that a strategy evolved because it had a certain adaptive function is little more than an imaginative evocation of the past. Whether or not the scenario actually occurred can never be decisively demonstrated because it cannot be replayed. As a result, so this critical argument runs, all such hypotheses should be regarded as efforts at reconstructive history rather than as scientific proposals. While there is a measure of truth in this, we would counter that the present can be understood only as an extension of the past: in the words of Theodosius Dobzhansky, 'nothing in biology makes sense except in the light of evolution.' After all, it was that living embodiment of scientific rigour, Karl Popper, who introduced the concept of 'useful myths' to develop ideas which, while not directly refutable, give rise to hypotheses which *can* be refuted, and therefore come into the category of scientific statements.

The eventual status of the group-splitting hypothesis of schizophrenia will be decided by the usual scientific means of progression – in particular by advances in genetics linked to developments in the behavioural ecology of mental disorder. There are certain crucial issues for research to decide, which may be listed as follows:

(1) Is there a graded genetic predisposition related to degrees of psychopathology in schizophrenia spectrum disorder (i.e. is there a differential predisposition to schizotaxia)?
(2) What life events influence the extent to which the predisposition is expressed in the life of the carrier?
(3) What evidence is there to support an association between group splitting and the emergence of charismatic leaders possessing schizotypal traits?

(4) Does a genetic loading for some degree of schizotaxia predispose susceptible individuals to become charismatic prophets?

(5) Is there any evidence that cult leaders are more frequently found among the relatives of schizophrenic patients than in the general population?

(6) Is there a tendency for such prophets to become frankly schizophrenic if their message goes unheeded and followers fail to materialize?

Of course, one cannot predict at this stage how long it will be before some or all of these questions may be answered. However, in the second edition of *Evolutionary Psychiatry* (2000), we have proposed one area in which the group-splitting or 'dispersal phenotype' theory of schizophrenia could prove to be of practical significance in guiding research into treatment of the disorder. It has already been demonstrated, through well-controlled randomized trials, that psychotherapeutic techniques are indeed able to modify the course of a schizophrenic illness, albeit to a moderate degree (Birchwood and Spencer, 1999). We suggest that greater success could be achieved if treatment programmes approached schizophrenia in the context of the biological function of the schizotypal propensity, so that instead of opposing this function by attacking it head on, therapists should make use of the energy available for the function's realization.

If our thinking is correct, then therapy needs to take account of the major factor distinguishing a successful cult leader from a schizophrenic patient, namely, that the leader is surrounded by a group of devoted followers who hang on his words and adopt his beliefs (however crazy they might appear to outsiders). By granting the leader enthusiastic validation of his ideas, the followers boost his self-esteem and help to prevent him from lapsing into a psychosis. Accordingly, one might anticipate a powerful therapeutic effect were it possible to provide each schizophrenic patient with a cultic group of devoted members.

Unfortunately, this would hardly be possible, even in the most generously funded research project! But it occurred to John Price that advances in computer technology could provide an intriguing alternative. Might it not be possible for each patient to be provided with a computer system within which to create his own group of followers

201

in 'virtual reality'? Could he not indoctrinate the robotic members of his cult with his own peculiar ideology and beliefs, sharing with them his visions, the hierophantic dictates of his voices, his neologisms, syntactical eccentricities and his mission? Then he might succeed in forming a network of inspired communication with 'part personalities' projected from the recesses of his own psyche through the miracle of silicon into a virtually existent world of his own devising. The consequent sense of gratification, rather than frustration, of his politico-religious ambitions could well prove therapeutic, especially in relieving the negative symptoms of the disorder. Research along these lines could determine how the patient's general behaviour may be affected, together with his relation to society as a whole. It is possible that even the relative social withdrawal necessary for the computer work to be done might be balanced by a rise in sociability as a result of increased self-confidence.

Another experimental possibility would be to give each patient a website on which he could publicize his ideas on the internet and invite the participation of actual people in the fulfilment of his mission. It is not unlikely that a proportion of patients would recruit real followers: the ensuing communications could be monitored by researchers to assess the clinical response of the patient. For those patients whose messages and world views were too bizarre or incoherent to attract followers, members of the research team could themselves visit the website and provide appropriate validation. In some cases, a combination of real and research followers might result in a more marked therapeutic effect.

There are, of course, important ethical issues involved in carrying through such a research project, but a cursory search would indicate that a number of schizotypal or schizophrenic people are already recruiting followers on the web. In these circumstances, a randomized controlled trial of website exposure in schizophrenia may prove to be ethically and practically feasible. Such a project could provide critical evidence for the validation or refutation of the hypothesis.

A matter of ethics

The old view that the principles of right and wrong are immutable and eternal is no longer tenable. The moral world is as little exempt as the physical world from the law of ceaseless change, of perpetual flux.   Sir James Frazer

Although it is true to say that a growing number of behavioural scientists are sympathetic to an evolutionary approach to the facts of human behaviour, many remain indifferent or hostile to it. They continue to be wedded to the Standard Social Science Model (SSSM), preferring to avoid biological thinking altogether and to insist that in human affairs cultural evolution has taken the place of biological evolution. There are several reasons for their anti-Darwinian prejudices, which have persisted for most of the past century, and which would account for the slow progress of the social sciences over the same period. Most prevalent of these objections has been the fear that acceptance of genetic influences on human psychology will be put to reprehensible 'right-wing' political ends, as was the case with Social Darwinism, which deservedly earned itself a bad name during the early part of the twentieth century. Those of us who have endorsed the evolutionary approach are often accused by those still stuck in the SSSM of wishing to promote just such a political agenda. Not only is this untrue of ourselves, but it is also untrue of those evolutionary psychologists who are known to us personally.

Instead of wishing to promote some political ideology, our more modest ambition is to work towards the provision of a firm, neutral scientific foundation on which our own speciality may be built. The irony has not escaped us that it is the *critics* of evolutionary psychology who are ideologically motivated: it is *their* strong left-leaning convictions that form the basis of their attitude to social and psychological issues rather than the scientific objectivity aspired to by the evolutionists. By denying their own political motives and projecting such motives onto others, these critics seem to be displaying that incipient paranoia which typically occurs when human communities divide! Our own apolitical contention is that evolutionary theories will prevail over non-evolutionary theories because they give a better explanation of the facts. Application of the usual procedures of em-

203

pirical science will decide the matter over the next few years, and we are content to abide by the outcome.

In the meantime, we persist in the belief that the psychiatric profession is destined to undergo a collective mazeway resynthesis. Thomas Kuhn himself made an evocative comparison between scientific revolutions and political revolutions which is strikingly compatible with our thesis. 'Political revolutions', Kuhn wrote, 'are inaugurated by a growing sense, often restricted to a segment of the political community, that existing institutions have ceased adequately to meet the problems posed by an environment that they have in part created. In much the same way, scientific revolutions are inaugurated by a growing sense, again often restricted to a narrow subdivision of the scientific community, that an existing paradigm ceased to function adequately in the exploration of an aspect of nature to which that paradigm itself had previously led the way. In both political and scientific development, the sense of malfunction that can lead to crisis is prerequisite to revolution' (p. 91). Paradigms, Kuhn insists, do not change through the mere collection of scientific data. They change as the result of 'a relatively sudden and unstructured event like the Gestalt switch' whereby a drawing of a pedestal is suddenly seen as a pair of profiles or a staircase is transformed into a cornice. 'Scientists then often speak of the "scales falling from the eyes" or of the "lightning flash" that flood-lights a previously obscure puzzle, enabling its components to be seen in a new way that for the first time permits its solution. On other occasions the relevant illumination comes in sleep. No ordinary sense of the term "interpretation" fits these flashes of intuition through which the new paradigm is born' (pp. 121-2).

A growing number of psychologists and psychiatrists are using the light that Darwin's luminous insight has cast on the human condition. To accept that genes exercise a powerful influence on human psychology and behaviour is not to argue that we are unconscious automata blindly programmed like marionettes to jerk through the routines of our lives. Our evolved capacity for consciousness not only enables us to monitor what is going on around us in the interests of survival and reproductive success but makes us aware of the *meaning* and *quality* of events as they occur, so that we may make ethical decisions about them.

10. Personal Afterword

The question of ethics is integral to the psychology of gurus and their cults. It is likely that the persistent materialism of our increasingly secular society will be conducive to a steady increase in their numbers. As this book has illustrated, the power of a charismatic leader can be truly enormous. Whether he proves to be a fount of wisdom or a wolf in sheep's clothing depends on the ethical stance adopted by his followers and himself. For this reason, all such leaders must be carefully scrutinized in the light of what we now know about them. Failure to watch, and when necessary restrain them, can all too readily result in another Adolf Hitler, Shoko Asahara, Jim Jones or Joseph Kibwetere rather than a Mohammed, Rudolf Steiner, Mother Theresa or Jesus Christ.

Notes

Preface

1. A 'paradigm shift' is occurring in contemporary psychiatry. The speciality is moving beyond the traditional medical model, with its emphasis on the diagnosis and treatment of dubious disease entities, towards an entirely new conceptual framework which defines the basic components of human nature in terms of their evolutionary origins and their essential developmental needs. For an account of these developments see Archer (1992), Barkow *et al.* (1992), Buss (1999), Gardner (1988), Gilbert (1989), McGuire and Troisi (1998), Nesse and Williams (1995), Pinker (1998), Stevens and Price (2000), Wenegrat (1984), Williams (1996), Wilson (1993).

2. For sex differences in mate preferences, sexual strategies and behaviour patterns see Bell *et al.* (1981), Buss (1989, 1994) and Wilson (1989).

3. The fundamental work on the human ethology of the mother–infant attachment bond was done by Bowlby (1958, 1969) and Ainsworth (1964). Bowlby's theoretical position has been integrated with Jung's theory of archetypes by Stevens (1982: revised edition in press).

4. The work of Daly and Wilson (1987) has established that parents make a greater emotional investment in their offspring than in less genetically close relatives, and that children who live with one natural and with one step-parent are more likely to be abused than children living with two natural parents.

Chapter 1 Charismatic Prophets and Their Cults

1. Report published in the *Otago Daily Times* (New Zealand) 26 March 1998 and reproduced in *Private Eye* (London) 15 May 1998.

2. The psychology of charisma has been investigated by Lindholm (1990), Oakes (1997) and Stark (1969).

3. One of the best researched and most informative of these studies is that edited by Marc Galanter (1989) for the American Psychiatric Association. Other sources on which we have drawn for general information about cults are Adas (1987), Allen (1986), Andres and Lane (1988), Barker (1990), Beckford (1985), Bromley (1981), Burridge (1969), Choquett (1985), Clark

(1983), Conway and Seigelman (1978), Cunningham (1984), Deikman (1990), Enroth (1983), Enroth and Melton (1985), Festinger *et al.* (1964), Firth (1965), Galanter (1982), Gratus (1975), Harrison (1990), Lanternari (1963), Levine (1979, 1989), Lewis (1986), Melton *et al.* (1982), Nelson (1972), Post (1978, 1986), Shaw (1994), Thrupp (1970), van Baalem (1960). Studies of specific cults are indicated where appropriate in the text.

4. For a more detailed account of messiahs and millenarianism see Olson (1982), Perez (1978), Tuveson (1974) and Wallis (1918, 1943).

5. Valiant efforts have been made to reconstruct the social ecology of hunter–gatherer groups living in the distant past. See, for example, Fox (1989), Leakey (1994), Mithen (1996) and Tudge (1995). There is fairly general agreement that our pre-agrarian ancestors lived in groups of about 100-150 people and that size of the population was effectively limited by the large hunting range necessary to sustain it.

6. See, for example, Foley (1996) and the discussion in Chapter 7 of this volume, especially pp. 128-30.

7. The tendency of groups to split after they achieve a certain critical size is by no means confined to groups of hunter–gatherers. It is seen in religious sects and political parties as well as professional organizations such as the various 'schools' of psychotherapists and psychoanalysts. It was apparent, for example, in the split in the Catholic Church between Eastern and Western divisions (the two Popes excommunicating one another), in the Great Schism between the Avignon and Roman Papacies, and in the split between the Protestants and Catholics at the Reformation. In politics the broad division between 'left' and 'right' gives rise to subdivisions within parties, for example, between the 'drys' and 'wets' in Margaret Thatcher's governments, between the pro- and anti-Europeans in the contemporary Conservative Party, and between the old left and 'new' Blairites in the Labour Party. The split in the British Psycho-Analytical Society between orthodox Freudians and the followers of Melanie Klein has been echoed by divisions within the original Jungian group in London with the result that there are now four separate Jungian organizations (Stevens, 1998a). The splits which regularly occur within college governing bodies, parish councils, etc. are too regular and too frequent to require description. A group has only to be in existence for some time for fissive pressures to build up within it.

Chapter 2 Thin Partitions: Extraordinary Abilities and Madness

1. The thin partitions between psychosis and creativity are explored by Boisen (1960), Claridge *et al.* (1990), Claridge (1997), Ellenberger (1970), Eysenck (1997), Keefe and Magaro (1980), May (1975), Peters *et al.* (1999), Rothenberg (1983), Storr (1972), Torry (1980) and Whiteside, (1981).

2. For the diagnosis of schizophrenia, DSM-IV lists the following criteria (which are grouped in three categories, A, B and C):

A. *Characteristic symptoms.* Two (or more) of the following, each present for a significant portion of time during a one-month period (or less if successfully treated):

1 delusions

2 hallucinations

3 disorganized speech (e.g. frequent derailment or incoherence)

4 grossly disorganized behaviour

5 negative symptoms, i.e. flattening of affect, alogia or avolition.

It is interesting that DSM-IV insists that only one Criterion Symptom is required if delusions are bizarre or hallucinations consist of a voice keeping up a running commentary on the person's behaviour or thoughts, or two or more voices conversing with each other. On this criterion alone, many prophets might be considered to be schizophrenic.

B. *Social occupational dysfunction.* For a significant portion of the time since the onset of the disturbance, one or more major areas of functioning, such as work, personal relations or self-care, are markedly below the level achieved prior to the onset of the condition.

C. *Duration.* Continuous signs of the disturbance persist for at least six months. This six-month period must include at least one month of symptoms (or less if successfully treated) that meet Criterion A.

3. DSM-IV describes people with *schizoid personality disorder* as exhibiting a pervasive pattern of detachment from social relationships and a restricted range of expression of emotions in interpersonal settings, beginning by early adulthood and present in a variety of contexts, as indicated by four (or more) of the following:

1 they neither desire nor enjoy close relationships, including being part of a family.

2 they almost always choose solitary activities.

3 they have little, if any, interest in having sexual experiences with another person.

4 they take pleasure in few, if any activities.

5 they lack close friends or confidants other than first-degree relatives.

6 they appear indifferent to the praise or criticism of others.

7 they show emotional coldness, detachment, or flattening of affect.

For the creative potential of people with a schizoid personality see Storr (1972).

Schizotypal personality disorder is described as 'a pervasive pattern of social and interpersonal deficits marked by acute discomfort with, and reduced capacity for, close relationships as well as cognitive or perceptual distortions and eccentricities of behaviour'. The criteria for establishing the diagnosis are met if five or more of the following features are present:

209

1 ideas of reference (i.e. incorrect interpretations of external events as having a particular meaning specifically for the person concerned);

2 odd beliefs or magical thinking that influences behaviour and is inconsistent with subcultural norms (e.g. superstitiousness, belief in clairvoyance, telepathy, or 'sixth sense'; in children and adolescents, bizarre fantasies or preoccupations);

3 unusual perceptual experience, including bodily illusions;

4 odd thinking and speech (e.g. vague, circumstantial, metaphorical, overelaborate, or stereotyped);

5 suspiciousness or paranoid ideas;

6 inappropriate or constricted affect;

7 behaviour or appearance that is odd, eccentric, or peculiar;

8 lack of close friends or confidants other than first-degree relatives;

9 excessive social anxiety that does not diminish with familiarity and tends to be associated with paranoid fears rather than negative judgements about the self.

Psychometric tests have been developed for measuring the presence of schizotypal traits (Bental Claridge and Slade, 1989; Raine *et al.*, 1995).

4. The healing aspects of mystical experience have been explored by Hood (1973), Horton (1973), Goodman *et al.* (1974), and Lewis (1971).

5. For an understanding of the meaning and religious implications of delusions and hallucinations see Cahill and Frith (1996), Clark (1980), Lenz (1983), Roberts (1991, 1992), Roth (1996) and Winters and Neale (1983).

6. A growing body of evidence indicates that schizophrenia is associated with abnormal changes in the brain, some of which are mentioned on p. 193 of the present volume. To prove acceptable, an ultimate theory of schizophrenia has to be compatible with any proximate theory (Price and Stevens, 1998). Even if it should be established beyond doubt, for example, that the disorder is due to a virus, this might well prove to be a form of symbiosis: it could be part of the 'extended phenotype' of the virus (Dawkins, 1989) to attack some specific part of the brain, thus converting a 'normal' genotype into a dispersal (schizotypal) phenotype. However well advanced research into the proximate mechanisms of schizophrenia may become, there will remain an overriding concern to explain this bizarre condition's ultimate cause – to understand why it evolved in the first place. For the integration of ultimate (evolutionary) and proximate (neurophysiological) approaches to schizophrenia see Crow (1995a, 1995b, 1996), Gottesman and Shields (1982), Jarvik and Deckard (1997).

Chapter 3 Spacing Out: A Natural History of the Prophet

1. For the relationship between paranoid ideas and charismatic leadership, see Robins (1986); for the link between paranoia and destructiveness see Storr (1991), and for the supersensitivity of paranoid patients to non-verbal cues see La Russo (1978).

2. This practice was carried to absurd lengths by Shoko Asahara who ordained twenty 'initiations' into Aum Supreme Truth, which consisted of making neophytes imbibe concoctions prepared from parts of his body. For example, 'Holy Hair Initiation' was his bizarre version of the traditional Japanese tea ceremony: clippings of Asahara's hair were brewed in boiling water and then drunk. His dirty bath water was bottled and sold to the faithful for $800 a quart. 'Blood Initiation' involved drinking a potion of DNA drawn from the Master's veins. This, he assured them, would grant them supernatural powers and guarantee rapid ascent up the ladder of enlightenment. It cost $7,000 a shot, and there was no shortage of takers (Kaplan and Marshall, 1996). Similarly, Aldebert, the eighth-century 'Christ', distributed hair-clippings and nail-parings among his followers, while Tanchelm of Antwerp, a self-proclaimed Saviour of the twelfth century, ordered his followers to drink his bath water as a holy substitute for the Eucharist (Cohn, 1970). These macabre ritualistic activities give strong testimony to the fantastic charge of 'mana' that charismatic leaders are perceived by their followers to possess.

3. For further insights into the creative process see Arieti (1976), Hadamard (1945) and Murphy (1958).

Chapter 4 Splitting and Revitalization: A Natural History of the Cult

1. Rich sources of this material are to be found in Barrett (1968), Bureau (1958), Hobsbawm (1971), Lanternari (1963), Lewy (1974), Littlewood (1984), Ribeiro (1970), Rotberg and Alia (1970), Thrupp (1970) and Wilson (1973).

2. Mazeway resynthesis is, admittedly, a rather clumsy term. Alternatives might be 'Damascene shift', 'reality reconstruction', 'altered *Weltanschauung*', or 'Gestalt transformation'. The existential psychologist, Binswanger (1958), introduced a similar concept to Wallace's 'mazeway' which he called the 'world design'. The term world design encapsulates an individual's conscious and unconscious attitudes and perceptions of the self and the external world. Binswanger viewed a delusion as a pathological distortion of the world design. We have chosen to retain 'mazeway resynthesis' because it has entered the literature and because we wish to give due acknowledgement to Wallace's seminal work on the subject.

3. For the role of cargo cults in facilitating cultural change see Christiansen (1969), Lawrence (1964), May (1982), Strelan (1977), Trompf (1977, 1990) and Worsley (1970).

4. In their meticulous record of the proceedings Joan's inquisitors wrote: 'The great danger was shown to her that comes of someone so presumptuous to believe they have such apparitions and revelations, and therefore lie about matters concerning God, giving out false prophecies and divinations not known from God, but invented. From which could follow the seduction of peoples, the inception of new sects, and many other impieties that subvert the Church and Catholics' (Sagan, 1996).

5. The Theosophical Society, of which Rudolf Steiner was originally a member, was founded by Madame Blavatsky in 1875. She claimed that she had been instructed in esoteric wisdom by a mysterious and never located 'Brotherhood of Masters' who were alleged to live somewhere in the Himalayas. Steiner broke away in 1910 but retained some of Madame Blavatsky's beliefs – e.g. that the universe was permeated with psychic ether (called *akasa*) which enabled people to use clairvoyance and telepathy.

Chapter 5 Leaders and Led: The Revolutionary Relationship

1. A striking illustration of this intensity is provided by the study of Baba and his sidewalk Ashram, published by Deutsch (1975, 1980, 1989).

2. For a discussion of the relative significance of conversion and brainwashing in cult recruitment see Barker (1984), Brown (1963), Galanter (1980), Lofland and Stark (1965) and Richardson (1989).

Chapter 6 Cult Politics: Power and Sex

1. The finding of Dr Emmanuele Peters and her colleagues that a larger than expected number of members of cults have schizotypal personalities conflicts with the reports of other researchers that cult members are no more abnormal than members of society at large. However, Peters counters that such studies have not used measures relevant to psychotic-proneness or schizotypy. Instead, they have focused on assessments of well-being and of life-satisfaction, and on neurotic symptoms such as anxiety and depression. As Roberts (1991) has shown, high degrees of life-satisfaction can be demonstrated even in chronically deluded patients.

Chapter 7 Schizotypal Dispersal and Genocide

1. Cognitive dissonance is the capacity to form and sustain in consciousness ideas and perceptions of fact which are objectively discordant or mutually contradictory. For an extensive discussion of this cognitive peculiarity see Festinger (1957).

2. See also Runciman (1986) on the tendencies of human societies to form varieties and Durham (1991) on genes, culture and human diversity.

3. For a much fuller discussion of these issues see Andreski (1964), Eibl-Eibesfeldt (1971, 1982, 1995), Fried *et al.* (1968), Ricoeur (1970), Stevens (1989), Storr (1991), Sumner (1913) and Wright (1943).

4. Allport (1966) made an interesting distinction between people who are either 'extrinsically' or 'intrinsically' religious. Extrinsics tend to be conventional, rule-bound and racially prejudiced; intrinsics tend to be more flexible, original and tolerant. This distinction finds echoes in that made between messianic prophets (who subscribe to orthodox doctrines) and charismatic prophets (who stand them on their head) made by Oakes (see p. 57). It also fits with our distinction between homopistic and heteropistic group splitting, hence the following table.

Homopistic splitting	**Heteropistic splitting**
messiahs	prophets
extrinsics	intrinsics
convention	subversion
tradition	revolution

5. Earlier migrations out of Africa have been described by Dawkins (1995), Stringer and McKie (1996), and many others.

6. 'When it was a question of an attack or defence against other tribes,' wrote the anthropologist G. Lindblom (1916), 'the Akamba (Eastern Bantu) were always united. But when no external danger threatened or prospects of booty did not bring about a union, perpetual internal quarrels and feuds prevailed.' The inner stability of the Roman Empire persisted right up to the time that its armies destroyed the greatest threat to the Empire's existence, Carthage; then inner dissensions and civil wars began. In the last 200 years, the countries which waged fewest international wars (like Spain, Portugal and the countries of Latin America) had the highest incidence of internecine strife and revolution. The Japanese, who were confined to their islands for most of their history by the military might of the Chinese Empire, had an unrivalled record of civil wars (Andreski, 1964).

7. On charismatic political leadership see Willner (1984).

Chapter 8 Apocalypse and Armageddon

1. Culture is itself the product of a long and complicated interaction between natural selection and social innovation (Boyd and Richardson, 1985; Durham, 1991; Lumsden and Wilson, 1981, 1983; Tooby and Cosmides, 1992; and Trinkaus, 1989). Our archetypal propensities determine the kind of cultures we form, and these in turn influence the reproductive strategies adopted by individuals living in them (Ridley, 1994). As a consequence, cultures impact on genes as surely as genes influence cultures, the personal psyche acting as an intermediary between them.

2. One of the first researchers to draw attention to these similarities was the nineteenth-century ethnographer Adolf Bastian (1826-1905). Collecting copious data from his travels all over the world, Bastian was impressed by the similarity he noted between the themes, motifs and rituals he encountered wherever he went. He noticed, however, that these universal themes, which he called *Elementärgedanken* (elementary ideas), invariably manifested themselves in local forms, peculiar to the group of people he happened to be studying at the time. These he called *Völkgedanken* (ethnic ideas).

3. Richard Dawkins (1976) has introduced the term 'meme' to describe the kind of motif or symbol which Jung ascribed to archetypes. Dawkins holds memes to be the cultural equivalents of genes. They are transmitted by teaching, initiation, imitation and learning, and, provided they achieve wide enough dissemination, do not die out when local populations become extinct. In this manner they constitute a 'meme pool' which, at the cultural level, corresponds to the gene pool at the DNA level. Susan Blackmore (1999) has carried this idea a good deal further. She argues that our brains do not create our own thoughts but act as meme receptacles. Memes, like genes, compete with one another and, she maintains, are subject to their own form of natural selection. However, not everyone is happy with the meme concept. Unlike genes, memes (ideas, motifs and symbols) are not true replicators. They are less stable than genes. They tend to undergo some degree of change every time they are transmitted from one mind to another. What gives them their relative stability are the archetypal structures responsible for their selection. The kinds of motifs and symbols that we favour and transmit are those best attuned to our archetypal biases.

4. They list an array of rules and behaviours implicated in relations between the sexes, religious rituals, healing practices, dream interpretation, the holding of property, the manufacture of tools and weapons, etiquette prescribing forms of greeting, hospitality, social deference, co-operating, and so on. A more recent study by Brown (1991) has stressed the need to give due acknowledgement to the diversity of human societies while at the same time studying the behavioural universals that underlie such diversity. The complex interaction between genetic programming and cultural diversity has been investigated by Durham (1991) and Lumsden and Wilson (1981, 1983). Thanks to the work of Eibl-Eibesfeldt (1971) and Ekman (1973), we know that certain facial expressions and social gestures correspond to specific emotional states independently of cultural differences.

5. Eliade's view is in harmony with empirical findings which suggest that innate propensities influence the content of dreams. The American psychologists Calvin S. Hall and Vernon J. Nordby (1972) collected dreams from a large number of subjects from various parts of the world. On the basis of their examination of over 50,000 dreams, they concluded that a number of typical themes are symbolically represented over and over again: 'These *typical dreams*, as we shall call them, are experienced by virtually every dreamer ... [they] express the shared concerns, preoccupations and interests of all dreamers. They may be said to constitute the universal constants of the human psyche.' They thus provide important evidence in support of Jung's hypothesis of a 'collective unconscious', although they do not themselves make this connection. What is more, their findings are in keeping with the overall perspective of evolutionary theory.

6. The earliest example of the apocalyptic theme in the Middle East is that involving Zoroaster, who lived in the sixth century BC. As a priest of the traditional religion of the Iranians, Zoroaster believed in one god, Ahura Mazda (Lord Wisdom), who was responsible for the creation and good order of the universe. Inevitably, Ahura Mazda was opposed by an evil figure, in this instance, Angra Mainyu, the spirit of destruction, lying and disorder. In common with other prophets, Zoroaster had wandered off on a spiritual quest which was rewarded with a vision in which he saw Ahura Mazda surrounded by six radiant figures. This convinced him that he was chosen to inaugurate a new religious teaching, namely, that the struggle between Ahura Mazda and Angra Mainyu would not go on for eternity (as was traditionally believed), but would have a finite end, after which peace and order would prevail unimpeded. The dead would be resurrected and all humanity united in a single community bound together by their shared worship of Ahura Mazda. This event Zoroaster described as 'the making wonderful' and it is the earliest recorded example we have of a millenarian prophecy. The fact that it went unfulfilled does not seem to have diminished the success of Zoroastrianism as a religion, any more than it did Christianity. Indeed, Zoroastrianism flourished in Iran and neighbouring lands until around 800 AD, and is still adhered to by the Indian Parsees.

Chapter 9 Love, Rank and Religion

1. For the evolution and psychobiological implications of religious belief and practices see Batson and Ventis (1982), Mithen (1996), Reynolds and Tanner (1983), Stevens (1986) and Wenegrat (1990). All agree that a group with a strong and intact religious belief system will outcompete a group with a weak religious affiliation or no religion at all, whether the competition takes the form of warfare, economic rivalry or the struggle for survival. It is not necessary to invoke group selection to account for this. It is quite simply advantageous for an individual (and his or her genes) to be a member of a religious group.

2. For the contribution of religion to the maintenance of social cohesion see Brown (1962), Durkheim (1965), Eliade (1958), Evans-Pritchard (1965), Johnson (1963) and Murray (1976).

3. For an exposition of the neo-Darwinist position on the evolution of moral behaviour see Ridley (1996) and Wright (1995).

4. Behaviourism and the 'Culture and Personality' school of twentieth-century psychology was able to account for certain very circumscribed forms of animal and human behaviour but failed when it came to the study of such complex capacities as the acquisition of language by young children. The new discipline of psycholinguistics only took off when Chomsky (1967) intervened with his neurobiological proposals that language development depends on the prior existence of 'deep structures' encoded in the brain. Recent advances in psycholinguistics have been eloquently presented by Pinker (1994).

5. Littlewood (1984, 1993).

6. Littlewood (1984) and Scholem (1973).

7. Miller (1987).

Chapter 10 Personal Afterword

1. 'A Sane Approach To Madness, Anthony Storr hails a fruitful development in psychiatric thinking', *Financial Times*, Weekend, November 23-24, 1996.

2. 'Leader Goes Ape', by Jonathan Hill, *Times Literary Supplement*, August 22, 1997,

3. 'Rebels with a cause', *The Lancet*, Vol. 335, pp. 694-5.

4. Wallace (1956a, 1956b, 1970, 1996).

5. Foulks (1977).

6. Littlewood (1984, 1991, 1993).

7. The most authoritative work on such altered states of consciousness is that edited by Tart (1972). For a detailed discussion of schizotypal access to the liminal state see Claridge *et al.* (1997).

Glossary

agonic mode: a mode of social interaction characteristic of hierarchically organized societies where individuals are concerned with warding off threats to their status and inhibiting overt expressions of aggressive conflict.

antinomian: from the Greek *anti* = against and *nomos* = the law.

apocalypse: derived from the Greek *apo* = away, from or off, and *kalyptein* = to cover or to hide. *Apokalypsis* therefore means to uncover what was hidden. The word has come to encompass the notion of a huge final catastrophe from which only an élite few will survive.

archetypes: innate neuropsychic centres possessing the capacity to initiate, control, and mediate the common behavioural characteristics and typical experiences of all human beings irrespective of race, culture or creed. In the Jungian scheme of things archetypes are the components of the *collective unconscious*. 'The concept of the archetype ... is derived from the repeated observation that, for instance, the myths and fairy tales of world literature contain definite motifs which crop up everywhere. We meet these same motifs in the fantasies, dreams, deliria, and delusions of individuals living today. These typical images and associations are what I call archetypal ideas. The more vivid they are, the more they will be coloured by particularly strong feeling-tones' (Jung, CW10, para. 846).

Armageddon: the site of the last decisive battle on the Day of Judgement as described in the Book of Revelation.

behavioural ecology: a discipline concerned with the functional analysis of behaviour in relation to the environment; particularly concerned with the costs and benefits of alternative strategies employed in environmental exploitation.

biosocial goals: the social goals for which we are biologically equipped to strive, such as care-giving, protection, love and status.

borderline personality: a concept applied to individuals whose abnormal personalities combine features of neurotic and psychotic symptomatology.

charisma: a Greek word meaning a favour specially vouchsafed by God; the term used by Max Weber (1947) to denote a certain quality of an individ-

217

ual personality by virtue of which he is set apart from ordinary men and treated as endowed with supernatural or exceptional powers or qualities.

cognitive dissonance: the capacity to form and sustain in consciousness ideas and perceptions which are objectively discordant or contradictory; a capacity particularly apparent in people with a *schizotypal personality*.

collective unconscious: a term introduced by C.G. Jung to designate the *phylogenetic psyche* (those aspects of the psyche which are inherited and common to all humanity).

cult: from the Latin *cultus* = worship; a group of individuals who have come together to share a common belief system, within a tightly knit community, based on devotion to the teaching and personal influence of a charismatic leader, who is believed to possess divine powers; new cults which have come into existence in recent decades are commonly referred to as new religious movements.

DNA: deoxyribonucleic acid; the basic hereditary material of all living organisms, making up the *genes* and located within the chromosomes.

delusion: a strongly held belief which is judged by others to be false.

ego: the part of the personality which one consciously recognizes as I or me.

enantiodromia: the propensity of all polarized phenomena to go over to their opposite.

ethology: the study of the behaviour of organisms living in their natural habitats.

flexible mutualism: a term introduced by Wenegrat (1989) to designate a tendency to form stable groups of individuals who co-operate with each other for their long-term mutual benefit.

folie à deux: the result of the process by which a psychotic individual succeeds in persuading a non-psychotic companion to share his or her delusional belief system.

free-rider: an individual who seeks to acquire an undue proportion of the group's resources without first satisfying the usual requirement of achieving appropriate social rank.

gene: the basic unit of heredity made up of *DNA*.

genome: the complete genetic constitution of an organism; the entire genetic programme characterizing the species.

genotype: the genetic constitution of the individual.

Gestalt: a German word meaning form, pattern or configuration; used in psychology to designate an integrated whole that is greater than the sum of its parts.

guru: a Sanskrit term meaning both 'weighty' and 'one who brings light out of darkness'; in India it is used to designate a Hindu or Sikh religious teacher.

hallucination: a false sensory perception formed in the absence of an external stimulus; characteristic of *psychosis* and may occur in any sensory modality.

hedonic mode: a mode of social interaction in which underlying dominance relations are not being challenged and agonic tensions are consequently absent, permitting individuals to be affiliative and to give their attention to recreational or task-orientated activities.

heteropistic splitting and dispersal: from the Greek *hetero* = other, and *pistis* = belief; the kind of group splitting in which a charismatic prophet plays a central role in gathering round himself a group of believers in whom he inculcates a set of unique beliefs. Since these are invariably at variance with those of the parent group the consequent clash of beliefs gives rise to intragroup conflict, fission and dispersal.

homeostasis: maintenance of balance between opposing mechanisms or systems.

homopistic splitting and dispersal: from the Greek *homo* = the same, and *pistis* = belief; the kind of group splitting and dispersal in which the charismatic leader is either redundant or of the messianic kind. After the split has occurred and the two groups separate they continue to retain the same belief system.

liminal state: term derived from the Latin *limen* meaning threshold or doorway; used in psychology to refer to psychic states experienced on the threshold between conscious and unconscious levels of awareness.

linking disorders: term used by Stevens and Price (2000) to designate that category of psychiatric disorders suffered by people who fear they will fail in competing for too highly valued social resources: attachment and rank. Linking disorders are therefore synonymous with 'disorders of attachment and rank'. They are to be distinguished from *spacing disorders*.

mana: a Melanesian word describing the exceptional power perceived as emanating from certain people, objects, or events; approximately equivalent to the Western sociological term *charisma*.

mazeway: term introduced by Wallace (1956a) to denote the mental image or *Gestalt* that each individual forms of the culture in which he or she lives: 'The mazeway is nature, society, culture, personality and body image, as seen by one person'; synonymous with Binswanger's (1958) 'world design'.

mazeway resynthesis: the reformulation of the *mazeway* which occurs in the mind of one charismatic individual at a time of social stress. A new ideological package emerges which seems to possess an internally consistent structure. Since this occurs suddenly and dramatically, the new insight is experienced as a revelation. The process might also be called 'reality reconstruction', 'Damascene conversion', or 'Gestalt transformation'. It bears many features in common with the abrupt formation of an intact and 'incorrigible' delusional system in a patient with schizophrenia.

Messiah: derived from the Hebrew word meaning anointed; the title conferred in the Old Testament on one divinely sent to deliver the Jewish nation; has come also to refer to an expected hero–saviour of an oppressed people or nation. When involved in group splitting, the Messiah tends to promote *homopistic* rather than *heteropistic* splitting.

module: a term introduced by evolutionary psychologists to describe a specialized component of the mind which equips it with the necessary 'intelligence' to deal with a specific 'cognitive domain' or a certain type of behaviour pattern. Examples are modules for acquiring language, intuiting the psychological state of others, classifying plants and animals, making and using tools, and dealing with the physical properties of the inanimate world.

narcissistic personality: people with this type of personality tend to be in constant need of reassurance that they are valued, appreciated and loved; their sense of self-importance and their hunger for admiration gives them a strong sense of entitlement, in that they entertain unreasonable expectations of especially favourable treatment from others as well as an automatic compliance with their wishes.

neurosis: term dating from the second half of the eighteenth century which originally meant a disease of the nerves. Since the work of Jean Martin Charcot (1825-93) and Freud on hysteria towards the end of the nineteenth century, however, neurosis came to be applied precisely to mental disorders which were *not* diseases of the nervous system. Although used less frequently than hitherto, neurosis remains a convenient term for a group of psychiatric disorders which do not involve hallucinations, delusions or loss of insight.

numinosity: a term introduced into psychology by C.G. Jung, who borrowed it from the German theologian, Rudolf Otto. Otto used it to describe what he regarded as the fundamental experience common to all religions – namely, the sense of awe and exaltation generated by the feeling of being in the presence of the Creator, an experience which Otto designated the *mysterium tremendum et fascinans*.

ontogenesis: the development of an organism through the course of its life cycle.

paradigm: term given a technical meaning within the philosophy of science by T.S. Kuhn in his *The Structure of Scientific Revolutions* (1962). Denying that scientific theories are mere products of induction from sensory experience, Kuhn argued that theories give meaning to facts rather than simply arising our of them. A paradigm is the theoretical framework within which all thinking in a given scientific discipline proceeds. A paradigm shift occurs when one theoretical framework is replaced by another.

paranoid personality disorder: people with this type of personality tend to be suspicious and distrustful of others and to attribute to them hostile intentions.

phenotype: the characteristics of an organism as a manifestation of the genes possessed by it. It is possible for organisms to possess the same genotype (e.g. identical twins) yet to have different phenotypes, owing to environmentally induced variations in their ontological development.

phylogenesis: the evolutionary origin and development of a species.

phylogenetic psyche: those psychic structures and functions which are characteristic of all members of the human species; synonymous with Jung's term *collective unconscious*.

prophet: from the Greek *pro* = for; *phētēs* = speaker: one who speaks for someone – especially for God (or any other deity) – as the inspired revealer or interpreter of his will; also one who foretells what is going to happen as a result of what has been revealed to him. When involved in group splitting, the Prophet tends to promote *heteropistic* rather than *homopistic splitting*.

proximate cause: term used in evolutionary psychiatry to denote an aetiological factor which operates on and through the *phenotype* (i.e. on and through the constitution and life experience of the individual).

pseudospeciation: term used by Erik Erikson (1984) to describe the propensity of members of one human community to treat members of another as if they belonged to a non-human species.

psychosis: a broad term used to cover those relatively severe psychiatric disorders in which hallucinations and delusions occur in people with relatively poor insight into their condition.

schizoid personality: people with this type of personality appear detached and withdrawn, express little or no emotion in such contact they may have with others, and prefer to engage in solitary activities.

schizophrenia: a severe *psychosis* characterized by relapses and remissions; acute phases of the disorder are marked by the so-called 'positive' symptoms – delusions and hallucinations, disorganized thought processes and bizarre forms of behaviour and speech. As the condition progresses 'negative' symptoms become more apparent, particularly poor personal hygiene, impoverished speech content and loss of motivation.

schizotaxia: a term introduced by Meehl (1962, 1992) to denote the genetic tendency to *schizophrenia*; he used the term *schizotypy* to denote the phenotypic manifestations of schizotaxia in non-schizophrenic individuals.

schizotypy: the manifestation of the genetic tendency to schizophrenia in non-schizophrenic individuals; characterised by magical thinking, unusual perceptions, and belief in paranormal phenomena.

shaman: from the Tungus word *saman* = one who is excited, moved, raised up; a priest–doctor among the northern tribes of Asia; has also come to be applied to the medicine man of North West American Indians.

spacing disorders: term used by Stevens and Price (2000) to designate that group of psychiatric disorders suffered by people who have difficulty in forming personal relationships and who deal with their inability to function appropriately in social groups by adopting a strategy of withdrawal. In the present work the term is applied to those who display a tendency to leave their natal group and who either move into another group or withdraw into an isolated existence.

splitting or *schism*: the term schism is derived from the Greek *schizein* = to split. The notion of splitting is one with which psychiatrists have made great play. Bleuler's (1911) redefinition of dementia praecox as *schizophrenia* was based on his observation that the disorder was characterized by a split or dissociation between thinking and emotional capacities. The idea of splitting was taken up by psychoanalysts in their discussion of the *narcissistic personality* (Kohut, 1971, 1977) when it was observed that people with this type of disorder were able to split or dissociate contradictory feelings, such as love and hate, from one another when they were experienced in relation to the same person. Our own use of the term in the present volume is restricted to the tendency of human groups to split along *homopistic* or *heteropistic* lines when they grow too big for their resources.

ultimate cause: a factor contributing to the structure of the human genome over millions of years of selection pressure.

Bibliography

Adas, Michael (1987) *Prophets of Rebellion: Millenarian Protest Movements Against the European Colonial Order (Studies in Comparative World History)*. Cambridge University Press, Cambridge.

Adler, Matthew (1997) 'Where do voices come from?' *Journal of the Royal Society of Medicine*, 90, pp. 28-32.

Ainsworth, M.D. (1964) 'Patterns of attachment behaviour shown by the infant in interaction with his mother', *Merrill-Palmer Quarterly*, 10, pp. 51-8.

Allen, John (1986) *Shopping for a God*. Inter-Varsity Press.

Allen, J.S., and Sarich, V.M. (1988) 'Schizophrenia in an evolutionary perspective', *Perspectives in Biology and Medicine*, 32, pp. 132-53.

Allport, G.W. (1966) 'The religious context of prejudice', *Journal for the Scientific Study of Religion*, 5, p. 447.

Andres, Rachel, and Lane, James R. (1988) *Cults and Consequences*. Commission on cults and missionaries.

Andreski, S. (1964) 'The origins of war' in *The Natural History of Aggression*, edited by Carthy, J.D., and Ebling, F.J. Academic Press, London.

Archer, John (1992) *Ethology and Human Development*. Harvester/Wheatsheaf, New York.

Arieti, S. (1976) *Creativity: The Magic Synthesis*. Basic Books, New York.

Babbage, S. Barton, (1937) *Hauhauism: An Episode in the Maori Wars 1863-1866*. A.H. & A.W. Reed, Dunedin, New Zealand.

Bainbridge, W.S. (1978) *Satan's Power: A Deviant Psychotherapy Cult*. University of California Press, Berkeley.

Balling, J.D., and Falk, J.H. (1982) 'Development of visual preference for natural environments', *Environment and Behavior*, 14, pp. 5-28.

Barker, E. (1984) *The Making of a Moonie: Choice or Brainwashing*. Basil Blackwell, Oxford.

Barker, E. (1990) *New Religious Movements: A Practical Introduction*. HMSO, London.

Barkow, J.H., Cosmides, L., and Tooby, J. (eds) (1992) *The Adapted Mind: Evolutionary Psychology and the Generation of Culture*. Oxford University Press, New York.

Barkun, Michael (1974) *Disaster and the Millennium*. Yale University Press, New Haven and London.

Barrett, D.B. (1968) *Schism and Renewal in Africa*. Oxford University Press, Oxford.

Batson, C.D. and Ventis, W.L. (1982) *The Religious Experience: A Social-Psychological Perspective*. Oxford University Press, Oxford.

de Becker, Raymond (1968) *The Understanding of Dreams or the Machinations of the Night*. George Allen & Unwin, London.

Beckford, James A. (1985) *Cult Controversies*. Tavistock Press, London.

Beit-Hallahmi, B., and Argyle, M. (1977) 'Religious ideas and psychiatric disorders', *International Journal of Social Psychiatry*, 23, pp. 26-30.

Bell, A.P., Weinberg, M.S., and Hammersmith, S.K. (1981) *Sexual Preference: Its Development in Men and Women*. Indiana University Press, Bloomington.

Bentall, R.P., Clardige, G.S., & Slade, P.D. (1989) 'The multidemensional nature of psychotic traits: A factor analytical study with normal subjects', *British Journal of Clinical Psychology*, 28, pp. 363-75.

Bigelow, R. (1969) *The Dawn Warriors: Man's Evolution Towards Peace*. Little Brown, Boston.

Binswanger, L. (1958) 'The existential analysis school of thought', in May, R., Angel, E., and Ellenberger, H.F. (eds), *Existence*. Basic Books, New York.

Birchwood, W., and Spencer, E. (1999) 'Psychotherapies for schizophrenia: a review', in *Schizophrenia*, edited by Maj, M., and Sartorius, N. Volume 2, pp. 147-214. WPA series 'Evidence Experience in Psychiatry'. John Wiley, Chichester.

Blackmore, Susan (1999) *The Meme Machine*, Oxford University Press.

Bleuler, E. (1911/50) *Dementia Praecox or the Group of Schizophrenias*, translated by Zinkin, J. International University Press, New York.

Boisen, Anton (1960) *Out of the Depths*. Harper, New York.

Bowlby, J. (1958) 'The nature of the child's tie to his mother', International *Journal of Psycho-Analysis*, 39, pp. 350-73.

Bowlby, J. (1969) *Attachment and Loss, Vol. 1, Attachment*. Hogarth Press and the Institute of Psycho-Analysis, London.

Boyd, Robert and Richardson, Peter (1985) *Culture and the Evolutionary Process*. Chicago University Press, Chicago.

Bromberg, Norbert, and Small, Verna Volz (1983) *Hitler's Psychopathology*. New York.

Bromley, David D. (1981) *Strange Gods*. Beacon Press, Boston.

Brown, Alan, Calvert (1963) *Techniques of Persuasion: From Propaganda to Brainwashing*. Pelican, London.

Brown, D.E. (1991) *Human Universals*. McGraw Hill, New York.

Brown, G.W., and Harris, T. (1978) *Social Origins of Depression*. Tavistock Publications, London.

Bibliography

Brown, L.B. (1962) 'A study of religious belief', *British Journal of Psychology*, 53. p. 259.

Bureau for Native Affairs, Hollandia, Netherlands New Guinea (1958) 'Anthropological research in Netherlands New Guinea since 1950', *Oceana*, 19, pp. 132-63.

Burkert, Walter (1996) *Creation of the Sacred: Tracks of Biology in Early Religions*. Harvard University Press, Cambridge, Mass., and London.

Burridge, Kenelm (1969) *New Heaven New Earth: A Study of Millenarian Activities*. Basil Blackwell, Oxford.

Buss, David M. (1989) 'Sex difference in human mate preferences: evolutionary hypotheses tested in 37 cultures', *Behavioral and Brain Sciences*, 12, pp. 1-49

Buss, David M. (1994) *The Evolution of Desire: Strategies of Human Mating*. Basic Books, New York.

Buss, David M. (1999) *Evolutionary Psychology: The New Science of the Mind*. Allyn & Bacon, Boston.

Cahill, C. and Frith, C.D. (1996) 'False perceptions or false beliefs? Hallucinations and delusions in schizophrenia'. In *Method in Madness: Case Studies in Cognitive Neuropsychiatry*, ed. Halligan, P.W. and Marshall, J.C. Psychology Press (Erlbaum), Hove.

Campbell, Joseph (1990) *The Hero's Journey*. Harper & Row, San Francisco.

Carter, M., and Watts, C.A.H. (1971) 'Possible biological advantages among schizophrenics' relatives, *British Journal of Psychiatry*, 118, pp. 453-60.

Cavalli-Sforza, L.L., and Cavalli-Sforza, F. (1995) *The Great Human Diasporas: The History of Diversity and Evolution*. Helix Books, Reading.

Cawson, Frank (1995) *The Monsters in the Mind*. Book Guild, London.

Chadwick, Peter (1992) *Borderline: A Psychological Study of Paranoia and Delusional Thinking*. Routledge, London and New York.

Chagnon, Napoleon A. (1980) 'Mate competition favouring close kin, and village fissioning among the Yanomamo Indians', in *Evolutionary Biology and Human Social Behaviour*, edited by Chagnon, N.A. and Irons, W., pp. 86-131. Duxbury, North Scituate, Ma.

Chance, M.R.A., and Jolly, C. (1970) *Social Groups of Monkeys, Apes and Men*. Jonathan Cape/E.P. Dutton, New York and London

Chance, M.R.A. ed. (1988) *Social Fabrics of the Mind*. Lawrence Erlbaum Associates, Hove and London.

Chomsky, Noam (1965) *Aspects of the Theory of Syntax*. Mit. Press, Cambridge, Mass.

Choquett, Diane (1985) *New Religious Movements in the US and Canada*. Greenwood Press.

Christiansen, Palle (1969) *The Melanesian Cargo Cult: Millenarianism as a Factor in Cultural Change*. Copenhagen Akademisk Forlag. John Wright, Boston.

Claridge, G., Prior, R., and Watkins G. (1990) *Sounds From the Bell Jar: Ten Psychotic Authors*. Macmillan, Basingstoke.

Claridge, G. ed. (1997) *Schizotypy: Relations to Illness and Health*. Oxford University Press. Oxford.

Claridge, G., Clark, K., and Davis, C. (1997) 'Nightmares, dreams, and schizotypy'. *British Journal of Clinical Psychology*, 36, pp. 377-86.

Clark, J.G. (1983) 'On the further study of destructive cultism', in *Psychodynamic Perspectives on Religion, Sect, and Cult*, edited by Halperin, D.A.

Clark, Robert, A. (1980) 'Religious delusions among Jews', *American Journal of Psychotherapy*, 34,1, pp. 62-71.

Clausewitz, C.M. von (1976) *On War*, edited and translated by Michael Howard and Peter Parritt (?), Princeton University Press, Princeton, NJ.

Cohn, Norman (1970) *The Pursuit of the Millennium: Revolutionary Millenarians and Mystical Anarchists in the Middle Ages* (Revised Edition). Oxford University Press, Oxford and New York.

Conway, F. and Seigelman, J. (1978) *Snapping*. Dell Publishing, New York.

Crow, T.J. (1995a) 'A Darwinian approach to the origins of psychosis', *British Journal of Psychiatry*, 167, pp. 12-25.

Crow, T.J. (1995b) 'Aetiology of schizophrenia: an evolutionary view', *International Clinical Psychopharmacology*, 10 (Supplement 2) pp. 49-56.

Crow, T.J. (1996) 'Precursors of psychosis as pointers to the Homo sapiens-specific mate recognition system of language', *British Journal of Psychiatry*, 172, pp. 289-90.

Cunningham, Loren (1984) *Is That Really You Lord? The Story of Youth With a Mission*. Kingsway Publications.

Dakin, E.F. (1929) *Mrs Eddy: The Biography of a Virginal Mind*. Charles Scribner, New York.

Daly, M., and Wilson, M. (1989) 'Evolutionary psychology and family violence', in Crawford, C., Smith, M., and Krebs, D. (eds), *Sociobiology and Psychology*. Lawrence Erlbaum Associates, Hove and London; Hillsdale, NJ.

Darwin, Charles (1859) *The Origin of Species by Means of Natural Selection*. John Murray, London.

Davie, M.R. (1929) *The Evolution of War: A Study of Its Role in Early Societies*. Yale University Press, New Haven.

Dawkins, Richard (1976) *The Selfish Gene*. Oxford University Press.

Dawkins, Richard (1989) *The Extended Phenotype*. Oxford University Press, New York.

Dawkins, Richard (1995) *River out of Eden: A Darwinian View of Life*. Weidenfeld & Nicolson, London.

Deikman, Arthur J. (1990) *The Wrong Way Home: Uncovering the Patterns of Cult Behaviour in American Society*. Beacon Press, Boston.

Deutsch, A. (1975) 'Observations on a sidewalk ashram'. *Archives of General Psychiatry*, Volume 32, pp. 166-75.

226

Deutsch, A. (1980) 'Tenacity of attachment to a cult leader: a psychiatric perspective', *American Journal of Psychiatry*, 137, pp. 1569-73.

Deutsch, A. (1989) 'Psychological perspectives on cult leadership', in Galanter, M.C. (ed.) (1989). *Cults and New Religious Movements*. The American Psychiatric Association, Washington DC.

Dieckmann, H. (1985) 'Psychological reflections on the nuclear threat', *Quadrant*, 18, 2, pp. 57-70. C.G. Jung Foundation, New York.

Dow, Thomas, E. (1978) 'An analysis of Weber's work on charisma', *British Journal of Sociology*, Volume 29, No. 1. pp. 83-93.

DSM-IV: *Diagnostic and Statistical Manual of Mental Disorders*, fourth edition (1994). American Psychiatric Association, Washington.

Durham, W. (1991) *Coevolution: Genes, Culture and Human Diversity*. Stanford University Press, Stanford.

Durkheim, E. (1965) *The Elementary Forms of the Religious Life*, Free Press, New York.

Edinger, Edgar (1999) *The Archetype of the Apocalypse*, Open Court, Chicago and La Salle, Illinois.

Eibl-Eibesfeldt, I. (1971) *Love and Hate*. Methuen, London.

Eibl-Eibesfeldt, I. (1982) 'Warfare, man's indoctrinability and group selection'. *Zeitschrift fur Tierpsychologie*, 60, pp. 177-98.

Eibl-Eibesfeldt, I. (1995) 'The evolution of familiarity and its consequences', *Futura*, 4, pp. 253-64.

Ekman, P. (1973) 'Cross-cultural studies of facial expression', in *Darwin and Facial Expression: A Century of Research in Review*, edited by Ekman, P., pp.169-222. Academic Press, New York.

Eliade, Mircea (1958) *Patterns in Comparitive Religions* (translated by Rosemary Sheed). Sheed & Ward, London and New York.

Eliade, Mircea (1964) *Shamanism: Archaic Techniques in Ecstasy*. Trans. Trask, W.R. Routledge & Kegan Paul, London, and Princeton University Press, Princeton.

Ellenberger, Henri (1970) *The Discovery of the Unconscious*. Basic Books, New York.

Ellis, Havelock (1904)

Enroth, Ron (1983) *A Guide to Cults and New Religions*. Intervarsity Press, Downer's Grove, Illinois.

Enroth, Ron and Melton, Gordon (1985) *Why Cults Succeed Where the Church Fails*. Brethren Press, Illinois.

Erikson, Erik H. (1984) 'Reflections on ethos and war', *The Yale Review*, Volume 73, 4, pp. 481-6.

Erlenmeyer-Kimling, L., and Paradowski, W. (1969) 'Selection and schizophrenia', *American Naturalist*, 100, pp. 651-65.

Evans-Pritchard, E.E. (1965) *Theories of Primitive Religion*. Clarendon Press, Oxford.

Eysenck, H.J. (1995) *Genius: The Natural History of Creativity*. Cambridge University Press, Cambridge.

Fest, Joachim C. (1983) *Hitler*. Penguin Books, London and New York.

Festinger, L. (1957) *The Theory of Cognitive Dissonance*. Evanston.

Festinger, L., Riecken, H.W., Schachter, S. (1964) *When Prophecy Fails*. Harper & Row, New York.

Feuerstein, Georg (1990) *Holy Madness: The Shock Tactics and Radical Teachings of Crazy-Wise Adepts, Holy Fools, and Rascal Gurus*. Arkana, Penguin, New York and London.

Firth, R. (1965) 'Introduction to "Religions of the Oppressed", by V. Lanternari,' *Current Anthropology*, 6, number 4.

Foley, Robert A. (1996) 'An evolutionary and chronological framework for human social behaviour', in *Evolution of Social Behaviour Patterns in Primates and Man*, edited by Runciman, W.G., Smith, John Maynard, and Dunbar, R.I.M., (pp. 97-117). Published for the British Academy by the Oxford University Press, Oxford and New York.

Foster, L. (1984) *Religion and Sexuality: The Shakers, the Mormons, and the Oneida Community*. University of Illinois Press, Urbana.

Foulks, Edward F. (1977) 'Schizophrenia and revitalisation in pre-modern societies', in *Psychiatry: Areas of Premise and Advancement: A Bicentennial Volume of the University of Pennsylvania*, edited by Brady, J.P., Mendels, J., Orne, M.T., and Rieger, W. Spectrum Publications, New York, pp. 137-44.

Fox, Robin (1975) 'Primate kin and human kinship', *Biosocial Anthropology*, edited by Fox, R, pp. 9-35. Malaby Press, London.

Fox, Robin (1989) 'Search for society: quest for a biosocial science and morality', Rutgers University Press, New Brunswick and London.

Fried, M., Harris, M., Murphy, R. (eds) (1968) *War: The Anthropology of Armed Conflict and Aggression*. Natural History Press, Garden City, New York.

Frith, C.D. (1992) *The Cognitive Neuropsychology of Schizophrenia*. Lawrence Erlbaum Associates. Hove.

Frith, C.D. (1994) 'Theory of mind in schizophrenia', in *The Neuropsychology of Schizophrenia*, edited by David, A.S., and Cutting, J.C. Lawrence Erlbaum Associates, Hove.

Galanter, M. (1979) 'The Moonies: a psychological study of conversion and membership in a contemporary religious sect', *American Journal of Psychiatry*, 2: pp. 36-42.

Galanter, M. (1980) 'Psychological induction into the large-group: findings from a modern religious sect', *American Journal of Psychiatry*, 137, pp. 1574-5.

Galanter, M. (1982) 'Charismatic religious sects and psychiatry: an overview', *American Journal of Psychiatry*, 139, pp. 1539-48.

Galanter, M. ed. (1989) *Cults and New Religious Movements: A Report of the*

Bibliography

American Psychiatric Association. American Psychiatric Association, Washington DC.

Gardner, Russell (1988) 'Psychiatric syndromes as infrastructures for intra-specific communication', in *Social Fabrics of the Mind*, edited by M.R.A. Chance. Lawrence Erlbaum Associates, Hove and London; Hillsdale, NJ.

Garety, Philippa A., and Hemsley, David R. (1997) *Delusions: Investigations into the Psychology of Delusional Reasoning*. Maudsley Monographs 36, The Psychology Press, Hove.

Gilbert, Paul (1989) *Human Nature and Suffering*. Lawrence Erlbaum Associates, Hove and London; Hillsdale, NJ.

Goodman, F.D., Henney, J.H. and Pressel, E. (1974) *Trance, Healing and Hallucination: Three Field Studies of Religious Experience*. Wiley, London.

Gosse, Edmund (1907) *Father and Son*.

Gottesman, I.I., and Shields, J. (1982) *Schizophrenia: The Epigenetic Puzzle*. Cambridge University Press, Cambridge.

Gratus, Jack (1975) *The False Messiahs*. Gollancz, London.

Gurdjieff, George Ivanovich (1950) *All and Everything*. Routledge & Kegan Paul, London.

Hadamard, J. (1945) *The Psychology of Invention in the Mathematical Field*. Princeton University Press, Princeton, NJ.

Hall, Calvin S., and Nordby, Vernon J. (1972) *The Individual and His Dreams*. New American Library, New York.

Harrison, Shirley (1990) *Cults: The Battle for God*. Christopher Helm (Publishers) Ltd. Christopher Helm (Publishers) Ltd. Bromley, Kent.

Harvey, Andrew (1991) *Hidden Journey: A Spiritual Awakening*. Rider, London.

Henderson, J. (1991) 'C.G. Jung's psychology: additions and extensions', *Journal of Analytical Psychology*, 36, 4, pp. 129-42.

Heston, L.L. (1966) 'Psychiatric disorders in foster home reared children of schizophrenic mothers', *British Journal of Psychiatry*, 112, pp. 819-25.

Hiden, J. and Farquharson, J. (eds) (1988) *Explaining Hitler's Germany: Historians and the Third Reich*, second edition. Batsford Academic and Educational Press, London.

Hobsbawm, Erich J. (1971) *Primitive Rebels*. Manchester University Press, Manchester.

Hood, R.W. (1973) 'Religious orientation and the experience of transcendence', *Journal for the Scientific Study of Religion*, 12, p. 441.

Horowitz, A.V. (1982) *The Social Control of Mental Illness*. Academic Press, New York.

Horton, P.C. (1973) 'The mystical experience as a suicide preventive', *American Journal of Psychiatry*, 130, p. 3.

Jackson, Michael (1997) 'Benign schizotypy? The case of spiritual experience', in Claridge, (1997).

Jackson, M., and Fulford, K.W.M. (1997) 'Spiritual Experience and Psychopathology', *Philosophy, Psychiatry, Psychology*, 4, pp. 41-65.

Jacobson, S. (1998) *The Hare Krishna Experience: A Theory of Motives for Embracing Krishna Consciousness.* Unpublished dissertation, Department of Anthropology, University College, London, WC1E 6BT.

James, William (1941) *The Varieties of Religious Experience: A Study in Human Nature.* Longmans, London and New York.

Jamison, K.R. (1993) *Touched with Fire: Manic-Depressive Illness and the Artistic Temperament.* Free Press, New York.

Jaroch, Matthias (2000) *Too Much Wit and Not Enough Warning? Sir Eric Phipps Als britischer Botschafter in Berlin von 1933-1937.* Peter Lang, Munich.

Jarvik, L.F., and Deckard, B.S. (1977) 'The Odyssean personality: a survival advantage for carriers of genes predisposing to schizophrenia', *Neuropsychobiology*, 3: pp. 179-91.

Johnson, B. (1963) 'On church and sect', *American Sociological Review*, 28, p. 539.

Jung, C.G. (1936) 'Wotan', *Neue Schweizer Rundschau*, Zurich, March, pp. 657-69. Published in English translationin Volume 10 of *The Collected Works of C.G. Jung (1953-78)*, edited by Read, H., Fordham, M., and Adler, G. Routledge & Kegan Paul, London.

Jung, C.G. (1953) 'Structure of the unconscious', *The Collected Works*, Vol. 7, pp.263-92. Routledge & Kegan Paul, London.

Jung, C.G. (1959) 'The concept of the collective unconscious', *The Collected Works*, Vol. 9i, pp. 42-53. Routledge & Kegan Paul, London.

Jung, C.G. (1960) 'On the nature of the psyche', *The Collected Works*, Vol. 8, pp.159-234. Routledge & Kegan Paul, London.

Jung, C.G. (1963) *Memories, Dreams, Reflections*, recorded and edited by Aniela Jaffe, Routledge & Kegan Paul, London.

Kaplan, David E. and Marshall, Andrew (1996) *The Cult at the End of the World: The Incredible Story of Aum.* Hutchinson, London.

Kaplan, Stephen (1992) 'Environmental preference in a knowledge-seeking, knowledge-using organism, in *The Adapted Mind*, edited by Barkow, J.H., Cosmides, L., and Tooby, J. Oxford University Press, New York and Oxford.

Karandikar, N.S. (1978) *Biography of Sri Swami Samarth Akkalkot Maharaj.* Bombay.

Karlsson, J.L. (1972) 'An Icelandic study of schizophrenia', in Kaplan, A.R. (ed.) *Genetic Factors in Schizophrenia.* Charles C. Thomas, Springfield, Il. pp. 246-55.

Kaufman, M.R. (1939) 'Religious delusions in schizophrenia', *International Journal of Psychoanalysis*, 20, p. 363.

Keefe, J.A. and Magaro, P.A. (1980) 'Creativity and schizophrenia: an equivalence of cognitive processing', *Journal of Abnormal Psychology*, 89 (3): pp. 390-8.

Kent, Stephen A. (1994) 'Lustful prophet: a psychosexual historical study of the Children of God's leader, David Berg', *Cultic Studies Journal*, Volume 11, No.2, pp. 135-88.

Kilbourne, B.K. (1989) 'Psychotherapeutic implications of new religious affiliation', in Galanter, M.C. *Cults and New Religious Movements*, The American Psychiatric Association, Washington DC.

Kohut, Heinz (1971) *The Analysis of the Self: A Systematic Approach to the Psychoanalytic Treatment of Narcissistic Disorders*. International Universities Press, New York.

Kohut, Heinz (1977) *The Restoration of the Self*. International Universities Press, New York.

Kuhn, Thomas S. (1968) *The Structure of Scientific Revolutions*. The University of Chicago Press, Chicago and London.

Laing, R.D. (1960) *The Divided Self: A Study of Sanity and Madness*. Tavistock Publications, London.

Lanternari, Vittorio (1963) *The Religions of the Oppressed: A Study of Modern Messianic Cults*. Macgibbon & Kee, London.

La Russo, L. (1978) 'Sensitivity of paranoid patients to non-verbal cues', *Journal of Abnormal Psychology*, 87 (5; October): pp. 463-71.

Lawrence, Peter (1964) *Road Belong Cargo: A Study of the Cargo Movement in the Southern Madang District*, New Guinea. Manchester University Press. Manchester.

Laxmi, M.Y. (1980) *The Sound of Running Water*. Rajneesh Foundation, Poona.

Leakey, R. (1994) *The Origin of Humankind*. Weidenfeld & Nicolson, London.

Le Bon, Gustave (1952) *The Crowd: A Study of the Popular Mind*. Ernest Benn, London.

Lenz, H. (1979) 'The element of the irrational at the beginning and during the course of delusion', *Confinia Psychiatrica*, 22, pp. 183-90.

Lenz, H. (1983) 'Belief and delusion. Their common origin but different course of development', *Zygon*, 18, pp. 117-37.

Levine, S.V. (1979) 'Role of psychiatry in the phenomenon of cults', *Canadian Journal of Psychiatry*, 24, p. 593.

Levine, S.V. (1989) 'Life in the cults', in *Cults and New Religious Movements: A Report of the American Psychiatric Association*, edited by Galanter, M.C. The American Psychiatric Association, Washington DC.

Lewis, I.M. (1971) *Ecstatic Religion*. Penguin Books, Harmondsworth.

Lewis, I.M.(1986) *Religion in Context: Cults and Charisma*. Cambridge University Press, Cambridge.

Lewy, Guenter (1974) *Religion and Revolution*. Oxford University Press, Oxford and London.

Lindblom, G. (1916) *The Akamba in British East Africa*, quoted by Quincey Wright (1943).

Lindholm, Charles (1990) *Charisma*. Basil Blackwell, Cambridge, Mass. and Oxford.

Littlewood, Roland (1984) 'The imitation of madness: the influence of psychopathology upon culture', *Socialscience and Medicine*, 19, pp. 705-15.

Littlewood, Roland (1991) 'Against pathology: the new psychiatry and its critics', *British Journal of Psychiatry*, 159, pp. 696-702.

Littlewood, Roland (1993) *Pathology and Identity: The Work of Mother Earth in Trinidad*. Cambridge University Press, Cambridge.

Loehlin, J.C. (1982) 'Are personality traits differentially heritable?' *Behaviour Genetics*, 12, number 4: pp. 417-28.

Lofland, J., and Stark, R. (1965) 'Becoming a world-saver: a theory of conversion to a deviant perspective', *American Sociological Review*, 30, pp. 62-75.

Lombroso, Cesare (1891) *The Man of Genius*

Loney, J. (1974) 'Background factors, sexual experiences and attitudes towards treatment in two "normal" homosexual samples', *Journal of Consulting and Clinical Psychology*, 38, pp. 57-65.

Lorenz, Konrad (1970) *The Enmity Between Generations and its Possible Causes*. The Nobel Foundation, Stockholm.

Lumsden, Charles J., and Wilson, Edward O. (1981), *Genes, Minds and Culture*, Harvard University Press, Cambridge, Mass.

Lumsden, Charles J., and Wilson, Edward O. (1983), *Promethean Fire: Reflections on the Origin of Mind*. Harvard University Press, Cambridge, Mass., and London.

MacLean, P.D. (1985) 'Evolutionary psychiatry and the triune brain', *Psychological Medicine*, 15, pp. 219-21.

May, R. (1975) *The Courage to Create*. Norton, New York.

May, Ronald L., ed. (1982) *Micronationalist Movements in Papua New Guinea (Political and Social Change Monographs 1)*. Australian National University, Canberra.

McClenon, James (1994) *Wondrous Events: Foundations of Religious Belief*, University of Pennsylvania Press, Philadelphia.

McGuire, M.T., and Troisi, A. (1998) *Darwinian Psychiatry*. Oxford University Press, New York.

Mead, M. (1961) *New Lives For Old: Cultural Transformation – Manus 1928-1953*. Mentor, New York.

Meehl, Paul D. (1962) 'Schizotaxia, schizotypy, schizophrenia', *American Psychologist*, 17, pp. 827-38.

Meehl, Paul D. (1992) 'Toward an integrated theory of schizotaxia, schizotypy, schizophrenia', *Journal of Personality Disorders*, 4, pp. 1-99.

Melton, J.G. Gordon, and Moore, R.L. (1982) *The Cult Experience: Responding to the New Religious Pluralism*. Pilgrim Press, New York.

Miller, R. (1987) *Bare-Faced Messiah: The True Story of L. Ron Hubbard.* Michael Joseph, London.

Milne, H. (1986) *Bhagwan: The God that Failed*, edited by Liz Hodgkinson. Caliban Press, London.

Mithen, Steven (1996) *The Prehistory of the Mind: A Search for the Origins of Art, Religion and Science.* Thames & Hudson, London.

Morinis, Alan (1985) 'Sanctified madness; the God-intoxicated saints of Bengal', *Social Science and Medicine*, vol. 21, no. 2, pp. 211-20.

Mullen, P. (1979) 'Phenomenology of disordered mental function', in *Essentials of Post-graduate Psychiatry*, edited by Hill, P., Murray, R., and Thorley, G. pp. 25-54. Academic Press, London.

Murdock, George P. (1945) 'The common denominator in culture', in *The Science of Man in the World Crisis*, edited by Linton, R. Cambridge University Press, New York.

Murphy, Gardner (1958) *Human Potentialities.* Basic Books, New York.

Murphy, H.B.M. (1967) 'Cultural aspects of the delusion', *Stadium Generale*, 20, 11, pp. 684-92

Murray, David Christie (1976) *A History of Heresy.* New English Library.

Nasar, Sylvia (1998) *A Beautiful Mind: A Biography of John Forbes Nash Jr.* Faber & Faber, London.

Nelson, G.K. (1972) 'The membership of a cult: the Spiritualist National Union,' *Review of Religious Research*, 13: p. 170.

Nesse, R.M., and Williams, G.C. (1995) *Evolution and Healing, The New Science of Darwinian Medicine.* Weidenfeld & Nicolson, London.

Neumann, Erich (1955) *The Great Mother: An Analysis of the Archetype.* Routledge & Kegan Paul, London.

Oakes, Len (1997) *Prophetic Charisma: The Psychology of Revolutionary Personalities*, Syracuse University Press, Syracuse, New York.

Olson, Theodor (1982) *Millenarianism, Utopianism and Progress.* Toronto University Press, Toronto and London.

Orians, Gordon, and Heerwagen, Judith H. (1992) 'Evolved responses to landscapes', in *The Adapted Mind: Evolutionary Psychology and the Generation of Culture*, edited by Barkow, J.H., Cosmides, L., and Tooby, J. Oxford University Press, New York and Oxford.

Otto, Rudolf (1917/1950) *The Idea of the Holy.* Oxford University Press, Oxford.

Pattison, E.M., and Ness, R.C. (1989) 'New religious movements in historical perspective', in *Cults and New Religious Movements: A Report of the American Psychiatric Association*, edited by Galanter, M.C. The American Psychiatric Association, Washington DC.

Perez, Leon (1978) 'The messianic idea and messianic delusion', *Mental Health and Society*, 5, pp. 266-74.

Peters, E., Day, S., McKenna, J., and Orbach, G. (1999) 'Delusional ideation in religious and psychotic populations', *British Journal of Clinical Psychology*, 38, pp.83-96.

Pinker, Steven (1994) *The Language Instinct*. HarperCollins, New York; Hamish Hamilton, London.

Pinker, Steven (1998) *How the Mind Works*. Allen Lane, The Penguin Press, London.

Popper, K.R. (1959) *The Logic of Scientific Discovery*. Hutchinson, London.

Post, J.M. (1978) 'Hostility, conformity, fraternity: the group dynamics of terrorist behaviour', *International Journal of Group Psychotherapy*, 36, pp. 211-24.

Post, J.M (1986) 'Narcissism and the charismatic leader-follower relationship', *Political Psychology*, 7, number 4: pp. 675-87.

Potts, R. (1998) 'Variability selection in hominid evolution', *Evolutionary Anthropology*, 7, pp. 81-96.

Price, J.S. (1967) 'Hypothesis: the dominance hierarchy and the evolution of mental illness', *Lancet*, 2, pp. 243-6.

Price, J.S. (1969) 'Neurotic and endogenous depression: a phylogenetic view', *British Journal of Psychiatry*, 114, pp. 119-20.

Price, J., and Stevens, A. (1998) 'The human male socialization strategy set: co-operation, defection, individualism and schizotypy', in *Evolution and Human Behavior*, 19, pp. 57-60.

Raine, A., Lencz, T. and Mednick, S.A. (1997) *Schizotypal Personality*. Cambridge University Press, Cambridge.

Rank, Otto (1961) *Psychology and the Soul*. Perpetua, New York.

Redlich, Fritz (1999) *Hitler: Diagnosis of a Destructive Prophet*. Oxford University Press, New York and Oxford.

Reynolds, V., and Tanner, R. (1983) *The Biology of Religion*. Longman, New York.

Ribeiro, R. (1970) 'Brazilian messianic movements'. In *Millennial Dreams in Action: Studies in Revolutionary Religious Movements*, ed. Thrupp, S.L. Shocken Books, New York.

Richardson, J.T. (1989) 'The psychology of induction: a review and interpretation', in *Cults and New Religious Movements: A Report of the American Psychiatric Association*, edited by Galanter, M.C. The American Psychiatric Association, Washington, DC.

Ricoeur, Paul (1970) *The Symbolism of Evil*. Beacon Press, Boston.

Ridley, Matt (1996) *The Origins of Virtue*. Viking, London.

Robbins, T., and Anthony, D. (1982) 'Deprogramming, brainwashing and the medicalization of deviant religious groups', *Social Problems*, 29, pp. 283-97.

Roberts, Glenn (1991) 'Delusional belief systems and meaning in life: a preferred reality?' *British Journal of Psychiatry*, 159 (supplement 14), pp. 19-28.

Roberts, Glenn (1992) 'The origins of delusion', *British Journal of Psychiatry*, 161, pp. 298-308.

Robins R.S. (1986) 'Paranoid ideation and charismatic leadership', *Psycho-history Review*, 15: pp. 15-55.

Rotberg, Robert I., and Alia, A. Mazrui, ed. (1970) *Protest and Power in Black Africa*. Oxford University Press, Oxford and London.

Roth, Sir Martin (1996) 'Commentary on "audible thoughts" and "speech defect" in schizophrenia', *British Journal of Psychiatry*, 168, pp. 136-38.

Rothenberg, A. (1983) 'Psychopathology and creative cognition', *Archives of General Psychiatry*, 40, pp. 937-42.

Runciman, W.G. (1986) 'On the tendency of human societies to form varieties', *Proceedings of the British Academy*, 72, pp. 149-65.

Sagan, C. (1977) *The Dragons of Eden*. Hodder & Stoughton, London.

Sagan, C. (1996) *The Demon-Haunted World: Science as a Candle in the Dark*. Headline Books, London.

Sargeant, William (1957) *The Battle for the Mind*. Harper & Row. New York.

Schlegel, A. (1991) *Adolescence: An Anthropological Enquiry*. Free Press, New York.

Scholem, G.G. (1973) *Sabbatai Sevi*. Princeton University Press, Princeton.

Seigel, A.M. (1996) *Heinz Kohut and the Psychology of the Self*. Routledge, London.

Shaw, William (1994) *Spying in Guruland: Inside Britain's Cults*. Fourth Estate, London.

Silverman, Julian (1967) 'Shamans and acute schizophrenia', *American Anthropologist*, 69, pp. 21-31.

Simonton, B.K. (1997) *Greatness: Who Makes History and Why*. Guildford Press, New York.

Spence, J. (1996) *God's Chinese Son: The Taiping Heavenly Kingdom of Hong Xiuguan*. HarperCollins, New York.

Spitzer, R.L., Endicott, J., and Gibbon, M. (1979) 'Crossing the border into borderline personality and borderline schizophrenia: the development of criteria', *Archives of General Psychiatry*, 36, pp. 17-24.

Stark, S. (1969) 'Toward a psychology of charisma, II: the pathology viewpoint of James C. Davies', *Psychological Reports*, 24: pp. 88-90.

Stevens, Anthony (1982) *Archetype: A Natural History of the Self*. Routledge & Kegan Paul, London; William Morrow & Co., New York.

Stevens, Anthony (1986) 'Thoughts on the psychobiology of religion and the neurobiology of archetypal experience', *Zygon: Journal of Religion and Science*, 21 (March), pp. 9-29.

Stevens, Anthony, (1989) *The Roots of War*. Paragon House, New York.

Stevens, Anthony, (1995) *Private Myths: Dreams and Dreaming*. Hamish Hamilton, London; Harvard University Press, Cambridge, Mass.

Stevens, Anthony, (1998a) *An Intelligent Person's Guide to Psychotherapy*. Duckworth, London.

Stevens, Anthony, (1998b) *Ariadne's Clue: A Guide to the Symbols of Humankind*. Allen Lane, The Penguin Press, London; and Princeton University Press, Princeton, NJ.

Stevens, Anthony, (1999) *On Jung*, second edition. Routledge, London; Princeton University Press, Princeton, NJ.

Stevens, Anthony and Price, John (2000) *Evolutionary Psychiatry: A New Beginning*, second edition. Routledge, London.

Storr, Anthony (1972) *The Dynamics of Creation*, Secker & Warburg, London.

Storr, Anthony (1991) *Human Destructiveness*. Grove Weidenfeld, New York.

Storr, Anthony (1996) *Feet of Clay: A Study of Gurus*. HarperCollins, London.

Strelan, John G. (1977) *Search for Salvation: Studies in the History and Theology of Cargo Cults*. Lutheran Publishing House, Adelaide.

Stringer, Chris and McKie, Robin (1996) *African Exodus: The Origins of Modern Humanity*. Jonathan Cape, London.

Sumner, W.G. (1913) *War and Other Essays*. New Haven.

Szasz, T.S. (1974) *The Myth of Mental Illness*. Harper & Row, New York.

Tart, C.T. ed. (1972) *Altered States of Consciousness*. Doubleday. Garden City NY.

Thrupp, Silvia L., ed. (1970) *Millenial Dreams in Action: Studies in Revolutionary Religious Movements*. Schocken Books, New York.

Tinbergen, N. (1951) *The Study of Instinct*. Oxford University Press, London.

Tooby, J., and Cosmides, L. (1992) 'The psychological foundations of culture', in *The Adapted Mind: Evolutionary Psychology and the Generation of Culture*, edited by Barkow, J.H., Cosmides, L., and Tooby, J., pp. 19-136. Oxford University Press, New York.

Torry, E.F. (1980) *Schizophrenia and Civilization*. Jason Aronson, New York and London.

Trinkaus, Eric (ed.) (1989) *The Emergence of Modern Humans: Biocultural Adaptations in the Later Pleistocene*. Cambridge University Press, Cambridge, New York. Port Chester, Melbourne, Sydney.

Trompf, Garry W., ed. (1977) *Prophets of Melanesia: Six Essays*. Institute of Papua New Guinea Studies and Institute of South Pacific Studies. Suva.

Trompf, Garry W., ed. (1990) *Cargo Cults and Millenarian Movements: Transoceanic Comparisons of New Religious Movements*. Mouton de Gruyter. New York. Berlin.

Tudge, C. (1995) *The Day Before Yesterday: Five Million Years of History*. Cape, London.

Tuveson, Ernest L. (1974) *Redeemer Nation: The Idea of America's Millennial Role*. The University of Chicago Press, Chicago.

van Baalem, Dr K. (1960) *The Chaos of the Cults*. Eerdemans.

Vayda, A.P. (1968) 'Hypotheses about functions of war', in *War: The Anthropology of Armed Conflict and Aggression*, edited by Fried, M., Harris, M., Murphy, R. Natural History Press, Garden City, New York.

Wallace, A.F.C. (1956a) 'Mazeway resynthesis: a biocultural theory of religious inspiration', *Transactions of the New York Academy of Sciences*, 18, pp. 626-38.

Wallace, A.F.C. (1956b) 'Revitalization movements: Some theoretical considerations for their comparative study', in *American Anthropologist*, 58, pp. 264-81.

Wallace, A.F.C. (1970) *Culture and Personality*, second edition. Random House, New York.

Wallace, A.F.C. (1996) *Religion: An Anthropological View*. Random House, New York.

Wallas, Graham (1926) *The Art of Thought*. Jonathan Cape, London.

Wallis, R. (1984) *The Elementary Forms of the New Religious Life*. Routledge, London.

Wallis, Wilson D. (1918) *Messiahs, Christian and Pagan*. Badger, Boston.

Wallis, Wilson D. (1943) *Messiahs, Their Role in Civilization*. American Council on Public Affairs, Washington DC.

Weber, Eugen (1999) *Apocalypses: Prophecies, Cults and Millennial Beliefs Through the Ages*. Hutchinson, London.

Weber, Max (1946) 'The sociology of charismatic authority', in *From Max Weber: Essays in Sociology*, edited and translated by Gerth, H., and Wright Mills, C. Oxford University Press, Oxford and New York.

Weber, M. (1947/64) *The Theory of Social and Economic Organization*, translated by A.M. Henderson and Talcott Parsons. Oxford University Press, New York.

Weber, M. (1968) *Economy and Society*, edited by Roth, G. and Wittich, C. 3 volumes. Bedminster Press, New York.

Webster, (1980) *Rua and the Maori Millennium*. Price Milburn, for the Victoria University Press.

Weisfeld G. (1999) *Evolutionary Principles of Human Adolescence*, Westview Press.

Wenegrat, Brant (1984) *Sociobiology and Mental Disorder*. Addison-Wesley, Menlo Park, California.

Wenegrat, Brant (1990) *The Divine Archetype: The Sociobiology and Psychology of Religion*. Lexington Books, Lexington, Mass.

Whiteside, M. (1981) 'Rare beasts in the sheepfold'. *Journal of Creative Behaviour*, 15, No. 2: pp. 189-98.

Williams George, (1966) *Adaptation and Natural Selection: A Critique of Some Current Evolutionary Thought*. Princeton University Press, Princeton, NJ.

Willner, A.R. (1984) *The Spellbinders: Charismatic Political Leadership*. Yale University Press, New Haven.

Wilson, Bryan (1973) *Magic and the Millennium: A Sociological Study of Religious Movements of Protest Among Tribal and Third-World Peoples*. Harper & Row. New York.

Bibliography

Wilson, Bryan (1975) *Noble Savages: The Primitive Origins of Charisma*. University of California Press, Berkeley.

Wilson, D.R. (1993) 'Evolutionary epidemiology: Darwinian theory in the service of medicine and psychiatry, *Acta Biotheoretica*, 41, pp. 205-18.

Wilson, Glenn (1989) *The Great Sex Divide: A Study of Male-Female Differences*. Peter Owen, London.

Winters, Ken, C. and Neale, John, M. (1983) 'Delusions and delusional thinking in psychotics: a review of the literature', *Clinical Psychology Review*, 3: pp. 227-53.

Wolff, T. (1956) *Structural Forms of the Feminine Psyche*, privately printed for the Students' Association, C.G. Jung Institute, Zurich.

Worsley, Peter (1970) *The Trumpet Shall Sound: A Study of Cargo Cults in Melanesia*. Paladin, London.

Wright, Q. (1943) *A Study of War*. 2 volumes. University of Chicago Press, Chicago, Illinois.

Wright, Robert (1995) *The Moral Animal: Why We Are the Way We Are; The New Science of Evolutionary Psychology*. Little, Brown & Co., London.

Zablocki, B. (1980) *Alienation and Charisma: A Study of Contemporary American Communes*. Free Press, New York.

Index

Aaron, 139
Abraham, 138
Adas, Michael, 207
affiliation, 48, 168-71
agonic mode, 169, 173-4, 187, 217
Ainu people, 134
Akamba people, 213
akasa, 212
alchemy, 164
Aldebert, 211
algorithm, 107
alienation, 175
Alister Hardy Research Centre, 34
Allen, John, 207
Allport, G.W., 213
American Naturalist, 115
Amos, 150
ancestral environment, 108, 142, 171, 173
Andres, Rachel, 207
Andreski, S., 212, 213
animal magnetism, 106
Anthony, D., 110
Antichrist, 9, 15
anti-cult activists, 109
antinomian teaching, 79-83, 217
apocalypse, 15-17, 71, 76, 83, 145-65; etymology of, 150; pre-Columbian versions of, 158-60; structural patterns of, 150-7; symbolism of, 148-56
apocalyptic disappointment, 2-3, 127, 160, 176
Apple white, Marshall Herff, 7, 198
Archer, John, 190, 207
archetypal symbolism, 148-56
archetype, 12, 17, 63-4, 145, 217; of the Apocalypse, 157; *see* apocalypse; of the Divine Child, 56; of the Enemy, 15; of Evil, 15, 76, 151-5; of the Father, 110; of Good. 151-5; of the Great Mother, 83-85, 110, 122, 154; of the Hero-Saviour, 63, 83-4, 122; of the Marshal Maid (or Amazon), 86; of the Medium, 86-7; of the Monster

(or the Beast), 15, 152-5; of the Predator, 152-3; of the Priest/Shaman, 83; of Religion, 184; of the Self, 110; of the Shadow, 76; of the Trickster, 83, 87-8; compared to 'memes', 214; mode of activation of, 83; possession by, 84
Aristotle, 21, 168
Arieti, S., 211
Armageddon, 11, 12, 17, 100, 127, 145-65, 217; symbolism of, 148-56
arousal, 179
Asahara, Shoko, 7, 10, 11-13, 52, 137, 143, 205, 211
attachment, 168-71; disorders of, 171-5
Aum Supreme Truth, 10, 11-13
avadhuta, 88
awakening, 56

Baba, 149, 212
Babbage, S., 159
Babel, Tower of, 129
Babylon, destruction of, 155-6
Bainbridge, W.S., 143
Baldur, 164-5
Balling, J.D., 161
Bama, Khepa, 89-90
Barker, E., 105, 207, 212
Barkow, J.H., 207
Barrett, D.B., 211
Bastian, Adolf, 213
Batson, C.D., 215
Beast, the, 15, 17, 152-3
Beautiful Mind, A, 25
Beckford, James A., 207
behavioural ecology, 189, 217
behaviourism, 215
Behemoth, 153
belief system, 131, 196; innate imperative to learn, 74, 106, 167-8; revitalization of, 69, 71, 76, 92
Bell, A.P., 120, 207
Bentall, R.P., 210
Berg, David Brandt, 116-17;

239

240

Index

de-programming, 109
Descartes, René, 52
detachment, 170
Deucalion, 147, 164-5
Deutsche, A., 149, 212
Dieckmann, Hans, 165
disorders of attachment and rank, 171-5
dispersal, 78-9, 125-43, 178, 197
Divine, Father, 57
Divine Light Mission, 129
DNA, 164, 218
Dobzhansky, Theodosius, 200
dominance, 170-3
Dow, Thomas E., 4
Dreaming Time, 182
dreams, 75, 145; compensatory function
    of, 195; culture pattern dreams, 75;
    and myths, 147; typical dreams of
    prophets, 76; universal themes in,
    214
DSM-IV, 25, 209-10
Durham, W., 212, 213, 214
Durkheim, Emile, 93, 215

Eccles, Solomon, 37
Eddy, Mrs Baker, 57, 87
Edinger, Edgar, 157
Eibl-Eibesfeldt, I., 212, 214
Einstein, Albert, 52, 183-4
Ekman, P., 214
Eliade, Mircea, 83, 93-4, 147, 181, 182,
    214, 215
Ellenberger, Henri, 64, 208
Eminent Theatre Journey Centre, 130
Emmerich, Count of Leiningen, 17
Empedocles, 48, 168
empiricism, 9
enantiodromia, 79-80, 218
'End of History, The', 16
Enroth, Ron, 227
epiphanic realization, 44
Erikson, Erik, 76, 100, 126, 131
Erlenmeyer-Kimling, L., 115, 119, 191
ethics, 203-4; and charisma, 103
ethnic cleansing, 76, 135
ethology, 188, 218
Evans-Pritchard, E.E., 215
evolutionary hypotheses, testability of,
    200
*Evolutionary Psychiatry, A New
    Beginning*, 171, 192, 193, 201;
    critical responses to, 190-1
evolutionary psychology, 64, 119, 145,
    189
evolved psychological mechanisms, 190
exhibitionism, 54
extraversion, 48
Eysenck, Hans, 208

Ezra, 150

Falk, J.H., 161
Falret, J.P., 23
Farquarson, J., 95
Father and Son, 3
Fatima, 85
Fechner, Theodor, 64
Feet of Clay, 8, 192
Fest, Joachim, 95, 102
Festinger, L., 127
Feuerstein, Georg, 79-80, 87-9
Firth, R., 208
fitness, 18
flexible mutualism, 74, 91, 105, 218
'flirty fishing', 117
flood, 76, 147, 156, 164
Foley, Robert, 133, 208
folie à deux 111, 199, 218
Foster, L., 108
Foulks, Edward F., 44-5, 194-5, 216
Fox, Robin, 91, 146, 208
free-rider strategy, 55, 62, 218
Freud, Sigmund, 54, 61, 64, 168
Fried, M., 212
Frith, C.D., 39, 210
Fukuyama, Francis, 16
Fulford, K.W.M., 34

Galanter, M., 105, 131, 192, 208, 212
Galton, Sir Francis, 48
Garden of Eden, 149
Gardner, Russell, 190, 207
Garety, Philippa, 36
Gauss, Karl, 65
generations, war of, 111-13
genocide, 76, 125-33, 135, 142-3
genome, 18, 28
genotype, 31-2, 218
George I, 21
Gestalt, 70, 218
Ghost Dance, 73, 159
Gilbert, Paul, 54, 190, 207
Gilgamesh, 153
God, 175, 184
Golden Temple, Order of, 7
Golgatha, 182
Good and Evil, struggle between, 151-5
Goodman, F.D., 210
Gosse, Edmund, 3
Gottesman, I.I., 123
Gratus, Jack, 208
Greatness, 22
Great Schism, 177, 208
Great Year, 164
gregariousness, 48
group splitting, 18, 77, 111, 137-8,
    148-9, 191, 193; ecology of, 18-19;

241

Index

rank, 168-71; disorders of, 171-5
Rank, Otto, 147
rape, 142-3
Rastafari movement, 82
Redlich, Fritz, 96, 99, 101
religions, 146, 167-85; definition of, 146; function of 146-7; origins of, 63; as psychobiological phenomena, 167, 215; universality of, 167
religious outlook, 183-6
research, 199-202
Restoration of the Ten Commandments of God, 10-11
revelation, 150; *see* awakening
revitalization movements, 70; *see* cultural revitalization
revolution, 104-13
Reynolds, V., 215
Ribbentrop, Joachim von, 100
Ribeiro, R., 211
Richardson, J.T., 109, 212
Richardson, Peter, 213
Ricoeur, Paul, 212
Ridley, Matt, 213, 215
Robbins, T., 100
Roberts, Glenn, 40, 212
Robespierre, 84
Robins, R.S., 210
Roots of War, The, 192
Rotberg, Robert I., 211
Roth, Sir Martin, 194-5, 210
Rothenberg, A., 208
Rua, 3, 119, 159
'rule-learning device', 168

sacredness, 66, 84, 179-83
Sagan, C., 154, 212
Sai Baba, 105
St John of the Cross, 149, 153, 155
St Luke, 44
St Paul, 37, 42, 66, 176
St Peter, 43
Samarth of Akkalot, 88
sannyasins, 59
Sargeant, William, 108
Schickelgruber, Maria, 101
schizoid personality, 26, 52-3, 221; diagnosis of, 209
schizophrenia, 24-5, 221; brain abnormalities in, 193, 210; computerized treatment for, 201-2; diagnosis of, 25, 209; in females, 121-2; genetic factors in, 30-2, 123-4, 193; low fertility in, 31; ultimate and proximal causes of, 39
schizotaxia, 193, 201, 221
schizotypal personality, 26, 51-2, 221-2; adaptive function of, 67, 174;

conspicuous among prophets, 51, 194; contribution to population dispersal and genocide, 125-43; in cult members, 122, 212; diagnosis of, 209-19; distinguished from borderline personality, 51; genetic factors in, 123-4, 193, 200-1; psychometric tests for, 210
Seigel, A.M., 53
Seigelman, J., 109
Self, the, 110, 180; projection of, 180
self-esteem, 54
Seneca, 21
Seneca people, 68-9, 75
Sevi Sabbati, 24, 80-1, 130, 173
sexual strategies, 119-21, 207
Shakespeare, William, 21
shamans, 45, 65, 93, 222; borderline personality of, 93
Shaw, William, 2, 80, 106-7, 129-30, 208
Shields, J., 123, 191
Shiva, 12-13, 89
Shouter Baptists, 82
Shree Rajneesh, Bhagwan, 7, 57-60, 130, 143, 152, 185, 198; 'awakening' of, 59; childhood of, 58; creative illness of, 58; psychological deterioration of, 60
sexuality of, 118
sickle-cell anaemia, 124
Simonton, B.K., 22
Slade, P.D., 210
Slater, Eliot, 191
Small, Verna Volz, 96
Smith, Hyram, 178
Smith, Joseph, 57, 130, 177-8; decrees polygamy, 178; visions of, 177
social attention holding power, 54
social cohesion, 107, 167, 173, 192, 215
social contract, 9, 91
Social Darwinism, 203
social hierarchy, 171-3
social homeostasis, 173
social isolation, 108; *see* spacing disorders
Soka Gakkai, 11
Southcott, Joanna, 85
spacing disorders, 47, 138, 171, 192-3, 222
speaking in tongues, 72, 129-30
Speer, Albert, 100
Spence, J., 14
Spencer, E., 201
Spencer, Herbert, 125
Spitzer, R.L., 51
splitting, 222; *see* group splitting
Spying in Guru Land, 2
Sri Ramakrishna, 89

245